Vera Volkova

Vera Volkova

Alexander Meinertz

Translated from the Danish
by
Alexander Meinertz and Paula Hostrup-Jessen

Foreword

by

John Neumeier

DANCE BOOKS

For Henry Danton

First published by Det Schønbergske Forlag, Copenhagen, in 2005

This edition published in 2007 by Dance Books Ltd
The Old Bakery
4 Lenten Street
Alton
Hampshire GU34 1HG

Copyright ©2007 Alexander Meinertz

ISBN: 978 185273 111 3

A CIP catalogue record for this book is available from the British Library

Produced by Jeremy Mills Publishing Ltd.
www.jeremymillspublishing.co.uk

Contents

Remembering Vera Volkova and Early Spring in Copenhagen
Foreword by John Neumeier

Never do I pass that spot on Kongens Nytorv without thinking of her. Walking towards the Royal Theatre that evening in 1964, she stopped suddenly near the corner of Hotel d'Angleterre and, interrupting our conversation, looked directly at me, saying, 'You – could be a choreographer'. It was the way Vera Volkova said 'you' – spontaneously, quietly emphatic, with the clarity and conviction of a surprising revelation – that burns in my memory.

She spoke with the same directness the first day I met her in 1963: 'You – are a dancer?' she asked. Her question made me smile with a secret pride – so full of respect and wonder was the word 'dancer' spoken – as if she, the world-famous teacher, had never before had the pleasure of meeting one. I had heard of this renowned teacher three years before actually meeting her. She was described in the souvenir programme for the 1960 American Tour of the Royal Danish Ballet as 'Vera Volkova, "the Great Teacher", regarded by many as the greatest instructor in classical and Russian styles...'. I had seen the Danish company in Chicago and was deeply impressed, particularly by the virile strength and dramatic intensity of the male dancers. It was also in Chicago that a friend introduced me to a New York City Ballet dancer with the exotic name of Dido. Thrilled to meet a 'real' professional dancer and confused by the next step in my own career, I asked her who was the 'best teacher for men in the world'. Although a Balanchine dancer, she answered without hesitation: 'Volkova!' It was the first time I had heard the Russian teacher's name spoken. Its sound was prophetic, striking in me a personal and fateful chord. I knew instinctively I had to find her.

'I spent the morning finding Vera Volkova at the Royal Theatre', I wrote in my diary on Saturday, 6 April 1963. The diary continues:

> I had letters of introduction but had no appointment, and was not even sure she was in Denmark, so I searched for the "Kongens Nytorv" in a state of extreme anxiety. It was not a disappointment – the Royal Theatre is impressive; it has a simple, almost quaint grandeur, and the patina of a theatre with a long tradition behind it.

Once at the theatre, I had a bit of trouble actually finding Volkova. Finally, a young blond boy in practice clothes took me to a room, which I think was the main rehearsal studio – there was a raised platform like a stage with ballet barres on two sides of it. Four girls were rehearsing on

the stage and several dancers watched. There was a short woman with
long brown hair and a vital Russian face: it was Volkova. She seemed
younger than I had imagined. I felt embarrassed as they stopped
rehearsing and everyone turned to look at me as I walked in. But Volkova
smiled immediately, took my hand and told me to sit down. I explained I
was American and wanted to study with her, and handed her my letters
of introduction. She read carefully, then looked up – looked straight at me
and said, 'You – are a dancer?' Whether question or statement, her words
defined me, and in those first minutes, without ever seeing me dance, she
seemed to recognise my very essence.

There followed, as a matter of course, precise plans: she noted carefully
in her calendar my arrival and departure dates and considered
immediately where and when we could work, as well as who would be the
pianist. I was beginning to know Vera Volkova – the practical, pragmatic
pedagogue who could at the same time communicate method through a
spontaneous and inspiring flow of verbal images. I was also soon to
discover a lightning-fast sense of humour.

I wrote that day: 'What I found interesting (and a comfort!) was the
fact that Volkova immediately and clearly was on "my side"! I felt she was
concerned from the beginning with helping me. It is early spring in
Copenhagen...' Why? Why would this legendary teacher, as a foregone
conclusion, care for a young, unknown student who happened to turn up
one day? I cannot explain it, but somehow these facts explain Volkova.
This meeting was a turning point – the early spring of my career.

I wrote after that first class:

> The next day was our first class. It began at 2:00 in the afternoon, but I left
> Madame Volkova at 9:30 that evening. Volkova is very active and animated as
> she teaches – I remember her clamping her own foot around my ankle to give
> me the feeling of *sur-le-cou de pied* position. She watches intensely, with great
> interest and concern. I felt immediately in that first class a relentless desire to
> communicate. Madame talks a great deal with such vital and fascinating
> inflections and uses such apt, vivid images in her corrections – how I wish I
> could record every word she says.

In the classes that followed, the stream of metaphors continued, each
word picturing the logical reaction to the shortcomings she observed.
Volkova was a poet and at the same time coldly analytical. In my diary I
observed:

> It's not like someone saying 'You must practise', but someone telling you
> exactly what to do. She explained for example: 'When balancing *à la seconde* or
> *passé* you must pull up on the opposite hip, as if you were a matador and the

bull were passing between you and the barre; this extra shift in the hip will level them and help the balance." Or later when I was having trouble with the turnout of my left foot and leg, Madame said, 'I should imagine there was an "eye" in that left heel, and that when the foot extends to *tendu*, it (i.e. the heel) must look at the wall! Also, if there were a gun in the heel, it would shoot at the wall, not into the floor!'

Although known for her eloquence, Volkova never used her facility with language to 'perform'. She was, in fact, a great teacher precisely because she could lose herself in the very act of teaching, becoming only the 'eye', the instrument to aid the pupil. Using her characteristic squint, the half-closing of her eyes, blocking unnecessary distractions in order to concentrate on the essential contours of her student's work, she analysed, diagnosed and prescribed without vanity.

My diary for that first day continues:

After class she invited me for tea and we went to a charming restaurant behind the Royal Theatre, Brønnum. We had tea and toast and Volkova spoke almost constantly of many things. She talked about how she had lost all the furniture in her London apartment by leasing it to a friend who died suddenly without leaving a will, how 'conservative' the Danish Theatre was and how they'd never asked her whether she wanted to stay for another season – it seemed to be a 'gentleman's agreement', nobody seemed to ask her anything! Her conversation however always came back to her true vocation – teaching. She explained how she'd struggled for two years to get an extra class for the girls just entering the company, the 'aspirants' who were not able to keep up in the normal company class. It was this which impressed me most – her sincere concern about education. She had organised this class outside union time and with no extra pay for herself, just so she could spend more time with these young dancers, could give them the corrections she hadn't had time to give in the company class. She confided that in twenty-one years of teaching, she'd realised what a very personal thing teaching really was, and what individual needs each dancer has. She admitted that she was actually 'sorry she found this out', as it made her less satisfied with her work, knowing that in a large class she was only giving each student 50% of what they needed. Talking on and on, the light changed, and she explained the beautiful concept of the French expression *l'heure bleu*. We ended up ordering dinner.

Volkova's conversations and interests were in no sense limited to ballet. Later in the evening she told me what I came to recognise as a typical Volkova story.

She spoke of how the American choreographer Ruth Page had given her 300 dollars when she volunteered to teach a class to the Chicago Opera Ballet

– and how she didn't want to accept it, but Ruth insisted, telling her to 'buy something foolish' with it, and so she did – she bought a coat she didn't really need for 280 dollars. Later, she met a hairdresser in Dallas who had never seen the sea – and wondered what colour it was. She also met two society ladies in Dallas who kept her waiting an hour and a quarter for a luncheon engagement, and talked about how one of them asked her to excuse her friend, as she was very artistic and therefore temperamental. Then Volkova, with her unique poetic logic, connected the three story fragments by asking me, 'Why couldn't one of those socialites or Ruth Page give that lady in Dallas the money to go to see the sea? The rich have no imagination.' At 9:30, we each paid for our dinner, but she treated me to coffee. Not one word was said about my paying for the lessons.

In the late summer of 1964, I returned to Copenhagen to study with Madame Volkova. I was just beginning to work after a foot operation performed in Århus by the well-known Danish 'Dancer's Surgeon' Eivind Thomasen. It was this doctor, in fact, who would later that same year operate on Volkova's knee. 'What a pity we were not here at the same time', she wrote to me from the Ortopædisk Hospital, Århus, in October 1964. 'I feel a society should be formed: "Dr. Thomasen's Brotherhood", with Flemming Flindt as an honourable member, he having been the first dancer to discover Dr. Thomasen.' At this difficult time, the care and caution exercised, the precise teaching plan that Vera Volkova developed for my recovery was treasured as an amazing luxury – and touched me deeply.

I wrote in my diary on 11 August 1964:

> I've started training again today and it was a most painful joy... joyful pain! My first class with Volkova – it only lasted about 20 minutes, in one of the beautiful studios in the Royal Theatre, late in the afternoon with only Madame, half-singing, half-counting for the simple exercises. I was so happy... I will always remember the five o'clock sun and the smell of new wood and Madame sitting on that chair and squinting at me. The Theatre was deserted and peaceful – there were beautiful diagonal shafts of sunlight streaming through the small round windows adding another cathedral-like quality to the cathedral quiet of the white room – Volkova said, 'When we do our barre we are very serious...'

I was not, however, Volkova's only private pupil that summer:

> Erik Bruhn asked Volkova if he could join my class today. What an honour! He was in Copenhagen after his holiday and wanted some extra work with her. It was truly quite thrilling for me having him there... I think there is no dancer I admire more. Watching him work was like seeing Volkova's words! I remember

especially the opening of the arms, shoulders and head, the noble expression of his face as he did *tendu* front, opening arms into third, then preparing for *pirouette en dedans*. Pointing *à la seconde* in preparation for an *attitude pirouette*, his foot seemed pointed from somewhere just below the ribs!

Then – on Wednesday, 26 August 1964 – I wrote:

Nureyev arrived today. The class was rather complicated for Madame as two other dancers, *étoiles* from the Paris Opera, Claire Motte and Jean-Pierre Bonnefous, also came to study with her. Erik Bruhn joined the class as well. It was hard for Volkova to juggle the whole thing, considering the various needs of the individual dancers – the French, just having returned from holiday, Erik Bruhn, seriously preparing for a coming performance, the sudden appearance of superstar Nureyev, and me, a near cripple! Although it was obviously difficult for Volkova to correct anything or anybody, confronted with such a wildly mixed bunch, she smiled through the whole thing...

The next day, I was a bit let down after the 'up' of my all-star class: 'Volkova segregated me from the whole lot of them', I wrote with a certain childish sense of disappointment at missing all the excitement. But I then concluded:

I am really quite touched that Volkova should have thought so much about my personal development to separate me from '*les enfants terribles*' as she calls them. It would have been so much easier just to lump us all together and let me struggle along, sink or swim, at the back. It's so typical of her completely serious approach to teaching – making a point of having me come early, so as to not be 'mixed with Nureyev and the French'.

The diary entries from the first few years of sporadic lessons in Copenhagen give a picture not only of an extraordinary teacher but also of a complex and unique woman. Although she spoke little about her past, situations and emotions from her Soviet background wove themselves from time to time into our conversations. On 15 August 1964, for example, I wrote:

...with Madame before her dinner engagement with Sol Hurok. She wore a black dress that she had bought in America – because of the tiny polka dot bows on the shoulder. She talked a little about Soviet Russia – about how her whole family had to live in one room, and how the thing she wanted more than anything was a room of her own – no matter how small. She laughed about the single little shelf she was given, and how she wanted that at least to be her own and kept just as she wanted. She said she screamed when her mother tried to put the winter blankets there, and that they didn't understand that even though it didn't look like there was anything there – she had to collect the things first – she wanted it to be hers, even to keep empty if it pleased her! I walked her to the Hotel d'Angleterre, where Sol Hurok was waiting for her outside...

I recall clearly that, in spite of Volkova's obvious devotion to teaching, she was a loving and loyal wife. Although enjoying an international reputation and being very much in demand as a guest teacher for major companies and private coach for famous personalities, Volkova was nevertheless deeply and genuinely concerned about her husband. I wrote on 15 August 1964:

> ... had tea after class this afternoon at Volkova's but she seemed preoccupied with her husband's dinner: she said she has a 'strong sense of responsibility' and that is quite obvious! It's one of the things that are so marvellous about her, this sense of order and responsibility that must hold her together in the midst of being carried away with her work – she has a husband who must be her first concern. I respect and admire the fact that she doesn't use her artistic calling, success and fame as a teacher as an excuse for a kind of easy 'Bohemian' existence. It seems her husband is that still point in her life around which the Erik Bruhns, Nureyevs and Sol Huroks revolve.

Writing now, I realise how very much there is to say about those precious lessons, those very special days with Madame Volkova, because, in fact, she did say so much! Not just nebulous fancy phrases, but words of sense and substance, precise instructions, communicated with her particular eloquence.

Her prophecy regarding my vocation, delivered in front of Hotel d'Angleterre, became reality. Later, I did in fact become a choreographer. In 1974, I was invited to stage *Romeo and Juliet* for the Royal Theatre in Copenhagen. It was an honour and a privilege for me to stage my first full-length work for this prestigious company, but it was the chance to bring my work home to Volkova that, in secret, was my greatest joy. She helped me discover the vulnerable Mette-Ida Kirk, a Juliet whom she coached with a critical love. Then she, who had spent so many patient hours in private classes always believing in me as a dancer, saw me dance Romeo, in her theatre. There was no doubt – my performance was for her. Not long after this, Vera Volkova died.

Today there is the sad perception that her teaching heritage is being slowly forgotten, as memories of her brilliant personality fade. I feel very fortunate – for me, she is ever present. Reading her words, she lives in these luminous images; and Vera Volkova lives, in fact, symbolically in many of my ballets. In Copenhagen, on 12 March 1975, I visited Madame Volkova for the last time. Entering the hospital room I experienced another face of Volkova, and was shocked at how pale and yellow, how small, lonely and frightened, she appeared. She was surprised to see me, and as I sat on her bed she took my right hand and pressing it firmly to her forehead with both her hands, said, 'You – do love me...' This spontaneous gesture, and the familiar 'you' remain unforgettable. You can find this simple, this strong gesture in several of my ballets – used at climactic moments when a deep, unconditional love must be communicated – Vera Volkova's eloquence is there, again.

Although I experienced Volkova intensely, it was, of course, through my very personal 'window' – the window of our classes, conversations and later correspondence. She was for me both pure inspiration and a down-to-earth woman. She taught me exactly how to open my arm nobly in the first position at the barre – with the same earnest directness with which she taught me always to peel the tomatoes when making an omelette.

Still, she is a mystery – there is so much I never knew, never asked about this enigmatic woman. Therefore, it is with intense curiosity, excitement and deep gratitude that I await this book, so long overdue!

Verotchka

'If only I could actually see you and talk to you about my pilgrimage', Vera Volkova wrote on 30 August 1967 in a melancholic letter to her friend, the British writer David Arkell. 'How can I explain what I felt', she continued, 'standing in front of my house on the Kutuzov Embankment?'[1]

Volkova, a Russian ballet teacher, had come home after almost 40 years in exile. She had followed a familiar route along the Neva from her hotel on her way to the house on Kutuzov, walking from the Hermitage, passing the French Embassy: 'I feel my life belongs to that river', she said. There on the Embankment she breathed the damp, salty air of the Baltic Sea that she remembered so well. Winter darkness had already enveloped the islands of Leningrad, and the twilight was painted with the streaks of grey and black she had not seen since she left Soviet Russia in 1929.

Volkova's return to Leningrad was an official visit: as the personal guest of the Artistic Director of the Kirov Ballet, Konstantin Sergeyev, she spent most of her time watching classes and performances at Leningrad's old Imperial Theatre. Sergeyev had invited her when the Kirov had performed in London the previous year.

Although Nikita Khrushchev had been deposed as Head of State in 1964, his new attitude towards the West – as a rival, rather than an evil to be ignored – had influenced the arts. The Soviet administration was keen to see the Royal Danish Ballet dance in Moscow and Leningrad. Volkova had worked with the Royal Danes for more than 15 years, and Sergeyev's invitation to her, a defector, was a gesture of goodwill that carried political weight and would pave the way for cultural exchange.

The Danish Government had negotiated a guarantee of her safe return to Copenhagen, but Volkova was still uneasy about going back: she did not trust the Soviet authorities. She had seen the full horrors of the Revolution, been a witness to Red Terror and suffered the consequences of Stalin's Great Terror. Recently, Nureyev's defection had brought back her old fears: since she had started working with the dancer in Copenhagen in 1961, she had been followed by KGB agents in the streets and received anonymous phone calls.

Her British husband, Hugh Finch Williams, had gone to Russia with her, but during their stay she revealed little of her feelings to him and he asked no questions. It was typical of their relationship. When he first met her in Shanghai in 1934, she was a stateless refugee in a desperate situation. He fell in love with her and saved her, but knew little about her. She had been reluctant to talk about her past, remained vague about dates and places, and hardly ever mentioned names. Now, though she showed him where she had lived as a child, she would disappear by herself in the mornings before going to class, or in the evenings after performances.

'My thoughts were as overwhelming and confused as the Neva itself in spring', she admitted in her letter to David Arkell.

> Suddenly the ice begins to melt and huge blocks with jagged edges are carried by the tide with tremendous speed and noise, pushing and overtaking and piling on top of each other, revealing dark cold water, while above it all the sun just mocks. As a child, a little frightened and very excited, I watched it all from that very house, sitting on my favourite place, the windowsill.[2]

Vera Nikolaeyvna Volkova, 'Verotchka', was born on 31 May 1905[3] in Tomsk, where her father, Captain Nikolai Volkov, was stationed with his regiment. Earlier that year, on Sunday 9 January, 150,000 civilians, including women and children, had been fired upon by Imperial troops outside the Winter Palace during a peaceful protest against the Empire-wide famine. Several hundred had been killed and news of the outrage had spread over the entire Russian Empire, which stretched from the Baltic and Black Seas to the Pacific Ocean, covering a sixth of the world's surface.

In February, the Tsar's army had suffered a surprising and humiliating defeat at the hands of the Japanese at Mukden; and, only a few days before her birth, on 27–28 May, the Russian fleet had been decimated at Tsushima. The Russian people's Imperial world was disintegrating.

Riots and unrest in the Volkovs' home city of St Petersburg had driven the pregnant Maria Vladimirovna to join her husband on the flat, forested West Siberian plain, with her children Irina and Lev. Her third child was born two months prematurely and, fearing that the baby would not survive, Maria and Nikolai had her baptised in haste in Tomsk's Bogoyavlensky Cathedral with Volkov's aide as witness. The child was given the name Vera from the Russian *vjero*, meaning faith.

In accordance with the ancient baptismal rituals of the Orthodox Church, Volkova was submerged in the font three times. The priest breathed on her forehead to exorcise the Devil and any evil from the child. Begging her guardian angel for strength and renouncing Satan on her behalf, he defiantly held her up towards the West, where the forces of darkness reigned, then towards the East and the light, before he anointed her with the oil of joy and wrapped her in white robes as a sign of miraculous rebirth and salvation.

Peace with Japan and the Tsar's promise of democratic reforms temporarily stabilised the situation and so, in 1906, Nikolai and Maria

Volkov took their three children home to St Petersburg. They settled in a fashionable area on what is now called Kutuzov Embankment, but was then known as Frantsusky Embankment: the French Embankment. The family lived in a first-floor apartment in a long, two-storey terracotta mansion, decorated with classical white capitals and pilasters. It had sweeping views over the River Neva to the first home that Peter the Great had built for himself after founding St Petersburg as his capital and 'window on the West'. On the opposite bank the Volkovs could also see the Peter and Paul Fortress, whose golden spire was a rapier pointed at the very heart of the capital. The Tsar's prisoners were held in that fortress, in cells so small that they could neither stand up nor lie down.

From the window whose sill would become Verotchka's favourite vantage point, one could also watch the heavy traffic crossing the Liteiny Bridge towards the city centre from the slums on the Vyborg side. In the evenings, the bridge would be raised, the noise of traffic around the house would lessen, and the sounds of the rushing river would fill the air.

Sometimes, on dark afternoons, Maria Vladimirovna would take her daughters to the Nevsky Prospekt, where they would drink hot chocolate in a fashionable café called Des Gourmets. Volkova never forgot the elegant ladies they saw on those outings: their veils, their heavy furs and the smell of perfume in the bitingly cold air. She also recalled her childish disappointment when she found that Grand Duchesses did not wear their tiaras on the street.

The Volkovs were minor gentry, owning lands south of Moscow. Having travelled extensively, fought in the Russo-Japanese War, and worked his way up through St Petersburg's central administration to the rank of Court Councillor, Nikolai Volkov had joined the class of ennobled bureaucrats created by Peter the Great. He was a slim, athletic man, with blue eyes and fair hair.

Volkova's mother, born Maria Vladimirovna Heine, had an artistic bent and had dreamt of a singing career, but married young and, her family thought, beneath her station. She was of German-Jewish descent, a great-niece of the German poet Heinrich Heine, whose work *De l'Allemagne* inspired one of the greatest Romantic ballets, *Giselle*.

Her grandfather, Maximilian Heine, came from a wealthy banking family and had studied medicine in Heidelberg. As an adventurous young man, he had travelled in the Middle East before joining the Russian Army as a surgeon. He served in the Balkans and in the campaign against the Polish uprising of 1832 before finally settling in St Petersburg. There he married Henriette, the daughter of Nicholas I's Physician-in-Ordinary, Nikolai von Arendt, famed for having attended Russia's national poet,

Alexander Pushkin, in 1837 as he lay dying of wounds sustained in his legendary duel.

In keeping with tradition, Maximilian Heine inherited his father-in-law's position and became a State Councillor and Physician-in-Ordinary to Alexander II the assassinated Tsar-Liberator. But he also had literary ambitions and wrote short stories, poems and travelogues, as well as medical articles. He was considered 'more stable and intelligent' than his artistic brother Heinrich, but 'unremarkable as regards mentality and temperament'.[4] A painting of Maximilian – destroyed during World War II, but surviving as a photograph – shows a portly, bemedalled military man with an impressive walrus moustache. Volkova, who identified strongly with the Heine family, believed that she had inherited her angular profile from Heinrich.

Many members of the Heine family's Russian branch were doctors. Maria's father, Vladimir, was affiliated to the Court as an ear, nose and throat specialist, and her son Lev studied medicine. The gene passed to Volkova; she was interested in science from an early age, and as a ballet teacher was noted for her knowledge of anatomy. She was convinced that, had she not become a ballet dancer, she would have become one of Russia's first female doctors.

The Volkov children had a French governess, Madame Lescard, who educated them according to strict French principles. They spoke French and read French literature. Volkova preferred Perrault's sophisticated, happy-ever-after fairy tales to the Grimm brothers' frightening stories. She also read Dickens, and inherited an interest in British culture from her father, who had visited Great Britain several times and dressed like an English gentleman.

At the age of nine, Volkova sat the entrance exam to St Petersburg's school for young noblewomen, the Smolny Institute, where her elder sister, Irina, was already a pupil. On 16 September 1914, she started in the seventh grade on a scholarship from St Petersburg's Assembly of Nobles, and experienced the last days of one of St Petersburg's great old Tsarist institutions.

Inspired by Madame de Maintenon's convent school in France, Maison St Cyr, Catherine the Great founded Smolny in 1765, envisaging an institution that would educate the daughters of the unruly and backward Russian nobility. She expected that the girls would exercise a beneficial influence on their husbands and sons.

The Institute's exalted aim was to 'change human nature from bad to good'. Cherry-picking what it saw as the best aspects of the European culture of the day, the school sought to endow its pupils with 'the demure comportment of an English Duchess', teach them to 'keep a good Russian table *à la française*', and stimulate them to develop 'the well-stocked mind of their German cousins'. Most importantly of all, a Smolny girl was expected to learn to 'rein in her spirits as she did a horse, sideways'.[5]

In the afternoons, the 600 Smolny pupils walked and played in the Institute gardens, which were tended by the Tsar's own gardeners. On Saturdays the girls, known in the capital as 'brides of the Tsar', worshipped in the spectacular, five-domed Smolny Cathedral, standing for stretches of up to five hours next to the grace-and-favour ladies who inhabited the old buildings surrounding the church.

The students' uniforms were unchanged since Catherine the Great's time: starched, white shoulder-capes over white blouses; white aprons, changed twice weekly; and heavy woollen skirts in different colours that denoted which class each girl was in. The Institute's patroness was the Grand Duchess Maria Pavlovna, who would be welcomed with great ceremony by row after row of girls curtseying very deeply.

Although Smolny focused on social formalities, its regime encouraged – demanded – iron self-discipline; and, in general, its alumnae grew up to be strong, energetic, independent and confident women. It was largely here that Volkova's personal values and morals were set.

In many ways the Smolny pupils led an extremely isolated and protected life, like little nuns, but the popular idea that they were delicate and spoilt was far from the truth. They were woken at six o'clock in the morning and studied until six o'clock in the evening: Russian and European literature, arithmetic, history, geography and architecture, as well as drawing, dance, music, needlework and home crafts. All lessons were conducted in French, and the children only spoke Russian among themselves in secret. Corporal punishment was prohibited, and the girls were treated gently. But they were taught not to be lazy, sad or moody – 'Chekhovian' – and were brought up according to a strict moral code incorporating concepts such as justice and honour.

One student later wrote in her memoirs that

the Institute's entire system sought to obliterate any kind of sentimentality, and to instil the restraint and suppression of any external signs of emotion.[6]

Among the pupils themselves, the qualities most prized were modesty and a well-balanced mind.

St Petersburg society made little allowance for childish temperament, and Volkova grew up quickly. She later said she had never really felt like a child.

A single formal portrait photograph of the Volkov sisters in Smolny Institute uniform has survived. In keeping with Russian tradition, the elder sister is seated. Irina, who with her broad features resembles her father's side of the family, seems at first glance younger than the standing Volkova. Looking more closely, though, one can see Irina's greater maturity in her careful pose, narrowed lips and strong, self-confident gaze. Volkova's expression is more vulnerable and tentative. Her mouth is slightly open, as if she is about to smile, but her hand is tense.

Temperamentally, the Volkov sisters were opposites. Irina was the driving force who dramatised everything, loved to paint but would give up in the face of a challenge. Volkova was the observant introvert who loved literature, and would persevere through difficulty.

Russia had entered World War I shortly after Volkova's enrolment at Smolny. 'St Petersburg' became 'Petrograd', in deference to anti-German feeling. As Volkova's second term opened, her father paid the sisters an unexpected visit; he had been promoted to Lieutenant Colonel and was in the capital on leave. Volkova remembered that he seemed tired and absent-minded. He checked the girls' marks, and gave each of them a box of chocolates before leaving. A few months later, in the spring of 1915, he was killed on the Galician front at the age of 37.

Disastrous losses in the war finally led to the February Revolution of 1917, the end of Imperial Russia, and the enforced abdication of Tsar Nikolai II, who believed himself divinely anointed and, to the end, laboured under the delusion that his people loved him.

Along with most other state institutions, the Smolny Institute was closed down. At the end of the spring term, the girls were sent home and Lenin – who had returned from his exile in Switzerland – took over the school buildings, turning them into the Bolshevik headquarters.

The British military attaché, Colonel Knox, happened to be near the Volkov home on Red Monday, and wrote in his memoirs:

> We stood a moment on the Quay, and looked back at the stream of troops now crossing the bridge to liberate the prisoners in the Krestovsky Prison.[7]

A Red garrison seized Liteiny Prospekt and set fire to the courthouse. White troops loyal to the Tsar barricaded themselves on the Volkovs' roof, while the bridge was raised in an attempt to keep the masses away from the city centre. Terror-stricken cadets sought refuge in the family's flat – 'two of them came and pleaded for us to hide them', Volkova remembered – while Maria and the children hid under mattresses beneath the windowsills.

Civil unrest continued even after the Tsar's abdication on 2 March, as Kerensky's Provisional Government clashed with the Bolsheviks. The journalist Harold Williams described a demonstration against Kerensky on the Liteiny Prospekt. 'It was a strange sight', he wrote, this grey, silent, moving mass in the dusk, with a blur of guns, the caps and bayonets of men on the lorries, and the bent figures of soldiers on artillery horses, all silhouetted against the pale sky ... Hour after hour crowds trudged the streets ... Soldiers and workers, workers and soldiers, in an endless, armed stream.[8]

October 1917 was windy, the sky grey and overcast. On 25 October, as gales howled through the streets and thrashed the treetops, Petrograd's inhabitants awoke to a city plastered with posters proclaiming the fall of Kerensky.

Amazingly, life continued as if nothing had happened. The trams ran as usual, the shops stayed open and there were no demonstrations in the streets. In the evening, the Maryinsky Theatre ballet danced *The Nutcracker* and Mikhail Fokine's *Eros* to Tchaikovsky's *Serenade for Strings*. But shortly after the performance started, shots were heard from the battleship *Aurora* on the Neva, the Bolsheviks occupied the Winter Palace, and the dictatorship of the Proletariat had become a reality. That night, while the Bolsheviks were taking over the Winter Palace to bring down the Provisional Government, the Congress of Soviets opened in the Smolny Institute's great white ballroom, where Volkova had taken her first tutored steps in dance.

The February Revolution had eliminated the monarchy. The October Revolution eliminated the upper classes, and the Volkov family was forcibly removed from the gracious apartment overlooking the river, to a one-room flat in the courtyard. 'When the real Revolution started, we thought it was just another strike', Volkova once told David Arkell, 'but when mother went to the bank and found it shut we knew it was different ...'

When the banks were nationalised in December 1917, the family immediately lost all sources of income. They were broke, and the rationing system largely favoured the working class. 'He who does no work shall not be fed', was the formal diktat. Like thousands of others, Maria Volkova began to sell their valuables on the street. The curtains went for a loaf of bread, the piano was used for firewood.

The author Isaak Babel described the mood in the city. He wrote about the empty markets, the people's increasingly desperate hunt for food, the shopkeepers' 'selfish blue eyes' that flickered over helpless crowds of women, soldiers in civilian clothes, and old men with leather galoshes.

A week ago I walked one whole morning through Petrograd, through the city of poverty and death. Fog, thin but forceful, whirled over the filthy cobblestones. Dirty snow was transformed into shining black puddles.

Babel was also horrified and frightened by the anarchy and violence that left the city's inhabitants paralysed by terror.

I went to the place where the dead are counted every morning – I enter the mortuary together with the guard. He raises the sheets and shows me the faces covered with black blood – the faces of people who have been killed several weeks ago.[9]

In August 1918, following a failed assassination attempt on Lenin, the Bolshevik government's secret police, the Cheka, launched the Red Terror: mass executions whose victims were selected by faith and social class. Petrograd was becoming a city of ghosts and shadows. Lenin moved the government to Moscow, taking the bureaucrats with him, and ordinary people fled Petrograd in their thousands. The city's population fell from 2.4 million in 1915 to 1.5 million by 1918.

Abandoned, Petrograd was a place of lawlessness and terror. When news reached the city in June 1919 that General Denikin's White Russian forces had taken Kharkov in Ukraine, Maria decided to try to send her children to safety. It was still relatively easy to cross the border, so in the autumn of 1919 Madame Lescard travelled to Kharkov with Vera and Irina. Maria and her son Lev remained in Petrograd.

In the 1950s, Volkova told David Arkell about the flight to Kharkov, and he recorded the conversation in which she described their dramatic experiences. She said that she and Irina lived 'a normal life' in Ukraine with Madame Lescard until they heard rumours that the Bolsheviks were approaching the city. The governess then abandoned the girls, fleeing to Odessa, where French warships were evacuating European citizens.

Volkova, aged fourteen, was put in a children's home, while sixteen-year-old Irina was placed with foster parents. Volkova would only say: 'It was quite an experience'.

The sisters decided to try to get back to Petrograd. 'We really didn't have a choice',[10] Volkova said, even though they had not heard from their mother for six months, and had no idea what they would find, if they ever reached home. In January 1920, they set out on their perilous journey, a few weeks after the Red Army had taken Kharkov.

'The traffic was only going from the North to the South, because everybody was running away from Leningrad', she explained.

Only the troops were going north... we planned this departure with taking lots of little things. Lots of food we saved, because we were told already by then that there was famine in Leningrad, but it didn't interest us, the famine, at the time. The only thing was to prepare ourselves, so we dried the mushrooms, put them on strings – they were hanging all over the place – and a few other things, cereals and things.

It was forbidden for children to travel without an adult; but the times were unusual, and at the train station the resourceful sisters found an old peasant woman whose destination was just a few miles outside Kharkov:

> ... we asked her to pretend that she was with us, that she was looking after us, and she agreed... With this poor woman, you know, we finally went in the train, and went as far as Moscow.

In the new capital, they learnt that all trains to Petrograd had been cancelled because of fighting along the line. Stranded at the Central Station, they faced another battle for survival.

> They were rounding up the urchins, you see, all the children who had no homes ... So we were terrified to be caught, you see, and put into, you know, the remand home, or whatever they are known as.

The sisters had no relatives in Moscow and very little money left, and lived from hand to mouth for several days.

> ... we didn't sleep much, and then we felt somehow it must come, that train. Really we were optimists and believed that the train would come, and the train would take us to Leningrad. And then it was announced that the train would come, but nobody could get on it except the troops.

A kind stationmaster allowed them to board the train. 'We finally arrived in Petrograd at five o'clock in the morning, but it was a great shock', said Volkova.

> It was a very grey and very sad city with shutters, you know, instead of shops, paper flying in the dirty, empty streets. The few people we saw looked sad and thin or very ill and bloated. We were frightened.

The city's famous wooden streets were rotting in the February slush and swimming in rubbish. Many houses had been abandoned: the population had fallen to 800,000, 35% of what it had been before the Revolution.

> We went to the old address and knocked on the door. It was about half past five in the morning and my poor mother was afraid to open the door because it was the time of day that people were often arrested. It was the thing she was the most afraid of, that one day she would have a knock at five in the morning ... We screamed, 'It's us! ... Mummy, it's us', and finally she rushed to the door and let us in and we were together again.

Secret Messages of the Flesh

Petrograd was a living hell. The civil war had broken down the Empire's infrastructure, and social upheaval in the provinces meant that little of the food still being produced reached the major cities. Famine struck, and even with rationing it was impossible to get enough food. The Volkovs froze during the long winter months and, like everyone else, were forced to burn their remaining furniture and steal wood from the streets to use as fuel.

As the family was penniless, Maria found work as a typist, but soon became exhausted and demoralised. The hardships took a heavy toll on Irina, who began to show the first signs of mental instability. Volkova suffered from anaemia – doctors recommended drinking a full glass of animal blood daily – but continued her education at the 23rd Workers' School in Petrograd's *premier arrondissement*. After school, she would walk to the other end of the city and queue for the family's soup ration at the Alexander Nevsky Monastery.

Later in life, Volkova liked to say she had become a dancer for the simple reason that dancers were privileged and were given extra food rations: ballet made her a breadwinner. But the truth was not quite as prosaic as she made out: she had loved dance since an early age. It had always been her passion, and it now became her salvation.

As a child, she had romantic ideas of dance as 'free' and dreamt of dancing with a veil[11] – perhaps because she had seen the American modern dancer Loie Fuller perform in St Petersburg. Fuller was immensely popular, and had toured throughout Europe and Russia before World War I. Stéphane Mallarmé, the Symbolist movement's leading poet, had described her dancing as 'the dizziness of soul made visible by an artifice'.

Dance had been on the curriculum at Smolny, to teach the girls proper deportment and social graces while giving them a little exercise. Once a week, an old French dancing master clad in the livery of the *Ancien Régime* – long-sleeved coat, knee-breeches and white silk stockings – taught the minuet, the gavotte and lancers in the white-pillared ballroom.

At Smolny, Volkova had particularly liked the gavotte, known as '*la danse classique*'. It originated in France during the Renaissance and had become very popular by the seventeenth century. It was dynamic, developing in expansive choreographic patterns, and involved flirtation, with the partners exchanging flowers.

Although the dances taught at the Smolny were court dances, they were closely related to the art of ballet. They shared many of the same steps, because classical ballet developed its language and aesthetics from the court dances of fifteenth-century Italy. Later, ballet evolved in France at the Court of Catherine de Medici, whose ballet spectacles were danced almost exclusively by amateurs: nobles who relished the opportunity to demonstrate their grace, dignity and culture. They performed in magnificent pageants on allegorical themes, which included not only dancing and music, but also declamation.

As a young man, the Sun King Louis XIV danced in ballets to music by Lully and Rameau. In 1661, he founded *L'Académie royale de danse* to train professional dancers. Pierre Beauchamps, the Academy's first director, established some of the basic principles that we recognise today, including the five positions of the feet with which most ballet steps and sequences begin and end.

Since then, almost all professional dancers have begun to train as children, so that their bodies can be properly aligned, moulded and developed. Muscle strength and flexibility must be built up gradually in the child over a period of a decade or more. As well as building power and mobility, ballet training develops the dancer's co-ordination, musicality and sense of space. It also aims to instil the ability to perform movements with precision and expression, following the scientific system described by the Italian ballet-master Carlo Blasis. In his *Traité élémentaire, théorique et pratique de l'art de la danse* (1820), Blasis analysed jumps, *pirouettes* and *batterie*, in the last of which the legs beat against one another in the air. This theoretical codification of classical steps continued throughout the century, as ballet developed as a dramatic art form.

After the Romantic era faded in Paris and Copenhagen, St Petersburg became the centre for the development of ballet in the last half of the nineteenth century. It was for the company attached to the Imperial Maryinsky Theatre that choreographer Marius Petipa created his magnificent and opulently staged ballets *La Bayadère*, *Swan Lake* and *The Sleeping Beauty*. Petipa was both a master of form and a bold innovator. Thanks to the Tsar's munificent patronage, no restrictions were placed on his creations. Imperial roubles enabled him to put hundreds of dancers on stage at once, commission music from composers such as Tchaikovsky and Glazunov, and order unimaginably lavish costumes and sets for his works.

But the Russian ballet began to stagnate from the beginning of the twentieth century. Petipa was nearing retirement and, although he continued to choreograph, his works were no longer felt to be innovative. The impresario Serge Diaghilev and his artistic collaborators infused the art form with new life when Diaghilev first presented his own company, the Ballets Russes, in Paris in 1909. It had arisen from the Imperial Maryinsky Ballet. Mikhail Fokine was Diaghilev's chosen choreographer, and Anna Pavlova, Tamara Karsavina and Vaslav Nijinsky his star dancers in the company's thrillingly original, shockingly sensual one-act ballets.

Volkova started her career as a ballet dancer in this transitional phase of the art form's development. She was a late starter – fifteen when she took her first lessons with Madame Erle, a retired dancer from the Maryinsky Theatre who lived in the same house as the Volkovs. She felt Volkova had a natural facility and encouraged her to pursue her passion for movement.

Petrograd's State Choreographic Technical School, the old Imperial Ballet School in Rossi Street, would only accept pupils under the age of ten. So Volkova had to choose between the Miklos School, in Princess Yurievskaya's house in Gagarinskaya Street, a few minutes' walk from her home, and the art critic Akim Volynsky's School of Russian Ballet at No. 6 Pochtamtskaya Street. The School of Russian Ballet was also known as the Baltflot School, because it was housed in the buildings of the Baltic Fleet, behind St Isak Cathedral.

The Miklos School was popular: it was housed in a glamorous building; it boasted a former mistress of the Tsar as one of its teachers; and Miklos himself was a reckless fantasist who bedded his dancers and often had to sell the school's accoutrements to make ends meet.

Akim Volynsky's School of Russian Ballet was by far the more ambitious of the two privately owned schools, and a much more serious proposition. Its staff included great artists who had danced with the Imperial Ballet, notably Nikolai Legat, Olga Preobrazhenskaya, Maria Romanova and Agrippina Vaganova. It was almost religiously devoted to an artistic goal set and policed by Volynsky himself.

Volynsky was one of Petrograd's most noticeable and controversial personalities, described by the musician and composer Dimitri Shostakovich as 'a short man with a large head and a face like a prune'. He looked like a cross between an undertaker and a prophet of doom, and described himself as reserved, impassive and far from physical. But his soul took flight when inspired by the beauty of classical ballet, and he was relentlessly demanding of the school's pupils, whom he regarded as servants in the temple of Terpsichore, the Muse of dance.

In the year in which Volkova started at the School of Russian Ballet, he wrote an open letter to Anatoly Lunacharsky, the Soviet Commissar for Education. He argued vehemently that there was a need for radically reforming the state ballet and providing the Maryinsky Theatre with a flow of new creative forces that have grown up in conditions of a different, higher type of culture.[12]

He sought a new vision of ballet in which the pupils of the future should learn not only to master the technique, but also to understand the idiom of classical ballet. 'The ballet must enter into the second stage of its development', he wrote, stressing that this would be possible only with a 'conscious attitude to this art'.[13] Volynsky proposed a new curriculum that would include the theory of movement, the aesthetics of classical ballet, choreographic principles from the ancient theatre, and various disciplines of a 'socio-cultural nature'. His curriculum was not approved for use at Petrograd's State Choreographic Technical School, but it was adopted at his own school.

Volynsky's closest ally among his teaching staff was the legendary ballet-master Nikolai Legat. Legat had been born in Moscow in 1869 into a dynasty of dancers. He and his brother Sergei had been trained at the Maryinsky Theatre by the Swedish teacher Christian Johansson, a pupil of the Danish ballet-master August Bournonville.

After a glorious career as a principal dancer – he had danced the Prince in the first production of *The Nutcracker,* and was both Anna Pavlova's and Mathilda Kchessinska's favourite partner – Legat became ballet-master and chief choreographer at the Maryinsky in 1903, when Petipa retired and Johansson died.

As a dancer, Legat was exceptionally lyrical; he was very much a product of the French school, and was considered the natural heir of Petipa and Johansson. But many saw him as a reactionary because he did not sympathise with choreographer Mikhail Fokine's less formal, more expressive approach. Professional frustration drove Legat to resign from the Maryinsky Theatre after 25 years of service. Immediately before World War I, he travelled to London with his future wife, Nadina Nikolaeva Briger, and danced in music halls there. When he returned to Petrograd there was no place for him at the Maryinsky Theatre, so he worked for a time at the Bolshoi Theatre in Moscow, where he felt like 'a small cog in a big wheel'.

Volynsky gave Legat renewed hope at the School of Russian Ballet, which both saw as the bearer of a sacred flame and a magnificent project whose radical new curriculum would offer a real alternative to the formulaic, one-dimensional teaching of the State Ballet School. They also hoped that, through the School, they could rescue the art, which they felt was being diminished to the point of destruction.

Another of the main pillars of strength in Volynsky's school was Agrippina Vaganova, who would become one of Volkova's most important teachers. She was less personally engaged in the school's mission, but Volynsky still regarded her as one of his disciples.

Like Legat, Vaganova was a pupil of Johansson. She had also trained with Legat himself and the ballerina Ekaterina Vazem. She became a member of the Maryinsky Theatre's corps de ballet in 1897 and was appointed a soloist in 1906; but it was not until 1915, only a year before she retired, that she was belatedly made a prima ballerina. She was known as the 'Queen of Variations', and the critic André Levinson considered her Nikolai Legat's finest pupil. Vaganova possessed 'an enormous formal talent in which she has no rival',[14] but developed slowly as an artist despite her fabulous technique.

Volynsky had been cool in his appraisal of Vaganova until 1912, when he began to see her with new eyes:

> [Vaganova] is a skilled soloist and talented in the themes of some variations ... Her firm toes allow her to tread lightly and quickly perform complex ballet figures and she possesses outstanding elevation.[15]

But to Volynsky the aesthete, she was not a 'beautiful dancer'. Having seen her in her first ballerina role in *La Source*, he decided she was not suited to leading roles because of the 'very sad impression made by the soft and fluid forms of her nicely proportioned body and big, hard head'.[16] Later he praised her for 'the "geometrical correctness" of the design patterns and a sense of mysteriousness'.[17]

Volynsky's criticism helped to develop Vaganova as a dancer. His reviews made her realise that the 'sweetness' of dance was not for her. 'Instead she must make her movements wider and freer.'[18] Volynsky's admiration grew daily, as he saw her progress. D. Talnikov writes in his book *Vaganova, The Dancer*:

> [Vaganova] smoothly bent her leg out to the side, even more courageously than usual, to the level of the waist. The cavalier (Legat) bent her body to one side and then to the other, making her own movements in the air freer. These big *battements* to the side precisely fitted the music, allowing nothing to be lost, not even the smallest detail. 'Every musical nuance is perfectly reflected in movement.'[19]

Spellbound, Volynsky concluded that

> to appreciate, in the correct way, the artist's art and to comprehend it as a whole with all the technical possibilities, it is necessary to see the dancer's performance of her variations separately from her cavalier. These variations performed by Vaganova will remain forever among the legends of ballet art. Moreover, it would be fitting to add the name of Vaganova to some of them in

order to immortalise her wonderful talent in these roles for future generations of ballet artists.[20]

The formal aspect was vital to Volynsky. He stressed that the beauty of Vaganova's dance was that it was always complete and perfect, her technique so deeply ingrained that she never had to make emergency improvisations. For Volynsky, technique was not simply a formal element of ballet, but the very medium through which the art expressed itself. That technique had to be learned; therefore it was almost inevitable that, after her performing career ended, Vaganova would become a teacher at his school.

Vaganova began to teach in 1918, shortly after her husband Andrei Alexanderovitch had committed suicide – shooting himself in front of the family's Christmas tree. Vaganova had to provide for her son and for her sister's two orphaned children; so, as well as teaching at the School of Russian Ballet, she took other small jobs, such as dancing in cinemas. Patriotic and, determined never to leave Russia, she turned down a well-paid job in Denmark.

Vaganova worked right from the start on the development of a method in which she analysed the old Imperial Theatre's two schools of thought and training: the French lyrical plasticity espoused by Legat and Johansson, and the ostentatiously acrobatic Italian style of which Enrico Cecchetti was the chief exponent. She tried to synthesise the best of both systems in a specifically Russian method that did not isolate the separate parts of the body, but trained the dancer to use the body as a harmonious whole. The teaching system's strength lay in its precise instructions for placing the body, based on her own studies of the skeleton and musculature.

Vaganova thought that the French school's graceful, understated movements were often unnecessarily decorative. The arms, for example, could be beautifully placed with soft, low elbows and elegantly extended fingers; but although they looked graceful, they lacked energy and – mannered and stiff – contributed nothing technically. The Italian school placed great weight on virtuosity and technique. Ballerinas, for instance, were drilled to execute thirty-two *fouettés* (whipping turns) on the spot. Dancers trained in this way had good balance, dynamic turns and strong feet, but often lacked artistry: the arms, for example, were 'broken' at the elbow or over-extended.

Alexander Pushkin, later to become famous as the teacher of Rudolph Nureyev and Mikhail Baryshnikov, was Volkova's favourite partner at the School of Russian Ballet. Apart from the lessons at the School, he and Volkova studied privately with Vaganova at the teacher's flat in No. 7 Bronnitskaya Street, across the Fontanka Canal in the Haymarket district where Dostoevsky's *Crime and Punishment* is set.

Vaganova taught Volkova and Pushkin at reduced rates in return for their help with her experiments, and it was in these that Volkova began to grasp the profound logic of Vaganova's developing method. 'She would give us what she called "Italyansky" *port de bras* with "Frantsusky" allegro steps in a search for a new formula', Volkova remembered, 'and if the combination didn't work she would moderate the idea or try something new.'[21]

Volkova also watched Vaganova give private lessons to the ballerina Olga Spessivtseva. They made an unforgettable impression.

> Vaganova composed an adagio for Spessivtseva, and when she had danced it Vaganova turned round and whispered to me: 'It should have been *pirouette en attitude en dedans*, not *en dehors*. It should have been *1st arabesque*, not *2nd arabesque*, but it was so beautiful that I didn't have the heart to stop her.'[22]

Later, Vaganova rehearsed Spessivtseva in a variation from the ballet *Esmeralda*, in which the ballerina dances with a hand-mirror. After watching the lesson, Volkova, fascinated, hurried home and practised the solo in the kitchen with a frying pan.

'I never saw her apprehensive or nervous',[23] Volkova wrote in a 1951 tribute to Vaganova, her great role model. Volkova loved to say that, as a young pupil at the School of Russian Ballet, she 'drank from the fountain'. Vaganova eventually became the Soviet Union's most famous ballet teacher, and her teaching principles have influenced ballet training all over the world, including Volkova's, since the 1930s.

'[Vaganova] had a natural dignity and authority and the only possible attitude to her was deep respect', Volkova remembered.

> From the moment she walked in, the classroom assumed the atmosphere of a cathedral with a ritual about to begin. She was patient, acutely attentive to detail and most methodical ... The most memorable thing about her appearance was her eyes. They were large, blue, unemotional – the eyes of a craftsman rather than of an artist. Her steady gaze seemed always to follow one about, missing nothing. Otherwise her appearance was unremarkable except for her elegant ankles and feet. Her large-featured face was the reverse of conventional good looks, but was infused with intelligence.[24]

To Volkova, Vaganova was both the scientist and the demanding teacher. She was inscrutable by nature and sparing with praise, but Volkova remembered a special smile that occasionally revealed her delight at a pupil's accomplishment.

> She had two smiles. One, the gracious one (at the end of the class) with which a Queen dismisses her Court; the other a smile of real happiness that

occasionally lit up her face when she saw in some pupil a movement of quality ... To see that strong face with its serious eyes transformed by a childlike smile, accompanied by an approving nod, was an experience not easily forgotten. She seldom praised anybody with words or went so far as to say, 'That is good.' Her greatest tribute to a dancer would be to say, 'You are now ready to do that step in public.'[25]

Volkova was soon convinced that Vaganova's teaching was based on sound principles:

Vaganova had the greatest respect for tradition. Often she would quote the masters from the past – a favourite comment was Johansson's 'On the *plié* and *relévé* is based the whole structure of the classical ballet'. Her comments were often unusual. Once she opened a new conception to me by saying, 'It is not enough to do an attitude, you must become an attitude.'[26]

'Vaganova was unpredictable but she was an experimenter', Volkova thought, 'and, perhaps because she was ugly, she admired beauty in others and loved to bring it to flower.'[27]

Volkova developed a close relationship with another of the School's teachers, Maria Romanova, a principal dancer at the Maryinsky Theatre. Besides dancing at the Maryinsky, renamed the State Academic Theatre for Opera and Ballet (the GATOB), Romanova also performed with her husband in Petrograd's cinemas in the intervals between film shows. Volkova often went along to accompany their daughter, Galina Ulanova, who was also a pupil at Volynsky's School and would become the Soviet Union's most famous ballerina.

Although Volkova thought Romanova's teaching less methodical than Vaganova's, she recognised that it inspired a great joy in dancing in her students and that Romanova had a rare ability to spot each pupil's individual talents. She was interested in line and the poetic quality of movement, which especially appealed to Volkova.

The dance had existential importance for Volkova, giving her a feeling of freedom and of being alive. The discipline required, the daily training that aims to give the pupil complete control over every muscle and every movement, became a fixed point in her chaotic world.

Igor Stravinsky observed that classical ballet represents 'the triumph of learnt understanding over what is casually acquired, rule over arbitrariness, and order over chaos.' It is clear, balanced and majestic, and, like few other art forms, driven by a striving for ideal beauty. It is, in many ways, a form of controlled escape: flight without the fear of losing touch with the ground forever. It aspires to something higher and, in dance, Volkova, artistic and profound, could express the inner voices of her body when words failed, or when she was afraid to put her feelings into words.

Dance communicated the secret messages of the flesh, everything the body remembered and spoke of. Though shy and intensely private, Volkova was not frightened by the means of expression dance opened up to her – it fulfilled her, precisely because it was at once private and public. Dance made food shortages, poverty and family crises fade into the background. With ballet as her focal point, she survived her teenage years believing that art would help her transcend the harshness and turbulence of the real world around her.

1. The Volkov family lived on what is now called Kutuzov Embankment, in a first-floor apartment in this long, two-storey terracotta mansion with sweeping views over the River Neva to Peter the Great's first home in his new capital, and to the Peter and Paul Fortress.

Photographer: Charlotte Munch Bengtsen.

2. Volkova (standing) and her elder sister Irina were pupils at the Smolny Institute, St Petersburg's school for young noblewomen, from September 1914 until it was closed in the October Revolution of 1917. This study of the sisters wearing the Smolny uniform is the only photograph to survive of Volkova as a child. It was probably taken in 1915.

Private collection.

3. The main building of the Smolny Institute for Noble Maidens. Trotsky and Lenin directed the October Revolution from the former school, founded by Catherine the Great, which they turned into the headquarters of the Bolshevik Central Committee and the Petrograd Soviet.

Photographer: Charlotte Munch Bengtsen.

4. Smolny girls were known as 'the brides of the Tsar' but the popular idea that they were delicate and spoilt was far from the truth. The school focused on social formalities, its régime encouraged – demanded – iron self-discipline; and, in general, its alumnae grew up to be strong, energetic, independent and confident.

Photographer unknown.

5. Volkova took her first dancing lessons at the Smolny Institute, from an old French dancing master clad in the livery of the Ancien Régime. Once a week he taught the girls the minuet, gavotte and lancers in the Institute's white-pillared ballroom.

Photographer unknown.

6. Akim Volynsky, philosopher, critic and founder of the School of Russian Ballet, was born a Jew, Haim Flesker, in 1861. He was educated at St Petersburg's Faculty of Law. By 1880, aged 19, he had already started his career as a critic.

Photograph courtesy of the St Petersburg State Museum of Theatre and Music.

7. Akim Volynsky with St Petersburg's most notorious poetess Zinaida Gippius. Volynsky and Gippius' husband, philosopher Dmitri Merezhkovsky, championed Russian Symbolism, a movement that revived themes from the Romantic era.

   Photograph courtesy of the St Petersburg State Museum of Theatre and Music.

8. Volynsky and Nikolai Legat, the Maryinsky Theatre's ballet master. Legat wrote: '...in Volynsky, I see a kind of Columbus in the field of classical ballet. I am absolutely convinced that future generations will acknowledge A.L. Volynsky as a theoretician who will stand higher than Noverre and Blasis!'

Photograph courtesy of the St Petersburg State Museum of Theatre and Music.

9. The School of Russian Ballet had nearly a hundred students, thirty of whom were boarders. This photograph shows Volynsky with the School's youngest pupils, the girls dressed in simple, Grecian-style tunics and wearing hair bands.

Photograph courtesy of the St Petersburg State Museum of Theatre and Music.

10. Volkova's class at the School of Russian Ballet. She is fourth from the left in the second row from the back. Her partner Konstantin Muller thought she was 'a lovely dancer, lyrical, beautiful in the Spessivtseva style'.

Private collection.

11. The School of Russian Ballet was housed in a building behind the House of Arts and performances took place in Volynsky's cinema The Bright Reel, an ornate 19th Century Neoclassical structure on Nevskii Prospekt and Bolshaia Morskaia Ulitsa. The film house still exists and is now known as the Barrikada Cinema.

Photographer: Charlotte Munch Bengtsen.

12. Physically, Volkova resembled her great idol, Olga Spessivtseva, and even copied the ballerina's characteristic centre-parted hairstyle. This picture, probably taken around 1925, is from a photograph of Volkova's class at the School of Russian Ballet.

Photograph courtesy of the Royal Ballet School Archives, the Vera Volkova Collection.

13. This portrait from Volkova's time at the School of Russian Ballet has something deeply melancholic about it, yet also something intense and erotic. One finger touches the pulse point at her throat, evoking an image of Leda and the Swan.

Photograph courtesy of the Royal Ballet School Archives, the Vera Volkova Collection.

14. In this promotional postcard from Shanghai, Volkova looks like a film star, playing the sensual diva to perfection. She gazes half over her shoulder, as if at something – or someone – following her. Half-smiling, she seems poised to run...

   Photograph courtesy of the Royal Ballet School Archives, the Vera Volkova Collection.

15. Volkova danced with Sergei Toropov and Georgi Goncharov as The Olympic Trio in Shanghai's most exclusive cabaret, at the Hotel Majestic in Nanking Road. The three Russians hoped to get to Europe and join Serge Diaghilev's Ballets Russes.

Private collection.

16. After the Olympic Trio broke up, Volkova worked in a dress shop and as a model to support herself and help her family in Leningrad. Georgi Goncharov started teaching. When Volkova visited one of his classes she made a great impression on one of his pupils, 11-year-old Peggy Hookham, who remembered that 'the vision she presented gave me my first inkling of what a ballerina should be'.

Photograph courtesy of the Royal Ballet School Archives, the Vera Volkova Collection.

17. A private photo of Volkova, Goncharov, the architect Emmanuel Gran and a woman friend speaks of Volkova's sadness and isolation in Shanghai. Toropov had returned to Russia, where he had been executed.

Photograph courtesy of the Royal Ballet School Archives, the Vera Volkova Collection.

The Petrograd Intelligentsia

Seeing their idols at the GATOB was the ultimate reward for the aspiring dancers of the School of Russian Ballet – experiencing the rapture inspired by the performances and being part of the excitement of the whole event. The Theatre had no box office: tickets were distributed through factories, organisations and associations, and sometimes pupils would be given free tickets. But there was also a lively black market at the Theatre's main entrance, for those who could scrape together the few kopeks for a ticket, and in this way Volkova managed to see her teacher Maria Romanova dance the Lilac Fairy in *The Sleeping Beauty*.

There were also countless small concerts in restaurants and cinemas, which Petrograd's 'desperadoes', young people obsessed by art, could attend. The great but ageing ballerina Olga Preobrazhenskaya, who also taught at the School of Russian Ballet, danced at the Philharmonic. One year, an impresario arranged a competition between four leading ballerinas and their partners at the Great Drama Theatre at Moika Canal.

Spessivtseva, whom Volkova had seen in *Giselle* and *La Bayadère*, was Petrograd's greatest, most individual ballerina. She lived as an ephemeral, divine figure in the city's romantically tinted imagination, and danced almost exclusively tragic roles. A woman of few words, she dressed like a nun in black robes that concealed her femininity and added to her mystery.

Dimitri Shostakovich was one of the charismatic dancer's many obsessive fans: 'I saw O.A. Spessivtseva in the box and I was stunned', he wrote to the critic Valerian Bogdanov-Berezovsky. 'Do you know who she reminded me of? A heroine out of Maupassant.'[28] To the smitten Shostakovich, she also brought to mind a character in a poem by Anna Akhmatova.

Even Volynsky had immediately been struck by Spessivtseva's beauty when he first saw her at her début in 1913. He noted her 'finely proportioned figure, the slightly long face surrounded by dark hair and the mat brilliance of her eyes under the thick eyelashes'. He appreciated her 'highly arched feet' and adored her personal style of dancing: 'dreamy and slightly over-refined ... redolent of Taglioni'.[29]

When he found that she, in return, was fascinated by him and his ideas about art – and was easily influenced – his enthusiasm redoubled, and the dancer and the critic became friends.

His credo, that ballet was a 'religious ritual', became hers as well; some believe it was this conviction that gave her dance its special quality. Against this, Spessivtseva's mother thought that Volynsky's influence was destructive, and feared that her dangerously highly-strung daughter would be driven to madness by his heady talk of God and the Devil, mysticism and the cosmos.

The Russian critic Yuri Slonimsky has written of Spessivtseva's definitive interpretation of her greatest role, Giselle, that from her first entrance she gave the audience an immediate, unforgettable sense of imminent disaster. 'She was in love', Slonimsky wrote 'and this passion was the cause of her suffering.'

> She fought for a love that sentenced her to destruction. Spessivtseva's eyes, which were wide open at the beginning of the first act, were closed at the end. A lonely, broken and traumatised being haunted the stage. In the second act Spessivtseva danced with half-closed eyes, as if she dared not see what was going on around her. The beauty of Spessivtseva's heroine grew simultaneously with Giselle's fight for happiness. Another person's happiness, not her own.[30]

Old photographs show Spessivtseva rising from the grave with her palms pressed against her body as if she is trying to protect her soul.

In 1921 Spessivtseva became involved with Boris Kaplun, a member of the secret police, the Cheka, and a dangerous, sadistic man. Kaplun persuaded her to inaugurate a Petrograd crematorium, and some said that he had forced her to watch the victims of the Red Terror burn there in the dead of night. Others believed that she, irresponsible, malicious and profane, had enjoyed the grisly spectacle, and informed against members of the aristocracy and bourgeoisie, receiving their jewellery in return for her treachery.

Jealous of their relationship, Kaplun forbade Spessivtseva to see Volynsky, and warned the older man to keep away from her on pain of death.

The gifted but troubled ballerina eventually escaped Kaplun and Soviet Russia to dance in the West with Diaghilev and the Paris Opéra Ballet, but her pattern of disastrous relationships with abusive men continued. Her mind shattered, she was admitted to a mental hospital outside Paris during World War II and never danced again.

Volkova finished her formal education at the 23rd Ordinary Worker's School in 1922 and became a full-time pupil at the School of Russian Ballet, which had just moved into new and bigger premises at 14 Gertsen Street, behind the House of Arts.

Spessivtseva's break with Volynsky directly influenced Volkova's future. Volkova, now seventeen, looked remarkably like Spessivtseva: she had the same mouth, the same eyes and the same line, all of which Volynsky noticed in his search to replace the disciple and physical ideal he had lost. Volkova even copied Spessivtseva's characteristic centre-parted hairstyle.

'Volkova's beautiful profile stands out, framed by gentle curls in a clever hair-style',[31] wrote Volynsky of his new protégée following a school performance, in which she had been one of the four little swans in a dance staged by Maria Romanova.

He also noted her potential as a dancer in a performance of an adagio choreographed by Romanova to Massenet's *Méditation*:

> [The work] is presented in a classroom manner, designed as such by Romanova. Again the execution of the work is disciplined, correct and harmonious, conceived without a break. All the dancers deserve warm praise: Ulanova, Prelatova, Thaisia Alekseeva, Shekulova and Kulagina. But Volkova and Nikolaeva are in a special category. Volkova is well suited for *pas de deux* work; she is supple and adept in all *développé* motifs and *renversé* turns as well as extended arabesques, attitudes and *tire-bouchons*.[32]

Equally importantly, he soon found that Volkova was not just intelligent, well brought up, strong-willed and talented – she was also still malleable. Both Spessivtseva and Volkova were fatherless and, like the young Spessivtseva, Volkova was receptive to the older man's spellbinding talk about art and its existential significance. She was hungry for it, and took it all in 'to bridge some of the yawning gaps in my education'.[33]

The world the critic opened up to his student added a new dimension to her daily training at the School. He visited her after class, and took her to concerts, lectures, debates and exhibitions. He was her guide to Petrograd's museums and, like her, he could talk about ballet for hours. The author Konstantin Fedin said that Volynsky's style when he lectured in that way was 'theatrical and pompous'. His language combined 'scientific discourse with mumblings about love, and laboratory analysis with religious ritual'.[34]

In their various ways, both were products of a lost age: Volkova with her Smolny background, Volynsky fascinated by nineteenth-century culture. Volynsky once praised Volkova's grace, which he attributed to her sewing lessons at school. He thought all girls should take lessons in sewing or weaving, so that they would learn to carry their necks gracefully as they bent over their work.

He gave Volkova her high standards. He had idealistic notions about the directions in which individual dancers could develop. Should that development not take place, he would make it painfully obvious, and it was often the most talented artists who felt his disappointment most keenly. Volkova inherited his rigour, though in a milder form. As a teacher, her ability to sense what the dancers she was working with could become was one of her most precious attributes.

Volynsky's knowledge and example shaped Volkova's aesthetics, and he became her primary influence, in many ways a greater one than her teachers, Romanova and Vaganova. But, like Spessivtseva's mother, Maria Volkova was worried about her daughter's connection with Volynsky, although more concerned for her safety than for her state of mind: she thought it dangerous for her to be seen with the critic, who was a well-known figure in Petrograd and had many enemies, both political and professional. Volkova's friends at the School also wondered at the relationship between their colleague and the School's director. Volkova insisted that their relationship was purely platonic, sustained by a young woman's fascination for her mentor.

The brilliant, inspiring Volynsky who came to mean so much to her was a loner and, perhaps, also lonely. He was a strange, complex man, full of contradictions, driven by a passion for truth. A rationalist who pined for spirituality, a philosopher who dreamed about dancing, he seemed almost to live in accordance with Friedrich Nietzsche's words: 'I do not know what the spirit of a philosopher could more wish to be than a good dancer. For the dance is his ideal, also his fine art, finally also the only kind of piety he knows, his "divine service".'

Volynsky was born Haim Flekser, a Jew, in 1861. He was educated at St Petersburg's Faculty of Law. By 1880, as a 19-year-old, he had already started his career as a literary and art critic. After his first book, *The Russian Critics*, he wrote a monumental study of Leonardo da Vinci, which attracted international attention and won him the Freedom of the City of Milan. He studied Renaissance art and Rembrandt, while working as literary editor to the Russian *Financial Times* and for two publishing houses, World Literature and Parthenon.

Alongside the philosopher Dmitri Merezhkovsky, Volynsky championed Russian Symbolism, a movement that revived themes from the Romantic era, and opposed Realism and Positivism. Based on an idealistic view of the world, Russian Symbolism was characterised by Romantic irony, mysticism and unfettered imagination, and had arisen as a reaction to the previous generation's lack of spirituality and creativity.

The Symbolists insisted that art was by definition symbolic in its quest to achieve the Absolute, the 'noumenal' in Immanuel Kant's philosophy. Their artistic motto was 'from the realistic to the super-realistic'. Some of the Symbolists were also inspired by the French authors Baudelaire, Mallarmé and Verlaine, and were fascinated by death and decay. At the beginning of the twentieth century they were known as the Decadents. Akim Volynsky was one of them.

His contemporaries were astonished by his theological interests, particularly his keen interest in Christianity, which developed in the

1890s when he wrote a series of long analyses of religious themes in Dostoevsky's work. In 1901, Merezhkovsky's wife Zinaida Gippius initiated a series of religious-philosophical meetings, and launched the journal *New Paths*. The journal published summaries of the discussions at the meetings, as well as works by various Symbolist authors, including Alexander Blok, Andrei Bely and Fyodor Sologub. Volynsky belonged to the circle.

At the beginning of the twentieth century, the Jewish Volynsky was a frequent visitor to one of the Orthodox Church's holiest places – the Greek peninsula of Athos. Only men were admitted to Athos, where the monks live a spartan life of religious contemplation. Volynsky spent long periods in a number of monasteries, studying Byzantine art and icon painting.

Later, during 1920–24, Volynsky was the Chairman of Petrograd's Writers Union, and a founding member of the Individualist Serapion Brotherhood, a group of talented young authors who insisted that they would allow no political interference in art. Volynsky believed that any artist's greatest talent is 'the ability to mould the materials of the outer world ... into images of a precisely apprehended inner world', and this is what the Brotherhood sought to develop. It took its name from a figure in E.T.A. Hoffmann's novel *The Sandman* in which the hermit Serapion appears, uninvited, in an unknown family's home and disrupts its idyllic existence. Serapion stands for the subconscious pushing its way into the foreground, and exemplifies Hoffmann's 'Serapiontic principle'.

Volynsky lived in the House of Arts, an artists' college in the old Eliseev Palace by the Moika Canal, with Osip Mandelstam and a number of the other great literary figures of the Russian Silver Age. The House of Arts became known as the Ship of Fools, because its days, and the days of everything it stood for, were numbered. One contemporary writer, Boris Eikhenbaum, thought that,

> in the House of Arts (on the Moika), which was then the Noah's ark for writers who had been saved from the Flood, Volynsky appeared to be Noah himself, the helmsman of this frail vessel which did not know where it was sailing ... [35]

The central heating had broken down and Volynsky lived in Madame Eliseeva's old room, one of the coldest. It was next to the library, which was never heated at all. Touching the books was like handling frozen iron but the collection was vast, so Volynsky and the other residents did not have to leave the house to do their research. When Volynsky was not writing, he stayed in bed all day, shivering and studying the sun, clouds, chubby cupids and long garlands painted on the ceiling. In the evening, he and the others would meet in the kitchen for endless debates with Efim, the Eliseev family's old servant – a clever and friendly man, though mainly interested in his pet pig, which scurried in and out between the aesthetes' legs.

Like Volkova, the author Nina Berberova was a frequent visitor to the House of Arts, where her future husband Khodasevich lived. Berberova remembered her visits there vividly.

> Aleksandr Benois (at that time with a large beard) and his brother, Albert Nikolaevich, sat at two concert pianos at different ends of the hall, and a Strauss waltz thundered out from the raised lids. Sun sparkled on the gilding, the four-hundred-pound chandeliers rang out and the Stroganov Palace looked in on us through the windows, a red flag over its decaying entrance... Akim Volynsky, lean-faced, frightfully slim, in a hand-me-down coat (or had he grown that thin?) kissed my hand. Gods dwelt here, and I was visiting gods. The gods played Strauss and ate biscuits. I danced among the gods, and Eliseev's cupids watched me from the ceiling.[36]

She described Volynsky 'as one of the most miserable figures of revolutionary and literary Petrograd'. He slept, she remembered, 'not only in a fur coat and fur cap but in galoshes as well'. Nonetheless, Volynsky gave Berberova the impression that

> he was still interested in women, in spite of his misery. He was an 'aesthete' and loved Beauty in the old (Symbolist) meaning of the word. And there was not much beauty left in Petrograd in 1922. Probably only the city itself, and the very young girls.[37]

Akim Volynsky worshipped *Sophia*, the divine concept of feminine beauty and wisdom, and found its most exalted expression in the female Russian ballet dancer, whom he compared to a swan.[38]

Rejection of ballet as an art form was widespread among the intelligentsia in 1920s Petrograd. Even Chekhov had said, 'I don't understand ballet. The only thing I know is that the ballerinas stink like horses in the intervals.' In spite of this trend, towering figures in the arts such as Mandelstam and Akhmatova continued to go to the ballet.

Volynsky had been introduced to ballet at the ballerina Kchessinska's fashionable salons. He did not begin to write about the art form until 1911, when he was 50, after attending performances over a number of years. Berberova remembered that at that time

> everybody was shocked that a philosopher had switched his interest to ballet. But he was very serious about it and did not argue with the 'Victorians' who did not think ballet a worthy topic.[39]

Volynsky applied himself to learning about classical ballet technique from Nikolai Legat and even took ballet classes with him, despite his age.

Based on his observations, he analysed the rules and vocabulary of classical ballet from an aesthetic perspective, drawing parallels with other arts and sciences, and formulating, for the first time, a prescriptive philosophy of dance. He imbued the ballet position *croisé* with the qualities of concentration and compression, and *effacé* with openness and freedom, pointing out how these opposing states also can be found in nature, psychology and human physiology.

On the same basis, he analysed positions and movements such as turnout, verticality, point work, *port de bras*, *battement*, *rond de jambe* and elevation in his quest for 'the Absolute Idea' underlying each movement.

Inspired by Kant, Volynsky believed in the power of 'apperception': a dancer had to have a degree of self-awareness in order to express an inner emotion through the external means of a dance movement. The inner spirit both inspires the movement and is expressed by it. Apperception is the spirit's instrument, and manifests itself, for example, in outwardly turned positions or in verticality.

'What we can discern about the hands, we can also see in the eyes', Volynsky lectured:

> They are always as if closed, looking inward, looking and not seeing what is happening around them. Then an act of will occurs, 'apperception' as it is called in psychology, and the eyes that were not shut, but not watching, open in actuality. They look and see.

He continued:

> Classical dance demands that all surfaces of the body be open. The face, the eyes, the hands, and even the back must discard the closed, the inward. If, in this sense, the face be open, but not the eyes, the overall impression of the dance will be imperfect. The eyes must always perceive and vitally penetrate the surroundings, nor may they remain in a state of passivity and indifference. Insofar as the body turns in every direction and opens 'outwards', it will be accessible to the rays of the spiritual, an instrument of ardour. In the dance, it plays constantly with its flaming tongues of fire.
>
> People with no understanding of ballet often say that it lacks emotion and temperament, which is, of course, a grave misunderstanding. As in no other art, one cannot, in the ballet, take even a single step without setting in motion the entire flaming mechanism, not of a lower, but of a higher nature. Only he can experience it, whose body glows as a fire, and who opens wide all the gates, windows and vistas of his soul, turning them 'outwards'. This is the true love of ballet, not the balletomania behind which are concealed profanation, viciousness and blasphemy.[40]

The Russian historian Vera Krassovskaya has written that Volynsky's 'absolute vigilance was in the same category as the absolute musical ear [perfect pitch]'. And even if dancers and choreographers often felt harshly treated or were angry with him, 'they always took note of his opinions'.[41]

In 1922 many ballet dancers, and probably many ballet-goers, found it extremely difficult to understand Volynsky's theories. Volkova, however, was fascinated, and it made a special impression on her when he explained his ideas by referring to Renaissance painters such as Raphael and Leonardo. She came to believe that classical ballet is as intensely technical as it is deeply personal. As a teacher, she used Volynsky's theories and analytical tools in her quest to bring out the individual expression of each of the dancers she worked with.

Legat also believed that Volynsky had grasped something essential, and wrote:

> ...in Volynsky, I see a kind of Columbus in the field of classical ballet. I am absolutely convinced that future generations will acknowledge A.L. Volynsky as a theoretician who will stand higher than Noverre and Blasis![42]

In June 1922, in an open letter to *The Life of Art* about Petrograd's State Choreographical Technical School, Legat wrote that

> particularly the teachers of classical dance do not possess enough knowledge for teaching ... I have myself observed that the school's pupils do not know even the most basic things. They do not know the classical laws ... The performance is flat, without *épaulement* ... I am personally convinced that the Maryinsky Theatre's school and the School of Russian Ballet should be united under Volynsky's leadership.[43]

Legat's letter did not lead to a merger of the two schools, though Fyodor Lopukhov, the GATOB's new Artistic Director, admitted that the dancers in his company and at the school were 'badly educated, even if they know how they should wear a ballet costume and conscientiously execute their steps'.[44]

Volynsky himself described the students of the GATOB's school as 'soggy lumps of sugar', provoking the Theatre's manager Leonid Leontiev to spring to their defence. Leontiev praised his budding dancers as 'little heroes who stoically bore the difficulties and deprivations of last winter',[45] and attacked Volynsky, calling him a 'bourgeois' who came to the Theatre

> in a sheepskin coat and felt boots when it was two degrees above zero, as was the case this winter, and is surprised that people on stage, half-dressed in thin

pieces of fabric, have become inert and out of tune, dancing without temperament or imagination.[46]

Volynsky retaliated with a criticism of Vaganova, who had left the School of Russian Ballet and become a teacher at the State Choreographical Technical School: 'Pedagogy is not her strong point: she was always too individualist.'[47] By then, Vaganova and Volynsky had parted ways; they had disagreed about technical questions of aesthetic and expressive importance.

Vaganova focused in her teaching on what is called allegro technique – the rapid execution of small, quick steps. As a dancer, she had excelled in the technique, and now said that

> dance's method lies there, in all its complexity and future perfection ... All dance builds on the allegro. The adagio is not enough for me.[48]

Volynsky took the opposite view: he saw 'the whole art of classical dance ... assembled' in the adagio. Like the eighteenth-century ballet theoreticians Noverre and Blasis, he believed that a dancer's range and potential were best revealed in an adagio:

> Adagio is the 'poem of love' in the sculpture composed by two dancing figures. The expressive aspect of ballet's plasticity demands an enormous inner creative power – the axis of all ballet. In the adagio, the 'sufferings' and psychological motives of the movements and images find expression. The dancer moves from the adagio to the variation, free of inner tension.[49]

Russians define 'plasticity' as the series of almost sculptural poses of ideal beauty that dance creates. Musicians endeavour to produce pure notes, to give sound clarity, strength, form, depth and colour. Dancers attempt to do the same with movement.

Plasticity is seen most clearly in the adagio, the structured but flowing execution of a series of steps in slow tempo that should be interpreted as a whole – as one might experience an adagio movement in a sonata.

Volynsky believed it was here that one could identify the essence of the art; one could master the allegro only after having first understood and gained complete control by way of the adagio. To retain plasticity and form in, for example, an allegro variation, and to avoid the type of dancing where arms revolve like windmills, it is essential for the dancer to acquire optimum body control. This complete mastery makes possible the perfect and expressive execution of every single step, and enables the dancer to preserve an intense understanding of it even in rapid step combinations.

Volkova was an adagio dancer, which Volynsky appreciated. But 15 years later, in England and Denmark, her teaching straddled her two mentors' views of art. Volkova was interested in the allegro and its virtuoso possibilities, but wanted her pupils to master the technique by way of the adagio, as Volynsky had recommended.

In this way, Volkova-trained dancers acquired an understanding of plasticity that distinguished them from all others. Erik Bruhn, Henning Kronstam and Margot Fonteyn were typical products of this aspect of Volkova's teaching, which also came to characterise and define the Royal Danish Ballet's unique Bournonville style in the twentieth century.

Warning Bells and Poets Dying

Opera and ballet had been regarded with suspicion as decadent forms of art since the October Revolution of 1917. During the first half of the 1920s the intelligentsia and the classical arts came under renewed attack, led by the Bolshevik organisation Proletkult, which harboured a strong iconoclastic faction revelling in the destruction of the old world. The Futurist poet Vladimir Mayakovsky stated, 'It's time for bullets to pepper museums',[50] while Vladimir Kirillov wrote, 'In the name of our tomorrow we will burn Raphael, destroy the museum, and trample over Art.'[51]

One of the advocates of a new proletarian culture, Platon Kerzentsiev, thought that 'opera and ballet in their essence are more appropriate to an authoritarian regime and to a bourgeois hegemony',[52] and in 1922 the Government in Moscow discussed a proposal to close the GATOB. The Theatre was now described as not only unnecessary, but also reactionary and harmful to the proletariat.

Soviet leaders could not care less whether the allegro or the adagio was the litmus test for perfection in ballet, but – as if by a miracle – Commissar Lunacharsky saved the classical dance in the USSR. In a famous letter to Lenin, Lunacharsky wrote that

> literally the entire labouring population of Petrograd treasures the Maryinsky Theatre so much, since it has become an almost exclusively working-class theatre, that its closing will be perceived by the workers as a heavy blow.[53]

Lunacharsky, a sophisticated critic and dramatist whose plays ranged from the visionary and the epic to historical dramas such as *Oliver Cromwell*, encouraged innovation in art as a metaphor for political change, and advocated both relative freedom of expression and stylistic pluralism.

In this politically charged climate, Volynsky not only maintained, with characteristic stubbornness, his position as a traditionalist and a defender of the classical arts; he also opposed the new dictates of Soviet culture – internationalist, collectivist and proletarian – and uncompromisingly criticised the choreographic experiments encouraged under the regime.

According to the ballet historian Elisabeth Souritz:

> Volynsky consistently fought for the preservation of classical dance in its academic forms, objecting to any penetration of what seemed to him extraneous elements. And Volynsky recognised the right to abstraction only

through these forms. He celebrated the beauty of the lines of the classical arabesque and protested against its distortion.[54]

The critic resolutely rejected Boris Romanov's anti-classical works, that diverged ever more sharply from the foundations of academic dance. He found Romanov's expressionist productions, with their emphasis on the grotesque, to be lacking in clear ideas and harmonious discipline. In 1922, Leonid Leontiev choreographed a version of the biblical drama *Salomé* to music by Alexander Glazunov, as well as a series of concert numbers that, according to Volynsky, 'were strewn over the accumulated snowdrifts of ballet material like unnoticed snowflakes, melting on the spot'.[55] He was equally scathing about the creations of Fyodor Lopukhov, the recently appointed leader of the GATOB, who, like other avant-gardists, had a desire to change 'everything', but also had a deep respect for the old masters, especially Petipa.

Surprisingly, Volynsky particularly disliked Lopukhov's ambitiously staged, innovative 'dance symphony', *The Magnificence of the Universe*, an attempt to create a new abstract ballet genre danced to symphonic music. Lopukhov was fighting, after all, for 'self-sufficient' dance; he wanted to present the classics in all the wealth of their forms, bringing out the internal meaning of each movement: 'His very intention showed Volynsky's influence.'[56]

Much of the imagery used by Lopukhov in the programme notes was almost identical to Volynsky's own; but, according to Elizabeth Souritz, 'the production itself did not correspond to the ballet theoretician's idea of a ballet with self-contained choreography'.[57]

The Magnificence of the Universe has since become legendary, although it was only performed twice: once in a rehearsal hall at the GATOB in September 1922; and then after a *Swan Lake* benefit for the Theatre's corps de ballet on 7 March 1923. The audience greeted the second performance with total silence. One of the dancers, Nikolai Soliannikov, recalled:

> Instead of the usual roar of applause there was the silence of the tomb. The audience didn't clap, didn't laugh, didn't whistle. It was silent.[58]

Volynsky introduced his review of the performance with the words:

> Once a mediocre scribbler, who had shown some talent, dreamed of the magnificence of the universe. After he woke up, he set about turning his nocturnal visions into the images of his favourite ballet. The result was a dance symphony, the likes of which the world has never seen.[59]

But the work was passionately defended by the avant-garde critics Asafiev and Sollertinsky, and by the young dancer Georgi Balanchivadze, who had danced in the production. Balanchivadze, who later became famous in the West as George Balanchine, used elements from *The Magnificence of the Universe* in his abstract ballet *Serenade*, which he created when he went to America in 1934.

Balanchivadze had only recently begun to choreograph and had several times fallen victim to Volynsky's sarcastic pen. For instance, Volynsky had dismissed one of his dance numbers by writing, 'He is treading the Petrograd stages in a specific type of piquant, unbridled dance.'[60]

Despite his youth, Balanchivadze could be as ruthless as the ageing critic, and retorted by reviewing one of the School of Russian Ballet's student performances in the magazine *Teatr*. Like Volynsky, Balanchivadze alluded to literature in his title, here to a character in Nikolai Gogol's comedy *The Government Inspector*, calling his review, 'The junior officer's widow – or how A.L. Volynsky whips himself'.[61] The angry dancer described the students as 'provincially saccharine shop clerks with pretensions to solo roles'.[62] He continued in a parody of Volynsky's own style: 'It lacks the basic rules of classicism ... It all creates a depressing impression.'[63]

Balanchivadze's attack on Volynsky was followed by another satirical article called 'The degeneration of the theatre. Terrible events at the ballet.' The article was a 'nightmarish tragedy' about the Maryinsky Theatre with Volynsky as Director.

On 23 October 1922, the GATOB's ballet company and representatives of its ballet school were summoned to a conference on Volynsky's criticism in Petrograd's theatre museum. At the meeting, GATOB Administrative Director I.V. Exkusovich concluded, predictably, that the Petrograd Ballet's performances

> had not lost anything in quality compared with pre-war standards, despite the extremely difficult conditions and unexpected complications.[64]

The continuing battle, known as the War of the Roses, was between the traditionalists, represented by Volynsky and Legat, and the reformists, personified by Fokine. It had been rumbling on since Petipa retired in 1903 and continued even after both Fokine and Legat had left the country.

Fokine had emigrated in 1918, and in the autumn of 1922 Legat admitted defeat when he finally realised that he would never become leader of the GATOB, and that there was no future for classical ballet, as he saw it, in the Soviet Union. He and his wife Nadina Nikolaeva left the country, and the disappointed Volynsky commented on Legat's exile in the *Petrograd Evening News*:

N. Legat and his wife N. Nicolaeva left this country and rushed towards the 'Yellow Demon' [Money]. It is regrettable that these two artists have left the country for good, as apparently they are not coming back. They will never be satisfied with their work abroad, for they will never find, in Europe, another country such as ours, where art is art, and one can work and live for art's sake. The money rush of the West has killed any possibilities of promoting art, and art is commercialised today like any other business.[65]

His words were prophetic: the Legats were restless and unhappy in Europe, where they finally settled in London and opened a ballet school. But it must also have seemed as if Volynsky's own fate had been sealed. Legat's exile and the loss of this respected ballet-master and ally significantly weakened Volynsky's position: he had lost all support at the GATOB, and there was no longer anyone to back his bid for a job at the Theatre or its ballet school.

Volynsky had gradually isolated himself not only from the political establishment, but also from a considerable part of the Petrograd ballet world. His life-consuming struggle for the understanding of ballet now seemed hopeless.

Apart from the staging of *The Magnificence of the Universe*, Lopukhov had revived Marius Petipa's magnum opus *The Sleeping Beauty* to music by Tchaikovsky. In an article entitled 'Lousy house painter' – a reference to Pushkin's words, 'It's not funny, when a lousy house painter ruins Raphael's Madonna for me'[66] – Volynsky poured scorn on Lopukhov's work as 'conservator', and on his revisions of Petipa's original choreography.

Volynsky knew the ballet inside out. He had studied it in 1914, and described in minute detail scenes from the old production.[67] He argued convincingly that

the entire picture was built on the *plastique* of the play of lines, on the combination of figures according to some specific principle, so that the smallest deviation from the picture described inevitably destroys the poetic effect of the whole act.[68]

Lopukhov was far less devoted to preserving the original work; his production became a watershed, creating a historical precedent. From then on, it became common practice to alter choreographic variations, or to cut or add entire new scenes and dances. At the time, there was no fully worked-out notation system in ballet, and choreography was simply handed down from dancer to dancer. What Lopukhov did was the equivalent of a composer's deciding to alter Beethoven's *Fifth Symphony*, and then destroying the original score. Volynsky felt Lopukhov had watered down Petipa's general vision, and felt compelled to react.

In the article 'Call an Ambulance!' he wrote that the task of reviving *The Sleeping Beauty* should have been entrusted to a first-class instructor such as N.G. Sergeyev (the ballet-master who later restaged Petipa's ballets for Ninette de Valois's Sadler's Wells Ballet in London). But:

> Sergeyev has been thrown out in recent years, cast off to some Riga by his self-styled pretentious replacement. All the variations in *The Sleeping Beauty* should be in their place. The soul must be returned to the corps de ballet numbers, the height of perfection and collective poetry in this choreographic creation, to achieve their harmonic effects.[69]

Volynsky again deplored Legat's departure. He, too, could have revived *The Sleeping Beauty*, but '[Legat] did not wish to work in the atmosphere of the current state ballet'. In Volynsky's opinion, the situation amounted to 'criminal neglect of primary obligations to the stage and art'. He regretted the loss of the many talented dancers who now worked for Diaghilev and other impresarios – 'travelling salesmen of commercial art' – on the European stages. But there was no indication that Volynsky himself would resign:

> Of course there's no point in folding one's hands. It is necessary to work. Sharp criticism should be turned on oneself.
>
> Great works are not done by means of diplomatic compromises or the well-intentioned smoothing of long-standing and useful conflicts with soothing conciliatory balms. One must hold the lash of criticism in one's hand when the lash of historical revenge already whistles over our heads. The moment is too serious, too tragic. It demands will, character and special action. For ballet is such an asset, such a unique and global pearl of Russia, that no one would ever forgive its loss from the nation's treasury. I speak now as a friend. There is nothing hostile in my words. But as a zealot of classical traditions, I insist on the necessary and immediate cleaning of the Augean stables of the ballet theatre. Seeing a falling hero, I call the ambulance.[70]

Misfortune followed misfortune. At the time of his confrontation with the public and the authorities regarding his criticism of the GATOB, he published a controversial anthology that included texts by Goethe, and the shunned writers Bely and Anna Akhmatova.[71]

A few weeks later, the House of Arts was closed, having, as Vladislav Khodasevich put it, 'sailed like a ship through darkness, storm and rain'. In September, several hundred intellectuals were expelled from Soviet Russia, and the residents of the House of Arts scattered in all directions.

Nina Berberova, Khodasevich and a number of other writers emigrated voluntarily. The old Symbolist Fyodor Sologub applied for an exit visa; when it was refused, his wife drowned herself in the Neva in despair and he stopped writing. Yuri Yurkin, Vladimir Narbut and Isaak Babel were executed, Mandelstam died in a Siberian prison camp, and other artists connected with the House of Arts, including Anna Akhmatova, were forbidden to write.

Those who survived and were allowed to continue their work, including Volynsky, struggled to make ends meet and to derive some meaning from the events around them. Later, Nina Berberova explained it as follows:

> I see now that the annihilation of the intelligentsia did not take a straight path but a crooked one, through a brief period of growth; the path was not simple, and some bloomed and perished at the same time ...[72]

Volynsky wrote three books elaborating his theories: *Problems in the Russian Ballet* was published in 1923, followed by *The Alphabet of Classical Ballet* (Leningrad, 1925) and *The Book of Exultation* (Leningrad, 1925). *The Alphabet of Classical Ballet* foreshadows Vaganova's *Fundamentals of the Classic Dance* (Leningrad, 1934), but whereas Vaganova's epoch-making work deals exclusively with practical issues of technique and training, Volynsky's books, which have never been published in their entirety in English, also seek to explain the expression and significance of dance. *The Book of Exultation* is dedicated to the pupils of the School of Russian Ballet, and is based on notes from the lectures Volynsky gave at the School, as well as his day-to-day notations.

In 1923 he opened a cinema in the block where the House of Arts had been. The cinema still stands, on the corner of Nevsky Prospect and Gertsen Street, and is now called the Barrikada Cinema. Volynsky named it the Bright Reel, and Shostakovich supplied musical accompaniment. Shostakovich's father had just died and the 18-year-old took the job for two months towards the end of 1923 to support his family.

He was, however, badly let down. Typically, Volynsky had no funds to pay him. When Shostakovich approached him deferentially about the problem the emaciated aesthete, glaring through his giant monocle, delivered a stinging reprimand: 'Young man, do you love art? Great, lofty, immortal art?'

According to Shostakovich, Volynsky then made him

> a beautiful speech, itself an example of high art. It was passionate, inspired, a speech about great immortal art, and its point was that I shouldn't ask Volynsky for my pay. In doing so I defiled art, he explained, bringing it down to my level of crudity, avarice, and greed. Art was endangered. It could perish if I pressed my outrageous demands.[73]

Shostakovich thereafter read Volynsky's 'high-flown articles on ballet and other exalted matters' with 'revulsion'.

The purpose of the cinema was to fund Volynsky's School of Russian Ballet, which was impoverished even after it acquired the status of a 'choreographic technical school' in 1924, becoming a state-approved institution on a par with the Petrograd State Choreographic Technical School. Since it had moved to Gertsen Street, off Nevsky Prospect, the School had grown steadily, and now had nearly a hundred students. Thirty were boarders, cared for by the mother of Volkova's classmate Inna German, who lived in a flat in the same street as the School.

Shostakovich and other of Volynsky's opponents derided the school as 'Volynsky's harem', but Volkova later said that she had presumed her mentor was homosexual and not attracted to his female pupils.

Photograph number 9 reveals that the acerbic critic had a softer side. It shows Volynsky with the School's youngest pupils, the girls dressed in simple, Grecian-style tunics and wearing hair bands. At first glance, the small, self-contained man in black seems to give nothing away. In keeping with his self-perception, he is *croisé*. And yet the photograph has a relaxed atmosphere, which could not have prevailed had a forbidding character been at its centre. The girls pose with coquettish grace and charm. Their expressions are open and trusting, and those on either side of Volynsky even have their arms linked through his.

Volkova's class is pictured in photograph number 10. She is fourth from the left in the second row from the back. Volynsky admired her profile. 'Her face is cut in sharp silhouette, particularly beautiful in profile or three-quarter angle',[74] he wrote. And she has deliberately placed herself with her 'best side' facing the camera. She is the most sophisticated-looking girl in the class, her hair parted in the centre in Spessivtseva style. The light falls so that she is partly hidden, but a closer study reveals an expression both alluring and enigmatic.

In a portrait photograph from the same period, she poses in profile with her chin resting on her hand. The picture has something deeply melancholic about it, yet also something intense and erotic. One finger touches the pulse point at her throat, creating an image reminiscent of *Leda and the Swan*, in which the swan drapes itself round Leda's neck. Clever Volkova was no doubt aware of this allegorical reference – and aware that her homage would appeal to Volynsky.

At a School concert, Konstantin Muller danced a *pas de deux* with Volkova, choreographed by Romanova and set to a sonata by Schumann. He remembered that all the boys wanted to dance with Volkova because she was beautiful and artistic. Muller thought Volkova was

a lovely dancer, lyrical, beautiful in the Spessivtseva style... She had a very good extension and a very pretty arched foot.[75]

Nevertheless, Volynsky gradually lost hope in Volkova as a dancer. In 1924 he wrote:

> Here is a girl who has been highly endowed with the gifts of a dancer's career. A well-shaped foot, stylish and classical, with lift and a sustained arch ... Her smile is welcoming, that of an artist. But for some reason we still have not had all that could be expected from this girl, in spite of four years of training. She is disadvantaged by a lack of musical sensibility and a certain atrophy of the subtler poetic nature. One particular plastic detail is easily noticed: it is a flaw that, if not constitutional, is caused by the failure to master bodily control and the basic disciplines of movement. The hip lacks symmetry, and this shows up in the shoulders and in the whole of the dance.[76]

Her limitations as a dancer did not erase her potential as an artist as far as Volynsky was concerned. He had important plans for her, and predicted with astonishing clarity that Volkova would become an exceptional teacher:

> Many of the girls in the Classe de perfectionnement aim at a teaching career ... Girls like Volkova and Sieff know how (and what) to teach. Experiments with Volkova in this respect have given most satisfactory results. If this poor and beautiful girl could be guided on the right path by an authoritative hand, we might get an entirely new kind of teacher in the sphere of ballet.[77]

The authoritative hand was, of course, Volynsky's own, and he foresaw Volkova as a 'bearer' of the School's ideals, a keeper of its traditions and 'heiress of all our hopes'.[78]

Volkova finished her training at the School of Russian Ballet in the spring of 1925, and on the Saturdays of 16 and 23 May she danced with 84 other pupils in performances at the Bright Reel Cinema.[79] After Lenin's death, Petrograd had been renamed Leningrad; so, on 11 June 1925, she received her diploma from what was now called the Leningrad Department for Professional Education. The document certifies that she had passed her exams in 'classical dance, character dance and historical dance' and also attended a course of lectures in 'the theory of dance (scientific, historical and aesthetic)'. This qualified her to work in all fields of dance, and on 19 June she received her membership card of the artists' trade union, RABIS.[80]

In July, Volkova toured Japan for two months with an ensemble that was run, like the GATOB, on a collective basis. Her first wages amounted to 2% of the total earnings of 73 roubles, or 1 rouble and 82 kopeks. In February 1926, she took part in another tour of Japan and Harbin, this time with an ensemble called The Flying Russian Ballet. It was organised by an agent named Stavrin, and led by a ballet-master named Sokolovsky.

According to the contract, Volkova danced solo parts and, with her colleague Georgi Goncharov, was responsible for the stage management.[81]

While Volkova was away on this second tour, Volynsky's political and artistic enemies finally won the battle against him. According to the Franco-Russian dancer and choreographer Serge Lifar, Volynsky was accused, among other things, 'of creating an art which did not conform with Soviet revolutionary principles'.[82]

Soviet historians claimed that the School of Russian Ballet had been closed for economic reasons. Today Boris Illarionov – Administrative Director of the Vaganova Academy in St Petersburg – says that in fact the School was not closed, but amalgamated with the Petrograd State Choreographic Technical School into the institution now known as the Vaganova Academy.

Volynsky died, aged 63, in August 1926, shortly after the amalgamation. When Volkova returned to Petrograd in the autumn of that year, she was given the official cause of death: a heart attack. But she never accepted it, maintaining to the very end that he had, like countless others, 'disappeared'.

If Volynsky died a 'natural' death, it was presumably nervous exhaustion and malnutrition that killed him. Shortly before his death he wrote in an autobiographical sketch,

> I look onto the street from my window under the roof, and I am filled with sickening indignation over everything. I reach for the newspaper – and it falls from my hands. There's not even a place in my soul for ridicule because there's absolutely nothing to jest about. I'd cry over the situation, but my eyes are dry from bitterness. In what can I invest my maternal feelings when everything around elicits not pity or conviction, but gestures of the greatest dispair. My soul wants to escape and hide somewhere under pure skies, where one can live and breathe. And I feel that in me my father is being resurrected in his moments of elemental rage. If only it were possible to find expression, to give vent to one's feelings in one loud cry of indignation and with it, and in it, die![83]

He died, however, without losing his belief either in the Symbolist dogma that new life and a new salvation will come from art, or in art's religious mission, the transformation of man, and publicly spoke out one last time:

> When the country is ruined and demeaned, or ravaged, the theatre is fatally going down. The stage shows carnival melodramas, gross farces and clowneries... At these fatal historical minutes the theatre turns into the warning bell of degeneration. It will form a crowd and unite it for a new good

fight. It will give them impulse for a new historical run. This is the way it has been, it still is and will be in any country, where the heroic spirit has not died under the burden of distress and lawlessness.[84]

Dimitri Shostakovich got revenge for his missing pay packets, and had the last word at a memorial evening in honour of Volynsky organised by the Writers' Union. 'I shared my memories', he wrote in his autobiography.

> The audience was in an uproar, and I thought, 'Even if you drag me off the stage, I'll finish my story.' And I did. And as I left I heard Sologub ask his neighbour, 'Who is that young bastard?' I bowed to him politely. For some reason, he didn't respond.[85]

The system that crushed Volynsky also defamed his character. Soviet ballet historians were licensed to portray Volynsky as a reactionary and power-crazy amateur, and he ultimately became a non-person in the Soviet Union, a victim of the ballet world's conspiracy of silence. But there were two noble exceptions: in spite of their differences, Fyodor Lopukhov and Agrippina Vaganova later stood up for Volynsky and recognised his importance to Russian ballet: 'While disagreeing with the critic Volynsky... I could not fail to welcome his explanation – the first such explanation – of the great essence of choreographic art',[86] wrote Lopukhov. In the face of official rejection of Volynsky, Vaganova acknowledged him in the preface to her book *Fundamentals of the Classic Dance*, describing him as 'the respected, loving art enthusiast A.L. Volynsky'.

In a sense, even Volkova rejected her mentor. She never spoke about her life in the Soviet Union after his death – those years remain undocumented and her best-guarded secret.

During the 1970s the Russian critic and historian Natalia Roslavleva repeatedly asked Volkova about *The Book of Exultation*, in which Volynsky had singled his pupil out as his heir. Volkova brushed Roslasleva's questions aside. She claimed ignorance of the work and insisted that she had left the Soviet Union before Volynsky had finished it, but that is not correct: *The Book of Exultation* was published in 1926 and Volkova did not emigrate until 1928.

'Dark is Thy Path, Wanderer'

Leningrad's trams had stopped running. There was no traffic. The city's boulevards resounded with the dirges of military bands and the footfalls of Red Army regiments slow-marching down 25th October Street. The *cortège* grew steadily as people from the side streets along the Moika and Fontanka canals joined it.

The city that Nikolai Gogol had described as 'a kingdom for the Dead where everything is wet, smooth, even, pale, grey and foggy' was burying Trotsky's second-in-command, Mikhail Lachevich – a ruthless hard-liner who had personally executed the Archbishop Andronicus and had been one of the Bolshevik leaders who decided the fate of the Tsar and his family in Ekaterinburg.

It was ironic that such a man should be given a state funeral by the old Imperial capital; but though he was a scourge of the Tsarist White Russians, in September 1928 Leningrad buried Lachevich as a beloved son. The old capital on the Gulf of Finland was dying. Moscow, the new, held Peter the Great's enchanted but cursed city in an iron grip of hate and distrust, systematically robbing it of vital resources and steadily crushing its intellectual life. The enervated city needed a hero and a defiant show of pomp and power. Lachevich's funeral came to symbolise the opposition, political and cultural, of a civilisation that was fighting for survival.

Volkova grieved for her own reasons. To her, Lachevich's funeral symbolised the final laying to rest of her own hopes of a future in the Soviet Union. Watching the procession from her window, she recognised some faces in the crowd. After breaking with Stalin, Lachevich had been exiled to Harbin where he had committed suicide or been assassinated – no one really knew which. His followers had taken his body to Leningrad; Volkova knew some of them from her days working as a dancer in the town on Russia's border with China. She went into the street to find them.

She carried herself like a dancer, and her friends were happy to see their 'Leningrad ballerina'. The precise weight she gave every step, and her straight back, were unmistakable signs of her classical ballet training, and the face she showed the world was one of great pride and dignity.

Privately, however, she was consumed by grief and frustration. Scattered information suggests that after Volynsky's death Volkova found it difficult to make a career in the Soviet Union. It is probable that her close association with Volynsky had destroyed her prospects in a system and a profession that wanted to forget the critic and his School of Russian Ballet, and she felt politically persecuted. Though she always denied it, it is equally possible that Volkova never reached the technical level required by the country's major ballet companies.

Among her comrades from the ballet school, Inna German and Konstantin Muller had been appointed to the opera house in Kharkov in the Ukraine, while little Galina Ulanova continued her training with her mother Maria Romanova at the GATOB school and went on to become the Soviet Union's most celebrated ballerina. Alexander Pushkin and Mikhail Georgievsky were offered jobs with the GATOB, and Vasily Koslov went to the Bolshoi Theatre in Moscow, where Volkova may also have tried to find work. She certainly lived there for a while and married a musician, Shura Vinogradov. The marriage was short-lived. After it broke up, Volkova began a relationship with a dancer from the Bolshoi Theatre, Serge Toropov, with whom she had decided to emigrate.

After Lachevich's funeral, Volkova announced her decision to her family. It was a blow and an unexpected and painful separation. 'Suddenly the engagement to travel with Serozya Toropov [came]; we thought one, two years, but it turned out otherwise', her mother Maria later wrote to her in Shanghai.

> How could we not foresee this! Sorry I am in such a mood today that I have been talking away! Everyone makes his or her own life![87]

Georgi Balanchivadze had left the country a couple of years previously. In his words, 'it was impossible to live in Russia, it was terrible – there was nothing to eat, people here can't understand what that means'.[88] He recalled that he:

> dreamed of moving anywhere at all, just to get away. To go or not to go – I never had the slightest doubts about it. None! I never doubted, I always knew: If there were ever an opportunity – I'd leave![89]

Maria Volkova believed that her daughter, too, had left because of the miserable daily conditions:

> Not even the poverty we lived in could tear me away, but it gave you the desire to make your own way, whatever the cost.[90]

Volkova often said later that she had planned to return, but she must have known it was unlikely to be possible. In 1928 the authorities viewed emigration as a hostile act and by 1931 it was classified as treason. Even among artists the emigrants were regarded with contempt, albeit often tinged with envy. Anna Akhmatova was one of the emigrants' most outspoken critics. She deemed it a mortal sin to leave one's native country, and cursed them with the powerful words: 'Dark is thy path, wanderer'.

Between 1917 and 1929, about three million Russians emigrated, creating a virtual nation in exile that stretched from Manchuria to California, and whose capital cities were Berlin, Paris and New York. They formed ghettos and, as is often the case when people believe they have been 'forced' to leave their native land, they felt that even if they could no longer live in Russia, Russia lived on within them. They clung to her language and literature, her religion and traditions, her cooking and her superstitions.

The poet Marina Tsvetayeva, who left Russia with her husband Serge Efron, described the separation as a kind of death, a separation of body from soul. She wrote, 'it is possible to live outside Russia and preserve it in one's heart'; but when Efron decided to go home, she went with him – and after his execution she committed suicide.

There can be little doubt that Volkova herself saw her emigration as a betrayal, but she did not enshrine Russia in her heart as Tsvetayeva did. It was a painful loss, which she tried both to forget and to come to terms with by creating a new life and a new identity. In the words of the Russian poet Alexander Griboedov, she fled without looking back, and sought a place in the world that could heal 'injured feelings'. Her departure, and the price she and her family came to pay for it, traumatised her so deeply that she drew a heavy veil between past and future, creating a divide that left its mark and haunted her for the rest of her life. It explains why talk of the Soviet Union or her background made her uneasy, why she never became part of the nostalgic Russian emigrant community and remained an outsider, not only in her adopted countries but even among her countrymen.

Volkova's long and solitary journey began on a Tuesday. All her family came to see her off at Leningrad's Moscow Station. The train to Manchuria left at 12.37, stopped at Sverdlovsk three days later, and arrived at Harbin the following Friday at 13.12. In 1929, the journey, which Volkova had already made twice previously, took 236 hours and 35 minutes, not quite ten days.

There was a dining car on the train, and it was possible to buy supplies at the stations it stopped at on the way, but passengers usually brought their own food with them for the interminable journey. It wound from European Russia, southwards past Moscow, eastwards past the Ural Mountains and across the Siberian plains to Asia.

Harbin had for a long time held a special status as Chinese territory under Russian administration, and had become a gathering place for White Russians. Almost a third of Harbin's 100,000 inhabitants were Russians, including a Russian regiment.

It was almost always winter in Harbin. Temperatures easily dropped to a numbing −30°C at night, and the Black Dragon River (Amur in Russian) froze solid to a depth of 12 feet. The horizon was dominated by the dome of Saint Sophia, the Russian Byzantine cathedral. The town's Russian quarter had Russian street names and cabs instead of rickshaws, while the Japanese quarter was characterised by trade, grain mills and the notorious Happy Villas where little boys and girls were sold in prostitution. Harbin's British quarter was crammed with abattoirs, where thousands of underpaid Chinese labourers butchered pigs, sheep and poultry for export to the USA.

The majority of the Russian emigrants who passed through the town on their way to the USA and Europe were members of the old aristocracy, professional classes and intelligentsia. They brought with them a level of culture and a taste for entertainment that made Harbin a centre for music and drama, with a nine-month theatre season, a symphony orchestra and a ballet troupe.

Volkova, who had already danced with the Harbin troupe in 1925 and 1926, joined the company once more, and went with them on a year-long Southeast Asian tour to Beijing, Singapore and Manila. In Shanghai, the last stop before returning to the Soviet Union, Volkova and Toropov abandoned the troupe. A third dancer, Georgi Goncharov, who was originally from Moscow, also defected. All three had hopes of somehow getting to Europe, where they would join Serge Diaghilev's Ballets Russes. Vaganova had told Volkova that he was always on the lookout for Russian dancers.

Shanghai, which the Russian trio intended to be a stepping-stone, resembled Harbin in a number of ways. Like the Manchurian capital, it was divided into international zones and had a large, well-educated Russian population that endowed the city with a touch of reckless glamour. But in spite of the Russians' love of grand gestures, the situation for most of them was hopeless. As Soviet refugees, all were stateless and many very poor. It was commonly accepted that the only way for a Russian woman to get to the West was through marriage to a French, English or American businessman. The Russian men's situation was equally bad, or perhaps even worse: they took whatever jobs they could find. Crime, alcoholism and drug addiction were rampant.

The city never saw snow, but had a lot of rain, culminating in the Plum Flower Rain season from mid-June to early July. The summers were hot and humid; at night, the city seethed with more than a hundred nightclubs, dancehalls and cabarets in the area between the waterfront (Bund) and the French Concession. The nightclubs were almost entirely staffed by Russians. The men acted as doormen and waiters, while the beautiful Russian women were taxi dancers, selling themselves as dance partners in clubs where Filipino or Russian orchestras played the popular tunes of the day.

In her biography of Margot Fonteyn, Meredith Daneman retold an old story that Fonteyn's mother, Hilda Hookham, saw Volkova dance in 'one of Shanghai's steamier nightclubs'.[91] It had grown, and piqued the prurient interest of many in the ballet world once Volkova, the Russian with the mysterious past, became successful in London. The truth is that Volkova, Toropov and Goncharov performed not in a steamy nightclub, but in Shanghai's most exclusive cabaret at the Hotel Majestic in Nanking Road, which seated 1,300.[92] It was a setting respectable enough to have been chosen a few years earlier by the Chinese leader Chiang Kai-shek for his marriage to May-ling Soong, the formidable Chinese First Lady, who became known as Madame Chiang Kai-shek, and who famously said that the only thing oriental about her was her face.

At that time, ballet dancers all over the world performed in music halls, vaudevilles and cabarets to survive: there was nothing unusual or sensational about it. In London, Balanchine was performing in Charles B. Cochran's 1931 Revue and Sir Oswald Stoll's Variety Shows with a troupe billed as George Balanchine's 'Sixteen Delightful Dancers'; and Legat had done the same.

The three Russian dancers in Shanghai were known as the Olympic Trio. They worked every evening, performing *pas de deux* from the classical repertoire – *Swan Lake*, *The Sleeping Beauty* and *The Nutcracker*. They also choreographed some dances of their own, sometimes introducing acrobatic tricks in the Bolshoi style.

A promotional postcard from 1930 (photograph number 15) shows the Olympic Trio in a passionate dance, probably inspired by Mikhail Fokine's Arabian jealousy drama, *Scheherazade*. Volkova, Goncharov and Toropov portray a love triangle in which Volkova has apparently surrendered to one of the men, Goncharov. He holds her by the waist and she arches backwards over his supporting arm. Her other suitor, Toropov, kneels in supplication, but she is holding him away with one foot. Goncharov's lustful attention is fixed on her, while she looks upwards, with the hint of a smile and unfocused eyes, as if consumed by her own pleasure and revelling in her erotic power over both men.

In another postcard (photograph number 14), Volkova looks like a film star, playing the role of sensual diva to perfection. She must have been twenty-five years old when the picture was taken, but seems older. She is not looking directly at the camera, but half over her shoulder, as if at something – or someone – following her. Her fur coat emphasises her

feline grace, and she is holding it closed as if she may be naked beneath
it. Half-smiling, she looks as if she is poised to run ...

Although the image is staged, it seems to tell us something about
Volkova's situation in Shanghai. Her future prospects were uncertain,
and she was disappointed to be stranded in a Chinese city, with no hope
of realising the artistic ambitions that had driven her to leave Russia. The
damp climate affected her health, and she gradually developed chronic
colitis, an intestinal condition that weakened her and made it almost
impossible for her to dance.

Serge Toropov was equally disillusioned and miserable. He looked into
the possibility of returning to the Soviet Union and was promised a visa
and safe conduct by the Consulate, but Volkova and Goncharov chose not
to go back. According to Volkova, Toropov was executed as soon as he
crossed the Soviet border.

A private photo taken the same year also speaks of Volkova's sadness
and isolation. In it, she still resembles Spessivtseva. Simply and stylishly
clad in a black dress, she is as slim as a bamboo rod and seems modest and
retiring in comparison with her three companions: her partner Georgi
Goncharov, the Russian architect Emmanuel Gran, and a woman friend
of his, who is being presented with a bouquet of flowers.

Volkova corresponded regularly with her family in Leningrad. Irina,
whose mental state had deteriorated after Volkova left, was improving in
health and wrote to her from a sanatorium:

> I'm enjoying the countryside like a child and not working, but in the autumn
> I'll think seriously about working and art. Such lovely weather after that
> frightful anguish and mental suffering at the hospital. What haven't I been
> through! The world seemed good to me, that is to say, the beautiful city of
> Leningrad with its islands and architecture. I feel more lively – more as you
> would like me to be. I'm calm and sensible again, am no longer restless and am
> very good to Mama. ... Verotchka, my good sister, is so far away; I think of you
> so much but don't know when you will visit us, or send for me!!!'[93]

Irina was willing to do any kind of job to get out of Russia, and
suggested becoming her sister's dresser.

The letters from Irina were painful reminders of life in Leningrad. They
put Volkova's own difficult situation in Shanghai into perspective, and
the correspondence reveals a complex relationship between the sisters,
embracing both love and jealousy. Irina was incapable of living in the
present. She was obsessed with the past, with memories of her childhood
and early youth with Vera. 'I'm sending you your little photos as you
asked. It is most precious – our simple, unsophisticated childhood. There

is my photo (where I am in Russian costume). I'm sure you would be kind enough to enlarge it for me ',[94] she begged.

She reproached Volkova for having made off with both sisters' share of happiness and success, but at the same time associated her with her dreams of a better life:

> Therefore, as you say in your letter, all hope rests with you, and I hope you will send for me. I am beginning to learn English in the most funny way, whereby I promise you to be good, good.

Later she repeated her request:

> Would you like me to come and stay with you? I feel much calmer now; on the whole I am a positive person and do not for a minute doubt that I would get both visa and residence permit.[95]

In contrast, Maria Volkova's letters revealed only a mother's unselfish love for her lost child. She was supportive of her daughter, realising that Volkova's life in Shanghai was probably not as easy as she tried to make it sound. But, consciously or unconsciously, Maria could not help but express her sorrow that she would not see her child grow up and develop: 'Your Chinese rose will soon surpass all flowers in growth, it is getting larger and larger, such a green plant', she reported with pride and enthusiasm. Volkova's gift to her mother had taken on a great symbolic significance for her and she sent her daughter tiny pressed flowers in return: 'Once I went to the Botanical Gardens, and sat and thought about you and Ira!'[96]

It becomes clear from the correspondence that Maria's life was unbearably dull. She saved her money so that she could buy coats and cigarettes for Irina and Lev, and declared that she herself wanted for nothing. The minutiae of her present life were often compared to experiences they had shared in the past – 'I will buy new, solid shoes, like I once did with you'. Finally, Maria exclaims: 'Write to me! When we write to each other it is like being together. Your letters mean everything to me.'[97]

When the Olympic Trio's engagement at the Hotel Majestic came to an end, Volkova found a job in a dress shop to support herself and her family. Georgi Goncharov started teaching; and when Volkova visited one of his classes one day, she made a great impression on one of his pupils, Peggy Hookham. Eleven-year-old Peggy was later to become Margot Fonteyn, Vera Volkova's most illustrious pupil.

'One day a tall, slender young woman entered through the wide double doors and into the front room/ballet studio where Goncharov was setting the *rond de jambe* exercise', Fonteyn wrote in her memoirs in 1975:

Goncharov, I thought, blushed slightly with pleasure at seeing her, and her presence brought an aura to which the little room was quite unaccustomed. In those days one would have said she looked Parisian, thus paying the highest compliment to her style of dress and her deportment. It was an extremely hot afternoon and she wore a very simple dress of printed silk with a flared skirt. Her face was not conventionally beautiful but attracted one with its oval shape, delicate nose and large eyes. The picture was rounded off by a wide-brimmed black straw hat ... The vision she presented gave me my first inkling of what a ballerina should be.[98]

Volkova's fortunes worsened in 1932 after the Japanese army bombed Shanghai's Chinese quarter and much of the international population fled, leaving the stranded Russians behind. As life returned to normal, an English businessman named Hugh Finch Williams visited the city for the first time.

Hugh Finch Williams was working for the trading company Messrs Dowdell & Company Ltd in Foochow, halfway between Shanghai and Hong Kong, a job he eventually gave up to study architecture in Shanghai.

At a cocktail party given by Volkova's friend Emmanuel Gran on his roof terrace, she was introduced to the twenty-eight-year-old aspiring architect, who recalled that Volkova had:

a classic profile, chestnut hair long to the shoulders and kind if shrewd eyes, not to mention an exquisite dancer's figure that in this model dress had a rare elegance ... She started to make me laugh and continued to do so to the end of her days. A born mimic, she caught the exact angle of life's little innuendoes or absurdities.[99]

He quickly noted and admired the empathy she radiated, and her incomparable ability to give every person she met her undivided attention and genuine interest. She was invariably polite and always had time for everybody, but as Finch Williams came to know her better he also observed her willpower and streaks of a 'ruthless anger', which she herself explained by saying that under her forbearing nature lay 'steel'.

Margot Fonteyn remembered Volkova as 'a perfectly trained product of the finest school in the world, who found the work incredibly taxing in the poor conditions and humid climate'.[100] Finch Williams, too, soon saw the gravity of Volkova's situation. She was extremely run down but could not afford medical attention, so he generously arranged for her to be sent out of town to a sanatorium, where she received treatment and gradually recovered her strength.

Their relationship developed into a love affair; and when he moved to Hong Kong in 1934, Finch Williams managed to procure Volkova a visa and send for her. On her arrival at the British Crown Colony, Volkova again fell very ill and again Finch Williams saved her by paying to have her admitted to hospital. In his opinion, her stay in Hong Kong was the turning point: it gave Volkova back her self-confidence and her belief in life. For Volkova, his solicitude meant that she owed him a debt of gratitude that she would spend the rest of her days repaying.

When she was discharged, the hospital staff secured her a place at the Helena May Institute, which had been founded in 1916 by a Governor's wife who wanted to create a 'home from home' that could provide young women with 'physical and moral protection'. Volkova's room on the top storey had a balcony and a magnificent view over the bay, which teemed with junks, sampans and ships of the British fleet. Her new home was within walking distance of the ballet school she then opened, and which rapidly became such a success that she was able to send for Georgi Goncharov from Shanghai.

When Hugh Finch Williams returned to England in the spring of 1935, he promised Volkova that he would try to get her to Europe. Exactly one year later he succeeded, and she sailed from Hong Kong on the German passenger ship *Scharnhorst* bound for England. A Russian citizen without a passport, she was not allowed to visit any of the towns the ship called at on the way. She felt, she said, like 'a dog in quarantine' on the six-week-long voyage, although she spent her time on board learning English and preparing herself for her new life in England.

Volkova arrived at Southampton in March 1936 after nearly seven years in Asia. Hugh Finch Williams met her off the ship, and later remembered how shy and insecure both had been at their reunion. They had not seen each other for nearly a year, and both realised that Finch Williams would have to support Volkova, and that she would be entirely dependent on him.

The couple agreed that Volkova should try to renew her passport at the Soviet Embassy in London, although they knew her chances of success were slight. As expected, her application was refused and so the only way for her to get a British passport was through marriage. Volkova and Finch Williams quickly resumed their life as a couple, in a flat in Judd Street, Bloomsbury, and decided to consult Finch Williams's brother David, a lawyer, about the legal implications of an eventual marriage and a later divorce.

Hugh Finch Williams had not yet told the rest of his family about his relationship with Volkova. His younger sister Elsa was the first of them to meet her formally. Many years later Finch Williams still had vivid memories of the occasion, and of his pride in his future wife.

Vera was wearing a very fitted Schiaparelli dress in dark blue angora wool, with the short puffed sleeves then fashionable, its ruched collar carrying a green scarab, her hair long to her shoulders. She was perched lightly on the arm of an easy chair and rose in a warm greeting as my sister came in.[101]

Volkova charmed Elsa, whose positive impression paved the way for an introduction to the rest of the family, and eventually they all came to the couple's wedding at Holborn Town Hall in 1937. It was a simple civil ceremony at which the registrar, as Volkova and Finch Williams recalled, seemed more concerned about catching her train home for the weekend than their marriage. Thinking Volkova's English inadequate, the registrar decided to conduct the ceremony in basic French – but, according to Finch Williams, it did not become any clearer as a result. At her wedding Volkova promised herself that Finch Williams would never have cause to regret the marriage. He felt that the first months of their life together as man and wife were in many ways their happiest. She never mentioned ballet. He had the impression that she had given up her artistic ambitions which probably suited his middle-class ideals. He found work as an architect for London Transport and continued to study painting, while Volkova tried to adapt to her new life as a housewife and worked to improve her English by reading Oscar Wilde.

According to Hugh Finch Williams, Volkova took to London immediately. She had had vivid ideas of the city since reading Charles Dickens as a child and loved the terraces of low brick houses. She was less impressed by London's more monumental side, which could not, in her opinion, match that of Leningrad. She regarded the English as a poetic people and admired their formality, as befitted a Smolny girl.

In the winter of 1936 Volkova thought she might be pregnant and visited a consultant at Queen Charlotte's Hospital, who confirmed the happy news. She was ecstatic and hopeful and shared her joy with her family in the Soviet Union.

'Happy New Year! This year will be so significant both for you and me – just think – a new little person will arrive, close, dear to us', Maria Volkova wrote to her daughter.[102] This was the beginning of a family correspondence that centred on the pregnancy, but soon revealed complications: 'You think so much and are so worried about the coming child, and that is bad for it', wrote Irina. 'Perhaps that is why it doesn't grow. Calm down and stop thinking about it, all your letters are full of it, you seem to be nervous...'[103]

Volkova was right to worry: hers was in fact a phantom pregnancy, a pseudocyesis, where the body exhibits all signs of pregnancy but there is no foetus. Further examination indicated that she would probably never be able to have children: the doctor assumed that her uterus had failed to develop correctly because of the famine in Petrograd during her teenage years.

Once a Dancer

According to Hugh Finch Williams, Volkova accepted the verdict that she would never be able to bear children 'philosophically', but he also felt that it plunged her into an existential crisis greater even than that she had lived through in Asia.

Volkova's correspondence with her sister indicates that her marriage to Finch Williams was also damaged, and Irina again pleaded with her to return to the Soviet Union:

> So many years have passed. I simply must see you. You have started to have troubles, so come back! By any means possible... The meeting with your family will revitalise you and you will want to stay. Don't be afraid.[104]

But remembering the fate of her Shanghai friend Toropov, Volkova had every reason to believe that it would be suicide to return. In the Soviet Union, Stalin's Great Terror had raged since 1934. The purges in the Communist Party, the central administration and the army had expanded into a campaign of terror against the general population: 681,692 people were executed in 1937–8. Between 500,000 and 1,000,000 died in the Gulags, Stalin's work camps. Rumours about the horrors flourished among Russians in exile; and while Volkova herself was safe, she was acutely aware of the dangers her family faced.

The tone of Maria Volkova's letters changed. 'It's good that you too know about our pilot heroes. Yes! Our country appreciates them, cares for them and spoils them', she wrote in a patriotic outburst doubtless inspired by the knowledge that the secret police read their correspondence. In an equally unlikely vein, she extolled the benefits of the Soviet system compared with capitalist England: 'It's a shame that in your case you have to work for a year before you can have a holiday, while with us it is – five months'.

One phrase stands out as a clear warning: 'Believe only me', she wrote, encouraging her daughter not to take Irina's unrealistic ideas at face value, but to read between the lines of her own letters for the truth.[105]

Without the hope of children and a family, it was clear that Volkova would never be able to reconcile herself to life as a housewife. She must have considered the possibility that she might begin to dance again, although she denied it when asked point-blank by Margot Fonteyn, then 18 and a promising dancer with Ninette de Valois's Sadler's Wells Ballet. Volkova had met Fonteyn's mother, Hilda Hookham, by chance and had been invited to dinner, where she explained that not only had she lost her technique beyond recall, but she would also find it hard to accept the calibre of work she was likely to be offered in London.

Although the Russian impresario Serge Diaghilev had revived interest in the art throughout Western Europe with his Ballets Russes, a void opened when the company broke up on his death in 1929.

British ballet was still in its infancy and London did not have a resident professional company, except perhaps for Marie Rambert's small group of dancers which first performed in 1926. Shortly after Diaghilev's death, the Carmago Society in London began to arrange performances with dancers like Olga Spessivtseva, and small ensembles began to form in Great Britain. Ninette de Valois's Sadler's Wells Ballet was one of the most enterprising and ambitious initiatives, but Mona Inglesby's International Ballet, and the Markova–Dolin Ballet, led by the dancers Anton Dolin and Alicia Markova, also attracted a London following. The Metropolitan Ballet, the Anglo-Polish Ballet, Ballet Rambert and Jay Pomeroy's Opera and Ballet Company mostly toured the provinces. Although Volkova had started to attend performances again, she could not see herself in any of these companies; many of the dancers were little better than amateurs and she was not impressed with the level of choreography being produced.

Nonetheless, at the dinner with Mrs Hookham (whom she dutifully asked for her Lancashire hotpot recipe), Fonteyn gave Volkova the address of a Russian ballet teacher, Igor Schwezoff.

Schwezoff taught in a studio on Gunter Grove, off the King's Road, 'according to the methods and traditions of the Maryinsky School, Petrograd'.[106] Like Volkova, Schwezoff had studied with Vaganova but considered one of the Maryinsky Theatre's male teachers, Obukhov, to be his mentor. After fleeing the USSR, Schwezoff had worked with the Original Ballet Russe de Monte Carlo and with Bronislava Nijinska in Paris, before settling in London.

Schwezoff and Volkova spoke Russian together, and the students at the school sensed there was some connection between them. One of them, Michael Bayston, knew that:

> both of them came to London via Harbin and Shanghai [but] neither of them ever said anything about the past [and] we often wondered if he [Schwezoff] had known Volkova before.[107]

Volkova and Schwezoff probably did know each other. Apart from having studied with the same teachers, they certainly had friends in common in the Soviet Union: Schwezoff had danced in Kharkov in the Ukraine with Volkova's classmates Inna German and Mikhail Georgievsky.

They both reached Shanghai in 1929; but whereas Volkova became stranded, Schwezoff had contacts there who were able to get him a European visa straight away. In spite of his relative good fortune, Schwezoff recalled that when he came to the West:

> I was called a communist and considered a pest wherever I went. At the time, I couldn't even get a passport or working papers.[108]

In 1934 he wrote a prize-winning autobiography, *Borzoi*, about his youth in St Petersburg both before and after the change of system in 1917. His reasons for flight were political only in so far as politics affected his work. 'I was actually indifferent to politics of any kind', he wrote.

> I only shared the disposition common to all artists that an artist is only an artist by virtue of his intensified individualism. A communist artist is actually a contradiction in terms.[109]

'An artist requires freedom to create', he said. 'Otherwise, he is not an artist at all.'[110]

When Volkova started taking classes at Schwezoff's school in the spring of 1938, she was nearly 33 years old. She had not danced for five or six years and was completely out of shape, but she still made an impression on Michael Bayston, who was her partner in class. According to Bayston, Volkova was not a great virtuoso,

> but she had line and style and some of the extravagances of Russian dancers. I partnered her in double-work; she was very light, had a good jump and a strong back, and she would alter what Schwezoff had set if she thought her way prettier.[111]

Schwezoff accepted Volkova's high-handed ways without a murmur and with a measure of respect. After a couple of months' training, Volkova took part in one of his school performances, dancing a solo she had choreographed herself.

She had chosen to set her dance to a piano study by the Russian composer Alexander Scriabin, his *Poème Tragique*, and she interpreted the music with fervour and intensity. Scriabin's piece, then unknown in Britain, recalls the enclosed forms and improvisatory atmosphere of Chopin's *études* and mazurkas. At the same time, the work's wide intervals and murky harmonies suggest the Scriabin of the composer's later, profoundly philosophical works.

Volkova's choreography reflected the music's yearning melodic fragments, the rush of drama apparent in the opening measures, and its almost theatrical trajectory thereafter. The piece hinted at grand passions, passions absorbed or transcended, in slightly more than three minutes. It was Volkova's first public appearance in the West, and, with a single exception, her last.[112]

Hugh Finch Williams recalled that the audience gasped when Volkova made her dramatic entry in a flimsy dress of flame-coloured chiffon. Her dance was a revelation to him: as she performed on stage, he saw a side of her character he had never experienced in their married life. Unlike the other dancers in the programme, Volkova did not present the usual kind of correct or conscientious spelling-out of classroom steps. Her dance was not an exercise, it was a statement: to Hugh Finch Williams, herself and the world. We can only guess at what private emotions fired her choreography, but both in its creation and its performance, *Poème Tragique* carried one overriding message: she had once been, and would always be, a dancer.

She briefly continued her training with Nikolai Legat, Volynsky's old partner. When he died, her last link with Volynsky and the School of Russian Ballet died with him, but her central interest would remain Russian ballet.

Colonel de Basil's Ballets Russes and the Ballet Russe de Monte Carlo of René Blum and Léonide Massine performed back to back in London in 1938, starring the three 'Baby Ballerinas': Tamara Toumanova (18), who danced with Blum's and Massine's company, and Irina Baronova (18) and Tatiana Riabouchinska (20) who were Colonel de Basil's stars. All three had been trained in Paris by Russian ballerinas from the Maryinsky Theatre who had fled to France after the Revolution, and Volkova wanted to experience their teaching also.

In Paris, she stayed in a cheap hotel in the rue Blanche, a narrow street that winds from the Opéra and *les grands magasins* up towards Montmartre, the artists' quarter perched on a hill. The hotel was three minutes' walk from Salle Wacker in the rue Douai where Olga Preobrazhenskaya taught, and just around the corner from the home of Lubov Egorova and her husband Prince Trubetskoi in the rue Rochefoucauld.

Of the two grand old ladies, Preobrazhenskaya was the more illustrious. Her career at the Maryinsky Theatre had been legendary; she was said to have the elegance of a duchess, the charm of a kitten and the temperament of a lion. She was also a spectacular eccentric: every morning before class, she would clamber up onto the piano to feed the doves on the windowsill. When her ancient tortoise could no longer walk, she had wheels fitted and trundled it around the classroom.

By 1939, the great Preobrazhenskaya, whose teaching had inspired Vaganova, was a tiny, hunched old woman, not much bigger than a child. But she was stubborn, determined and relentlessly demanding of her students. She would not hesitate to grab a student from the back and shake her to push her further in the quest for perfection: 'It's good for you to cry. Now we'll try again', she would say brusquely if someone broke down.

Enrico Cecchetti had been one of Preobrazhenskaya's teachers, and in essence she taught the Italian school. The classes were rigidly structured, with a half-hour barre. Unlike Vaganova, Preobrazhenskaya did not use *épaulement* or exercises for the torso during class; her focus was primarily on the legs and lower part of the body.

Lubov Egorova's classes were also pre-Vaganova – old school, but French rather than Italian. She gave the same basic barre every day; the arms were held close to the body, *à la seconde*. Egorova's exercises were simple and rhythmic. Unlike Preobrazhenskaya, Egorova was a very gentle woman; quiet and reserved to the point of shyness, she never raised her voice or touched the pupils. A renowned beauty in her youth, and still supremely elegant, Egorova wore her long grey hair wound into a bun at the nape of the neck, and gloves to hide a skin complaint.

As a student, Egorova had been in the same class as Mikhail Fokine. She became a technically brilliant dancer, famed for her interpretation of Princess Florine in the ballet *The Sleeping Beauty*, which she had danced with Nijinsky as the Bluebird. A Russian critic wrote about her, in praise, that when she danced it was like 'a light that glows but gives off no heat'.

To Volkova, Egorova's classes were a greater inspiration than Preobrazhenskaya's. They reminded her of her old teacher Romanova at the School of Russian Ballet. Egorova remained seated throughout the class until the last exercise, when she would get up and dance. 'Now, the *adage*', she would say, with great reverence, to her Russian pianist, Madame Marie, who always played Chopin.[113] The adage was not an exercise, it was a performance: long, lyrical and stylised. Volkova believed Egorova improvised the dance, her students copying their teacher's movements behind her. Now, dancing, every step had *épaulement*; Egorova's emotive choreography covered the whole room, searching, striving and longing for something intangible. It was *plastique*, sculptural, and ended with a pose of supplication, like a prayer.

Volkova also studied with one male Russian teacher in Paris, Boris Kniaseff, who was notoriously temperamental. The students who attended his class in Salle Pleyel could never be sure whether he would turn up or not; but when he did, the regime was relentless. Kniaseff had been married to Olga Spessivtseva, and claimed that his teaching was based on the exercises Spessivtseva herself had used. The classes lasted two hours and were regarded as the longest in ballet history. The dancers would spend an hour at the barre, and an hour in the centre, doing exercises without the support of the barre.

Volkova was fascinated by Kniaseff's magnetic personality, though perhaps not by his teaching. He hypnotised his pupils. It was like watching a cobra dance. He shouted and spat out his instructions like acid; there was never any doubt what was expected of his students, but on occasion he liked to take off his shoes and socks to demonstrate a point, or perhaps it was just to proudly display a foot with only four toes.

Kniaseff intended to start a ballet company and invited Volkova to join it, but when Volkova consulted Egorova the old lady advised her not to get involved in Kniaseff's venture. 'I have spoken to Madame Egorova about the possibility of joining Kniaseff's company but her advice is against it', Volkova wrote to Hugh Finch Williams in London.

> He is rather irresponsible in paying the money and difficult to work with. In her opinion I must stick to what I decided to do, work hard, exploit the opportunity of being in Paris and improve my work. The rehearsals will take too much time and energy. She was very nice about it and I am doing what she advised me.[114]

In Paris, Volkova met again a Dutch bank employee, Tommy, whom she had known in Hong Kong. 'Quite unexpectedly Tommy arrived in Paris as soon as he got my letter', she wrote to Hugh Finch Williams in London.

> He spent five days and left this morning by airplane as he got a telegram from his bank in Amsterdam. I hope you don't mind this. He entertained me quite a lot and my knowledge of nightlife in Paris is considerably enlarged.
>
> Last night we went to see a play by Jean Cocteau, *Les parents terribles*. I enjoyed it very much. Good acting and some interesting dresses, which I will describe to you when I will see you. The play is a drama and some situations are forced but the idea is good. It is for the first time in my life that I have seen a play in spoken French. I have been in Casino de Paris where Maurice Chevalier is the main attraction. Altogether it is a very good show of this type, of course a lot of double-meaning jokes and even a sort of lesbian dance with two women kissing each other and so on. But everything so elegant and well presented. The Théatre du Grand Guignol was rather disappointing, very vulgar and stupid. The place itself is rather an amusing place, used to be a chapel and afterwards atelier of a painter, now it is a tiny theatre less than for 300 people.[115]

Volkova used to eat every day at a Russian bistro on the rue Fromentin, around the corner from her hotel. There she met David Arkell for the first time. Arkell was a young British journalist who was working as an editorial secretary on the *Continental Daily Mail*. A Russophile (and

Francophile), Arkell often had dinner in Russian restaurants, then the cheapest in town. He was very shy, and it was Volkova who initiated the conversation that would lead to a lifelong friendship.

The writer's artistic interests included a passion for ballet; drama, music and dance ran in his blood. His grandfather was an organist and musicologist; his father, a popular playwright and novelist; his mother, an actress and dancer. And his much-admired Uncle Teddy, Edwin Evans, was a music critic and friend of Diaghilev, Stravinsky, Poulenc, Ravel and Picasso. As chairman of the Carmago Society, it was Edwin Evans who had invited Spessivtseva to dance in London, and Volkova's resemblance to Spessivtseva must have struck Arkell immediately.

Arkell had just published his first book, *Paris Today*, a charming and entertaining guide. He was thinking of writing a novel, *Portrait of Mimosa*, which he told Volkova about at that time but wrote 20 years later. Arkell was, first and foremost, the quintessential romantic. In a foreword to one of Arkell's later books, the biographer Claire Tomalin described him as a 'literary detective', who enjoyed discovering lost data. He was always dreaming about a France that had long since vanished, and 'had the ability to write about the personalities that interested him as if they were old friends he had just run into round the corner'.[116] In 1979 he published *Looking for Laforgue*, a book about the French symbolist Jules Laforgue, who had influenced T.S. Eliot. And in 1986 he published a biography of the French author Henri Alain-Fournier, *A Brief Life*, that in several ways bound him to Volkova.

Arkell loved Alain-Fournier's novel *Le Grand Meaulnes* [My Great Friend] about youthful longings, first passion and tragic disappointment. And in many ways, the story of the narrator, fifteen-year-old François, and the beautiful Yvonne de Galais resembles that of Arkell and Volkova.

Arkell fell in love with Volkova:

> Never had I seen such charm united with such seriousness. Her dress revealed the slenderness of her waist – slender to the point of fragility. She got down slowly and came into the shop, removing a brown cloak from her shoulders – the most serious of girls, the most fragile of women.[117]

He soon realised, however, that his feelings were not requited; but he continued to admire her and draw inspiration from her beauty, her courage and her wisdom. As in *Le Grand Meaulnes*, their relationship developed into what Alain-Fournier called 'a friendship more moving than a great love'. Arkell never saw Hugh Finch Williams as a rival in a struggle for Volkova's heart, because, rather than on any man, her eyes were fixed 'on some distant object'. Yvonne de Galais's words could be Volkova's own:

But most of all, I would teach those boys to be sensible. I'd impress upon them a kind of wisdom I do know something about.

Paradoxically, while Arkell idolised the past, Volkova – whose life encompassed all the elements of mystery, fate and tragedy that so intrigued him – was decidedly focused on the future. She became his muse.

They explored Paris together. He would often meet her after class with Egorova, and he recalled that at one point the choreographer and ballet-master Léonide Massine asked her to travel to South America with him. And that the French poet and novelist Jean-Louis Vaudoyer, who had penned the libretto for one of Fokine's most famous ballets, *Spectre de la Rose*, spoke about reconstructing the ballets in Molière's plays for the Comédie-Française, with Volkova as ballerina.

'Like all other dancers Volkova worked like a slave at her training', Arkell later wrote, 'but Paris meant far more to her than simply dancing.'[118]

In April 1939 they saw Jean-Louis Barrault play the leading role in a production of Laforgue's *Hamlet*, and Knut Hamsun's *Hunger* at the tiny Montmartre Théâtre de l'Atelier on Place Dancourt. Volkova found Barrault's body language expressive, but was challenged by Laforgue's text. After the performance, at a café on the square, they found themselves sitting at the next table to Barrault and his friends. Arkell and Volkova listened to the conversation all ears, but were too diffident to introduce themselves.

On another occasion, though, Volkova was more direct. She had long admired the Dutch painter Kees van Dongen, who worked in Paris. A Fauvist, Van Dongen had painted Anna Pavlova and Ida Rubinstein in 1909. When Arkell pointed out the painter's studio one day, Volkova resolutely rang the bell. Van Dongen invited them in and they spent the afternoon discussing painting. When Volkova asked Van Dongen what he thought of the Northern Lights, he replied that he preferred electric lighting!

Arkell was fascinated by Volkova's personality. One day, when she was to meet Hugh Finch Williams's parents at the Gare du Nord, she conscientiously arrived much too early for the train. So she sat down on a porter's trolley and began to read Aldous Huxley's *Point Counterpoint* – a novel about British intellectuals searching for harmony in the difficult inter-war period. Carried away by the book, Volkova forgot the time, read the novel from cover to cover, and missed her in-laws' arrival.

When Germany invaded Poland in September 1939 and Great Britain declared war, Volkova immediately returned to London. She and Hugh Finch Williams again tried to make a life together, and moved to the suburb of Putney where they rented a two-storey flat with a small studio in Swan Studios, Deodar Road. Volkova became increasingly introverted. Williams watched her working with fanatical concentration in the garden, which ran down towards the Thames. She scurried around like a little mouse among the fruit bushes and yellow roses in their quiet garden while the world fell into ruins around her.

In a letter from Irina, Volkova learnt that the Great Terror had struck her family. Maria Volkova had been arrested.

> Most of those who are arrested are given the opportunity of leaving the big cities and living in the wilderness! Our Mama will presumably also be among those poor souls.[119]

The victims were taken away by the secret police, locked up in Lubyanka prison and brought before a three-man court, which – as a matter of form – would sentence them to lengthy prison terms or dispatch them to work camps. In 1939, there were 2.9 million Russians living in Gulags.

Lev and Irina were terrified:

> Do not write to her but write to me at address Moscow 93 Poste restante, and you should not mention my surname and Ljova's name either, because he is in a panic, but the best thing you could do is to come back. Think it over. Firstly we could all be relieved that all this is not because of you and it would be a colossal moral support for Ljova.[120]

Lev Volkov had prepared himself for forcible removal to the provinces and had begun to sell his furniture but Irina continued to bombard Volkova with questions and pleas:

> Perhaps you will find connections in Moscow and we could all find out what was the reason for this? So sweet Verotchka, it is long ago since I have heard from you, but if you write poste restante I will receive your letter. I am waiting impatiently, for a letter and then for you. All this should be considered. Your husband will not of course give you permission, while all our family may be annihilated for this reason.[121]

In May 1940, the Germans arrested David Arkell in Normandy. He was interned in a civilian prisoner-of-war camp in Saint-Denis, just outside Paris, for the duration of the war. Hugh Finch Williams was called up, given the rank of Major and sent overseas to India.

Volkova volunteered for the Red Cross, and then the St John's Ambulance Brigade, but she was rejected: Since the Molotov–Ribbentrop Pact between the USSR and Germany, all Russian citizens were viewed with suspicion as possible enemies and traitors.

World War II, West Street and Sadler's Wells

In her solitude, doing class every morning again became the fixed point in Volkova's life. The logic, purity and beauty of the physical exercises sustained her. The steps and movements demanded an absolute concentration that kept real life at bay for a while and cleared her mind. Rising on *pointe* gave her a feeling of control; keeping her balance, a breadth of view. In jumps, she loved to leave the ground and float free in the air. Landing again, she was strengthened.

This depth of meaning and understanding imbued Volkova's movements with a unique quality that the British ballerina Diana Gould sensed immediately when she first saw Volkova training with Lydia Sokolova:

> Although she was no longer in the first flush of youth, I was galvanised at what I saw and for the rest of the morning watched her like a lynx, for here in every pose, in every line and angle, in the elegant turn of the head, the sensual shoulders, in the stretch of the arms and the liveliness of the hands, in the perfect turn-out, the control of the hip and back was what I remembered having only once seen when I was a child at a performance (her last) of *Swan Lake* by Olga Spessivtseva.[122]

And Gould was not easily impressed. She had been trained by Marie Rambert in Notting Hill and was an awe-inspiring, dynamic woman. The choreographer Frederick Ashton had been a fellow pupil and had created one of his first ballets, *Leda and the Swan*, for her in 1928. Serge Diaghilev proclaimed her 'the only young woman I would like to marry', while the British critic Arnold Haskell described her as 'the most musical dancer England has produced.'

In 1944, Gould married the violinist Yehudi Menuhin and entered into a symbiotic relationship with him, giving up her career to support him in his. 'If one performing artist marries another', she wrote in her autobiography, *Fiddler's Moll*, in 1984, 'it is obvious that one of the two must dissolve his or her persona in the other.'

Before Gould adopted her role as Menuhin's protector, she danced as prima ballerina with Jay Pomeroy's Russian Opera and Ballet Company. When Volkova rented a ballet studio in Basil Street, off Sloane Street in Knightsbridge, in 1941 and began to teach, Gould instantly became a student and brought her fellow soloists from the company with her.

Volkova's teaching was a revelation to Gould, because:

she had the ability to make one conscious of one's whole body as a musical instrument and not as a piece of technical mechanism: under her tuition one became a conduit through which passed the rhythm and the melody, not just a muscular gymnast ... I, who as a child had never known gentle teaching, would say that it was a combination of a loving heart, a generous mind and a passionate desire to give to her pupils all that she herself had so assiduously learnt from her own great teachers.[123]

Gould was soon so convinced of Volkova's gifts that she offered her a job as ballet mistress with the Company when it was performing at the Cambridge Theatre. Volkova hesitated, not sure she would be up to the job; but in spite of her uncertainty she was also reluctant to turn down the challenge. Volkova had no reason to doubt herself, Gould insisted, and was proved right:

She brought out – as only she could – this wonderful sense of physical style and what I would call spiritual grace in the company. Just as the Eastern religions do not separate soul from body, so the real Russian teaching incorporates the whole being: mind and heart, intellect and emotion, and so animates one's entire being and will that it summons from one a depth of intent one was not oneself aware of.[124]

Volkova never raised her voice, and even dancers who often played truant from morning training began to come to classes:

How could a dancer give less than all he had to a teacher who gave him all she had? How could one not strain to the utmost in homage to one who taught so lovingly, so warmly and so ever-patiently? For above all she was a natural teacher, an organic one – no steely theorist with a structure worked out once and for all. Oh no! She was a divinely gifted communicator. Walter Pater said, "the way to perfection is through a series of disgusts". Vera knew how to help one through this morass, for in her mind was a permanent vision, that of the perfect dancer and with that lighting her way she moved forward taking us all with her on her illuminated path.[125]

In the summer of 1942, her success with Gould's company prompted Volkova to open her own school in West Street, a side street that ran from Shaftesbury Avenue at Cambridge Circus to Upper St Martin's Lane. West Street is mostly known as the address of one of London's most celebrated restaurants, The Ivy, and for St Martin's Theatre, diagonally opposite the restaurant. In 1942, comedies by J.B. Priestley and Noël Coward were playing at the theatre: today, Agatha Christie's *The Mousetrap* is in its Nth year.

Less well known is the Queen Anne building halfway up the street, once a chapel where the Methodist John Wesley preached for more than

50 years. Wedged in next to that old church with its regular frontage is a sooty, narrow little redbrick building with pointed windows. It was here, at number 26, that Volkova made her reputation as one of London's best ballet teachers.

Volkova taught every day from 10 to 11.30 a.m., and again from 11.30 to 1 p.m. The dancers who attended morning classes passed through the neo-Gothic front door and then, turning sharp right, stepped directly into the rehearsal room: a claustrophobic space with flaking pink walls, uneven wooden floors and three grimy windows facing West Street.

At the opposite end of the room was another door leading into Wesley's chapel and, facing the windows, a platform from which the pianist, Kathleen Keep, looked down on the class. Next to the stage was the entrance to the girls' cramped changing room. No one really seemed to know where the boys changed. The West Street studio had a washbasin, but no baths or showers. Barres ran along three of the walls, and two full-sized, gold-framed mirrors were propped up against the fourth.

Volkova was often the last to arrive. Making an entrance worthy of a star, she was always very elegantly dressed and made an impression on the men in the class when she stepped through the door. Richard Ingram, boyfriend of dancer Peggy Ayers, often watched classes. He remembers Volkova as 'a central presence whenever she appeared': a 'strikingly black-haired, long-nosed, dramatically mannered woman', who spoke 'with deep guttural Russian murmur between words' and lit endless du Maurier cigarettes with a wheel-and-flint petrol lighter.'[126]

Volkova shed her chic street clothes behind a curtain, and when she reappeared was a different woman: she often wore odd ballet shoes or odd leg-warmers, and was not embarrassed to change them in front of her fascinated admirers. Her persona would change as radically as did her appearance – the self-controlled, reserved Russian lady metamorphosed into a soul on fire.

Gilbert Vernon, a Sadler's Wells dancer who took classes in West Street, was 'electrified' by her and remembers how she, in turn, focused intensely on her dancers. Her mobile face conveyed her thoughts and feelings as expressively as an actress's, her figure was still splendid, and:

> on her head she wore a silk turban in the style of the times. Ends of it seemed to constantly be coming loose and she would tuck them in but to little avail. For much of the class there was a cigarette in her mouth but she never quite seemed to get a chance to light it.

She was constantly getting up to demonstrate a step or correct bad placement.

At the time Volkova still spoke English badly and with a strong accent. She made up for it with emphasis and speech music:

> *Up* and *up* and *forward* and *back*. *Poosh* on that *shöllder* – *Harold*! And *up* and *down* and *shoosh* – finish! Now you do *failli-glissade-jeté-failli* ... Peggy – your head – you know – yes? ... Margot – your heeps – peench – you know what I mean?[127]

Leo Kersley, a principal dancer at Sadler's Wells Ballet, thinks it important to remember that dancers learn most from those who dance in front of them, 'and Volkova demonstrated all the steps herself!'

Although Gilbert Vernon had never seen Volkova perform on stage, he regarded her as a ballerina: 'She would have been a great Giselle, I think, if she had had the strength. I can't see her doing the Swan Queen, especially Odile, and I can't see her doing Aurora. She could act; she had feeling, her feeling showed all the time. The way she conducted the class, it was a living experience in acting. When you think back on it, that's what it was.'

Richard Ingram watched fascinated and quite transported with joy for the first time:

> as Chopin poured from the hacked old upright, injecting great waves of romance into the incredible turns and leaps of these vigorous, concentrated athletes... Here there were no smiles at the audience... In front of my eyes, only a few feet away, the most stunning human bodies, clad only in bits of knitted wool and tightly bound vests and pants, flew and dived at the extremity of their energy, catapulting into the corners of the room as their *enchaînements* forced them to finish right against the wall.

The critic Fernau Hall was also one of those who came to watch the classes in West Street. He noted that:

> Volkova, accustomed to the grand manner, almost weeps to see English dancers performing steps without passion or excitement, as if they were slicing bacon. ('No, no, no, no – you must be geroic [heroic]. So – ee *ya* ta ta ta. You do – oom. You must do – OOM!'). She is particularly strict with the men, who tend to be excessively fussy. ('Alexis: all your dancing is with your mouth open. At the end you look like dzeece – men never do flowery things. Henry – just extend your arms – don't flap them!'). She demands vitality, fire, simplicity – not swooning heads and affected arms.[128]

'I don't want to see any exertion', Volkova chanted to her disciples. 'Remember shoulders, down, down ... Stretch knees ... Bend over as if you were picking flowers from the meadow ... Never forget, balance is everything ... the most important thing if you want to be great dancers.'[129]

It was at West Street that Volkova finally came to an understanding of where her true artistic gift lay. As she relinquished her hopes of a career on the stage, she began to fulfil Volynsky's prophecy that her future would be as a communicator, interpreter and catalyst. Her students were witnesses as she accepted the vocation that had been waiting in the background all that time.

This made the war years among the most important in Volkova's life. They were also among the happiest, despite her uncertainty about the fate of her family in Russia and the fact that Hugh Finch Williams was serving in India. To those around her, Volkova was happy and friendly but remained enigmatic. Pamela May, a principal dancer at the Sadler's Wells Ballet, worked closely with her but never lost sight of the fact that Volkova's private life was private. She did not share her inner world. Volkova appeared to be so devoted to her work that not even a world on fire could shake her off course.

Leo Kersley was in no doubt that Volkova had 'embarked on a mission'.[130] George Bernard Shaw noted that ballet greatly helped to keep up morale during the war, a truth Kersley sensed evening after evening at the stage door after performances. Leaving the theatre, the dancers would find themselves 'surrounded by a crowd of men and women on leave from the services or from the hospitals and factories'. They wanted to shake the artists' hands and thank them for making life in the blacked-out city more bearable.

Kersley recalls that 'the rations, the bombs, the endless touring, the eight or nine performances a week with a change of programme at every performance and the rehearsals that entailed were bearable because we all had a mission led by our leaders: Helpmann, de Valois, Volkova and Fonteyn'.[131]

During the war, Sadler's Wells Ballet toured the country non-stop, and Henry Danton, who was on the road with the company, remembers how:

> it was incredibly difficult. We used to change towns every week, we sat on the trains all day on Sundays. Sometimes we sat in a siding for half a day, waiting for troop transports to pass. We usually arrived late at our new destination, we often had no digs, and were bundled out of the train, with our bags, out into the black-out, to go from door to door trying to find a place to sleep. Our suitcases were really heavy, because we were on tour for months on end. We just got what we were given to eat. Bread and potatoes, one egg a week, two slices of bacon, one egg, one day meat, no butter.
>
> This went on week after week, and of course we were rehearsing new ballets during the day. I don't know how we survived.

Fonteyn worked harder than anybody. She would dance *Coppélia* in the afternoon and *Swan Lake* in the evening, and the Corps de Ballet worked terribly hard too. *Dante Sonata* was emotionally very exhausting for me ... We also did *The Wanderer* and *Façade*. It was a hard training ground. All the time I was trying to gain more technique and learn more, so going back to London and to be able to study with Vera was such a joy.

In 1943, Ninette de Valois hired Volkova to teach at the Sadler's Wells Ballet School in Rosebery Avenue. Audrey Harman, a student at the school, remembered that Philip Chatfield knocked on the door of the girls' changing room one day and shouted: 'Come, quick, Veronica Lake is taking class!' The students' old teacher, Nikolai Sergeyev, had left to join the International Ballet as ballet-master, and Volkova took over his job.

According to Harman, there was a world of difference between Volkova's teaching and Sergeyev's:

> Sergeyev was the old Russian School, his classes were very heavy. We used to start with 32 *battements*, before doing *plié* ... His problem was that he didn't speak much English. She had a rich Russian accent, but she did speak English. That was part of the fun of the class... We were all rather terrified of the older teachers, but Vera you could talk to and she gave you such a joy of dancing. We had mixed classes then, and the boys still talk about those days ... She had a special connection with the boys, they loved her.

Volkova was cheeky enough to say things like: 'Put your pelvis forward, Gordon, it's rude but it's correct.' Harman remembered Volkova demonstrating a *développé* to one side, lifting her leg very high, far beyond what was respectable, and casually remarking: 'Don't mind the suspenders, boys!'

Volkova taught in a small studio under the Theatre roof, but she was reluctant to interrupt classes even when the air-raid sirens sounded. 'We all had to go down under the stage, but Vera would say, "No, Michael [Boulton], you don't want to go down, do you?" and she would keep him for a private lesson.'

Volkova also gave morning class to the company proper and quickly came to play such a central role in the young organisation that Kersley and others came to view her as one of its 'leaders', although she was only hired by the hour.

'She worked with our technique, but she always took our repertoire into account, and we were not used to that', remembered Pamela May, who also appreciated that 'she always came and watched the performances... She didn't teach us the same things, she would change things and steps if something looked better on me. Some things suited Margot better, some things suited me better.'

Ninette de Valois was less enthusiastic about Volkova's work with the company and about her relationship – professional and personal – with Margot Fonteyn. In terms of establishing classical ballet as an art form in Britain, de Valois proved herself a visionary and earned her place in history. She was also an egomaniac who wanted complete control over the company she had founded – and for Volkova to gain respect and influence was therefore a threat. The only competition de Valois could endure was from her own protégées, and as Pamela May explains: 'She wasn't trained by de Valois, de Valois didn't discover her.'

Volkova was quickly sidelined, left to teach only the Ballet School pupils; and even at the School, de Valois took every opportunity to lecture her in public on questions of style and technique. But Pamela May believed that the lack of professional sympathy was not solely on de Valois's part: Volkova was aware that she also needed the freedom to develop her own ideas – and when de Valois told her to give up West Street or leave Sadler's Wells, she chose the latter option. When that happened, De Valois strictly forbade the dancers to take classes with Volkova but, led by Margot Fonteyn, they followed her to West Street, and relations between de Valois and Volkova worsened.

Beryl Grey, another of the company's ballerinas, thinks: 'Ninette possibly took it as an indirect attack on her methods – that people felt she wasn't good enough and other teachers offered more than she could.'[132] One of the company's soloists, Julia Farron, is convinced that 'by that time I don't think she could have done much about stopping Margot. Vera did absolute marvels for her, and Margot couldn't move without Vera guiding and helping her. Vera was marvellously Russian – but without the carry-on: absolutely pure. The best teacher Margot ever had, without any doubt at all.'[133]

Fonteyn herself put the dancers' feelings into words in an interview with a women's magazine: 'She has every quality a teacher needs. I think it is as much a gift to be a great teacher as it is to be a great dancer or a great choreographer ... I think perhaps it is her absolute, almost child-like concentration and enthusiasm which makes her so wonderful to learn from.'[134]

'We needed her', insisted Pamela May.

When de Valois found out that one of the soloists, Henry Danton, was among those attending Volkova's classes against her wishes, she lashed out: 'I will not have you going to that tuppenny-ha'penny teacher round the corner!' Danton would not back down in the face of de Valois's anger. He knew what kind of teaching he needed, and he was no longer getting it at Sadler's Wells.

By 1946 Audrey Harman had graduated into the company, was dancing solo roles with The Sadler's Wells Theatre Ballet and danced with Sadler's Wells at The Royal Opera House. She remembered Frederick Ashton coming up to her as they were all standing on the stage before the curtain went up on *The Sleeping Beauty*, quietly saying, 'I hear you've been a naughty girl, going to Volkova's classes!' But Ashton himself attended Volkova's classes: she fondly called him her 'fat sylph'. He came to her because he found Ninette de Valois's classes too constricting and Volkova, who was always eager to encourage choreographers, let him 'do his business' at the back, experimenting.

Every day Volkova singled out Fonteyn at the morning classes in West Street. Audrey Harman recalled that after the barre there was a moment's silence before Volkova would say, in her pronounced Russian accent: 'Margoot, you know, opposite mirror.'

Fonteyn herself felt uneasy about all the attention she got in West Street: 'After the war, Volkova's studio attracted all the top foreign dancers who passed through London. It was almost like attending a morning levée, with eminent critics and guests coming to watch. It is not very enjoyable being observed in class, though doubtless good for the soul.'[135]

In her memoirs, Fonteyn compared her partnership with Volkova to that of the romantic ballerina Marie Taglioni and her father Filippo:

> I worked so hard in Volkova's class that I used to wish I could faint, as the great Taglioni is reported to have done every day at the end of two hours' training with her father. Anyway, though I felt sick and ready to die, I remained, to my annoyance, conscious and quite healthy-looking.[136]

The Volkova–Fonteyn collaboration was, in the best sense of the word, an exchange: a working relationship, and a way of working, that was both professional and personal and greatly stimulated Volkova. In Fonteyn, Volkova found a dancer who had not only ability, but also the will to make every second of her training count: a kindred spirit who recognised the obligation that comes with talent and was prepared to give her all to fulfil it. It became Volkova's ideal template.

The relationship was one of trust. Henry Danton believes that it was stronger and more intimate than most people realised, extending far beyond the rehearsal room. To him they seemed more like sisters than teacher and pupil.

Their personal closeness allowed room for experimentation, failure and uncompromising honesty in their professional life. Gilbert Vernon remembers that 'One day she set a very difficult *adage*. When it was done, she looked quizzically at Margot and said, "You know, Margot, that was what the French call *moche* – rubbish!" Margot agreed.'

Volkova and Fonteyn also worked privately for two hours every afternoon on Fonteyn's roles for Sadler's Wells, and on a detailed and purposeful analysis of Fonteyn's full potential as an artist: 'Be elegant. Be aristocratic. Inspire awe and affection. That is *your* style', Volkova decided.[137]

> Often ... I would think I had made a little progress on a step, only to hear Volkova say regretfully, with her head slightly on one side, 'Yes. Well, somehow it didn't quite come out, isn't it?' She had a beautiful way of getting her colloquialisms mixed – 'Here and then' instead of 'Here and there' – and imaginative descriptive phrases such as, 'Head is like you are smelling violets over right shoulder'; or, 'Arms are holding delicate flowers you must not crush'. I was greatly charmed by 'Leg does not know is going to arabesque'. It gave me a new perspective on my limbs as though they were independent of me. I was reminded of another teacher who really unnerved me by saying, 'Don't trust your right foot,' Fonteyn recalled.[138]

Volkova said to Gilbert Vernon that it was a joy to teach Robert Helpmann. He got everything right away... but he had always forgotten it by the next day! With Fonteyn it was different: like 'dripping water on a stone: it takes a long time, but once it's there it is there forever'.[139]

Volkova also learned from Fonteyn. 'You can't impose your personality on a great dancer – I learned that with Margot', she said. 'What I tell [the dancers] is, do it convincingly, do it your way.'[140] Most of all she appreciated Fonteyn's musicality: 'I had problems in class with the timing of a particular step', Gilbert Vernon remembers, 'so Volkova suggested that I should stand behind Fonteyn and follow her.'

Fonteyn had already danced the leading parts in the great classical ballets like *Swan Lake* and *Giselle* before the outbreak of war, but Leo Kersley does not think that Sadler's Wells finally claimed her as its own ballerina until 1946, when the Royal Opera House reopened after the war: 'Vera's and Margot's mission was complete'.

Fonteyn's dancing had changed fundamentally. She had pared it down to the bone and penetrated to the heart of each step. She cut out all mannerisms and affectation. She removed 'dancing' from dance and *became* dance. Ashton had previously described Fonteyn's feet as 'pats of butter', but the critics remarked that her *pointe* work had become stronger.

Gilbert Vernon agrees that Fonteyn was transformed after her intense training with Volkova: 'Photographs from before World War II show Margot's beautiful line, but the hands are like claws. Vera Volkova in the classroom and Frederick Ashton in the rehearsal room helped to eliminate the tension and create what were surely the most expressive hands in ballet.'[141]

In her biography of Fonteyn, Meredith Daneman claims that it was the architects of British ballet who created Fonteyn: Ninette de Valois, Sadler's Wells Ballet's Musical Director Constant Lambert and choreographer Frederick Ashton. But it was Ashton and Volkova who worked with Fonteyn to make the dream come true.

To Michael Somes, Fonteyn's partner, some of his 'fondest memories' of those years were 'of going with Margot, and often with Sir Frederick to West Street, in the afternoons after classes were over, and going through all the classical *pas de deux* in detail for hours and hours'. To Somes, Volkova 'seemed tireless and so completely absorbed. She transmitted a way to work which I have always remembered.'[142]

Fonteyn had Ashton in her mind when she trained with Volkova: 'She had an absolutely unwavering vision of the ideal, from which nothing distracted her. I worked hard every day to be prepared for the time when Ashton would return to the company and make new ballets for me ...'[143]

To Pamela May it was obvious that there was a clear line from Volkova's classes to Ashton's choreographic work. They were artistically related: 'There was always a quality, every movement had a quality ... Ashton needed that, and Vera helped him through us. She prepared us to be ready to work with him when he wrote his ballets.' Ashton and Volkova loved to discuss and talk, 'and she often came to rehearsals when he was creating new work'.

Audrey Harman remembered that when Fonteyn and May returned from training with Preobrazhenskaya in Paris, Volkova was eager to know what they had learnt. She noted a particular step and drew Ashton's attention to it. The choreographer later used it in one of his ballets.

The Sadler's Wells Ballet built its reputation in the 1930s and 1940s on its staging of the great classical Russian ballets in which Fonteyn excelled, but the remainder of the repertoire consisted mainly of works by Ninette de Valois, Robert Helpmann and Frederick Ashton. When Ashton was in the RAF during World War II, Helpmann's ballets came to dominate the repertoire: theatrical ballets such as *Hamlet* and *Adam Zero*, which focused on death, destruction and the uncertainty of the future. But it was Ashton, a classicist, who was chosen to create the opening ballet for Sadler's Wells Ballet's season at Covent Garden when the building was re-opened as an opera house in 1946.

Ashton's new work was *Symphonic Variations*. A highly distilled abstract ballet for three couples to music by César Franck, it had been inspired by the visions of St Teresa of Avila and St John of the Cross. It was not originally intended to be abstract, but during rehearsals it developed from the latter's *Spiritual Canticle*. Following the theme of the eclogue – in which the bride, representing the soul, searches for the bridegroom, representing Christ – it became a deeply personal, almost spiritual, statement about the power of faith, the victory of civilisation over barbarity, and the enduring power of classical ballet in the face of modernism. The central strand of St Teresa's mystical thought throughout all her writings – the struggle for the ascent of the soul – pervades the ballet.

Volkova visited Ashton at his country house while *Symphonic Variations* was being conceived. 'I retain a vivid image of him', she later wrote:

> ...his face lit by the open fire of his little retreat in Datchet, as he outlined to me his ideas and described, in his inimitable way, many of the beautiful movements he had in mind for a future ballet. I was familiar with most of the choreography he had so far achieved. This clearly was a new side of his many-sided talent.[144]

Ashton's train of thought struck a chord with Volkova and touched on much of what Volynsky had preached at the School of Russian Ballet. Ashton himself 'was afraid that if I put my thoughts into words, even to myself, I might deflect myself from creating the work in terms of dancing',[145] but he discussed the ballet with the designer, Sophie Fedorovich, and with Volkova.

Ashton's biographer Julia Kavanagh detects a 'Russian' influence in *Symphonic Variations*, which she ascribes to Volkova, and Margot Fonteyn remembered that:

> Vera Volkova often came to the rehearsals, and tiny details were discussed and reworked as though they were part of an architectural plan for a building that would last forever. The final pose in particular was unresolved for several days while different versions were tried.[146]

Pamela May added that Volkova 'always had suggestions, and she made them in the nicest way'.

Ashton's ballet was a work where, finally, technique was not just a formal element: it was the medium through which the art expressed itself, and realised Volynsky's ideal in moulding 'the materials of the outer world ... into images of a precisely apprehended inner world'.

'More abstract than hitherto, Ashton's limpid choreographic inventions transcended the prose style', Volkova later wrote, 'and with Sophie Fedorovitch's green cathedral of a décor achieved a sense of atmosphere rare in works of this kind.'[147]

After the destruction of war, with London bombed, with millions dead, and in the face of bestiality, Ashton's dancers seemed to find the still centre of themselves that could confine these things: a state characterised by a blissful peace and such ecstatic flights that the bodies were literally lifted into space. They reached out to each other and found some sense of peace; holding hands they came to a place of understanding that involved the audience in a very powerful way.

Symphonic Variations ends as it opens, with the dancers lifting their eyes, awakening at the climax of the mystical experience. Again, in Volynsky's words:

> ...the eyes that were not shut, but not watching, open in actuality. They look and see.

'The Eyes of a Fanatic'

When Volkova opened her studio in 1943, one of her first students, Tommy Linden, a dancer in West End musicals, brought his friends Henry Danton and Peter Wright with him to West Street. Wright, who danced with Kurt Jooss, and later became a choreographer and Director of the Birmingham Royal Ballet, remembers how Danton, whom he now describes as 'a bit of a rebel', was immediately taken with the Russian teacher: 'He was obsessed by her.'

Danton was a promising member of the Sadler's Wells Ballet but had started late as a dancer. His father had been killed in the Great War, leaving his widow to bring up a daughter and two sons alone. Both his great-grandfathers had been army generals, one of them Chief of Police in India and the man who imprisoned Gandhi for his own protection. From the age of 9, Danton was educated on a King's Cadet Scholarship at Wellington College in Berkshire, a military public school, and later at the Royal Military Academy, Woolwich. He was commissioned as a Second Lieutenant in the artillery in 1939. When World War II broke out, he was promoted to Captain at the age of 20, responsible for four howitzers and the men who operated them, but Danton was desperately unhappy in the Army and was, by his own admission, not cut out to be a soldier. During one exercise on Salisbury Plain, he succeeded in losing himself and all his men, most of whom were 'old sweats' who had been called home from the colonies.

Sent home on leave to recover after a fall from the platform of a lorry during a troop transport, Danton determined to abandon his family-instigated army career and pursue a secret dream instead. Once a week he sneaked away from home to join a class with Judith Espinosa, a teacher of the French school: 'In the first class, she had me stand at the barre in first position, then lift my leg in the front and carry it around to the back', Danton remembers, the joy of that first experience still evident in his voice.

> She said, 'Are you sure you've never taken a ballet class before?' So I said, no, and then she called the secretary in and she called someone else in and said, 'Just look at this, this boy, he can do this right away.' And it was simply because I had done a lot of skating, you know, we did spread-eagle, which is of course turned out in second position, and I lifted my leg on skates in *arabesque*, so, you know ... '

Just a year after taking up dance, Danton started his professional career with the Allied Ballet and Mona Inglesby's International Ballet before joining Sadler's Wells, where Ninette de Valois immediately dubbed him 'the New Boy'. 'I was the New Boy for at least two years', says Danton. 'She never bothered to learn my name, or she knew it and just didn't say it, in a sort of beating-down process.'

Classes at Sadler's Wells were taught by Ninette de Valois herself, or by Peggy van Praagh, 'a dyed-in-the-wool Cecchetti dancer', according to Danton.

> She had big, heavy legs and was completely shut in the legs. She had sufficient technique to dance *Coppélia*, but they had to put her in a long skirt because she had such over-developed legs.

When Tommy Linden first took him to West Street, he was desperately looking for a teacher outside the company to guide his training and develop his style, and he fell in love first with Volkova's dancing. 'She showed me exercises and positions I had never known before', he remembers.

> Everything about her seemed correct, and she was correctly placed. Since what I wanted more than anything else was to learn, I would naturally be attracted by her.
>
> I knew there was a reason why I wanted to dance, but the goal – to be able to express the entire register of human feelings with one's body and in movement – had never been formulated in classes. This I found with Vera, all in one parcel containing technique and style and the lot.
>
> Everything I achieved with her led logically further to the next step. There was a development; there was a form of progress that I had never experienced in other classes, which were not thought out with the same foresight. Her classes appealed to my own sense of logic and cause and effect. Perhaps the most important thing of all: one had the impression that Vera was concerned about her pupils and genuinely interested – that she wanted them to learn and become better.

She stimulated and inspired Danton:

> I was painfully aware that there was much too much I couldn't do, and I told her so one day. 'I'm sorry to hear that,' was her ambiguous reply. I don't know if it was her intention, but with that remark she cast petrol on the flames!

Volkova chuckled at the end of her answer, which surprised Danton: 'She did that after everything she said. No matter whether it was something funny or sad – a bit like a child.'

She had the most fabulous legs. When she taught class, she wore a three-quarter-length black cotton skirt, and stockings which she put on especially for the class ... sort of flesh colour.

Anyway, she would pull the skirt up, tuck it into her panties, so that the whole leg was seen. And she had these fabulous legs! I mean, she would do *developpé* unfolding this fabulous leg with this enormously beautiful instep on the end, and then she would step up into *arabesque* on a big half-toe, like an arrow going into the floor, and hold the position. She was really wonderful, wonderful to watch!

Volkova returned Danton's admiration, and she respected his integrity, his insatiable hunger for learning and his great natural talent, though one West Street dancer, Yvonne Cartier, remembers her also saying, 'Hasn't Henry got a lovely body?' And she is not sure Volkova was only talking about its facility for ballet.

Danton felt there was an 'almost mystical connection' between them, and he talked about her incessantly. At 40, she was still attractive in her dramatic, feline way. Danton says, 'She had an oriental way of moving her head. She was exotic, elegant and mysterious; she was Mata Hari.' Volkova was also still sexual, and her husband had been on active service for some years by the time she met the man who was to become her lover. As well as marking his good looks and the flattering attention he paid her, Volkova had noticed that he had 'the eyes of a fanatic'. She saw in those eyes a passion for the dance that matched her own. Although her secret admirer did not know it, she was equally attracted, as a story Danton tells makes clear.

One day Danton thought he spotted his teacher in a crowd. On an impulse he followed her, although he would never have dared to approach her. When he made eye contact with the woman he had been trailing, he realised he had been mistaken and turned away sheepishly – whereupon he ran straight into the real Volkova, who had been following him. Naturally, they merely greeted each other politely and hurried off in opposite directions.

On 20 February 1945 a group of dancers from the Sadler's Wells Ballet went to entertain Allied troops in Belgium and France. When Danton was in Paris, he took classes with Viktor Gsovsky, one of the city's many Russian teachers. Danton was sway-backed (he had an abnormally concave lumbar spine). Using a method of radical stretching very much in opposition to Volkova's usual training, Gsovsky solved the problem in less than two weeks. When Danton returned to West Street in April, Volkova noticed immediately:

I went back to class with Vera and she took one look at me when I stood at the barre and said, 'What have you done with your body? She was just amazed that my sway-back had disappeared completely in the time that we had been away. I told her I had taken classes with Gsovsky, and she said, 'You have to tell me all about it.'

She invited me to her home to have dinner with her. She lived out in Putney, across the river. And we had dinner, and we talked about it, and we stayed up all night talking about dance, and I described the class to her, in detail, exactly how he gave it. Because Gsovsky was very, very musical. I think I learned a great deal about rhythm and the musical composition of steps from him. Vera had a little trouble with music, I thought. She had a pianist, a nice, round English lady, Kathleen. She sat up on the platform and played the piano like she was pumping an organ for the Queen. She would play whatever she knew, and sometimes it just didn't help you do what Vera was asking you to do ... It was always a sort of bone of contention between us that I felt that the music was not adequate there.

Anyway, she was always most interested in seeing what other teachers were doing, and the next morning, in class, she started trotting out what I had told her. Gsovsky had a set barre, he taught the same barre every day, and I had told her exactly what the barre was, and out she trotted these exercises. And she kept walking past me saying, 'Is that right, is that right?' But she got it all right.

In that class there was another Russian dancer called Nina Tarakanova, and she had been with the de Basil company and had danced with Massine and was Russian-trained ... When the class finished, I went outside and there was Nina waiting for me and she gave me hell! She said, 'Why don't you leave Vera alone? We all know what Gsovsky teaches. We want to know what *she* has to say.' So I really got it in the neck from her. Of course, she was right.

The night of the Gsovsky conversation, Danton had stayed in Putney. Volkova had given him a guest room, and they both went to bed exhausted, but Danton could not sleep and was still awake when the door opened and Volkova came in with a lighted candle, like a phantom: 'I was terrified', he recalls.

When their relationship became physical after such a long time of denial and restraint, an overwhelming passion was released and Danton quickly moved into Volkova's house. The couple lived together for almost a year: a scandalous thing to do in those days, and one that could have ruined Volkova both socially and professionally. Marie Rambert, one of Volkova's friends, remarked that something about Danton had changed. She thought he had had an affair with the dancer Celia Franca: 'Look what Celia has done for Henry', she said to Volkova. 'Isn't it wonderful that she has turned him into a real, manly dancer?!'

He remembers that he and Volkova used to meet secretly for lunch:

Between the last morning class and the afternoon class, she would go out and have lunch and relax and then go back and teach again. People were always buttonholing her after the class to talk to her, because she was a personality. People came just to see Volkova. She was the first Soviet dancer who had ever been seen in England. She did have a marvellous personality on top of that, and she was a wonderful teacher ... Anyway, she was always trying to escape. She would get out of the class as soon as possible. We had a little Greek restaurant run by a guy called Nick. It was in the basement, at the top of Shaftesbury Avenue, a short walk. He was very nice, always had very good food, used to have steaks and all kinds of things from the black market. So we had this arrangement that we would meet there, and have lunch and talk, and sometimes we would go out afterwards and go for a walk.

We would walk like any two people who like each other, hand in hand. She had such sharp eyes, she'd obviously been well trained in Russia to see danger when it's approaching. We would be walking along hand in hand and then she would see somebody from the company, or someone she knew, and she would shake my hand off in such an abrupt way and assume a pose two steps in front of me. So funny. It made me laugh so much.

They were discreet, but their affair could not remain secret for long in their small world of ballet. They would take separate trains into town, and were careful never to arrive at classes at the same time, but according to Gilbert Vernon everyone knew about it. Frederick Ashton discovered it when he met the couple by chance in Regent's Park and thoroughly disapproved. He was attracted to Danton but had been rejected so he tried to stir up trouble, advising Volkova to end it and making bitchy remarks to Danton about the mole on Volkova's upper lip.

Ninette de Valois accidentally spotted the lovers in a pub where they had thought they were in no danger of being discovered.

Volkova and myself, we were already there eating our lunch, and in walks Ninette de Valois. As far as she was concerned I was still the New Boy, some insignificant, useless little dancer, who she didn't like particularly much because she couldn't dominate me. So she said, 'Oh Vera, there you are', and pulled up a chair and sat down and started talking with Vera. I was absolutely sweating with nerves because we were trying to make sure that no one would know what was going on, because Vera was married, after all. I remember I was eating soup, I tried to get the soup up to my mouth, and I couldn't get it, I was shaking so much I shook the soup all over the place, all over me, all over the table, and Ninette said, 'What's the matter with you, Boy?' I remember that was the most terrifying luncheon I've ever had. I sat there like some nonentity while she talked shop with Vera. It was absolutely horrible! I couldn't get the fork, I kept missing my mouth and digging the fork into my cheek.

The only person Volkova confided in was Margot Fonteyn, who was herself involved in a complicated affair. Late in the summer of 1945, Fonteyn went on holiday with Volkova and Danton to the Cornish coast, where Danton's mother and sister had rented a house. Fonteyn's mother, Mrs Hilda Hookham, went with them and tormented Fonteyn with attempts to manoeuvre her into a romance with a famous film director in whom Fonteyn had no interest. (Moira Shearer was filming *The Red Shoes*, and Mrs Hookham had ambitions for her daughter to become a film star, too.) The younger generation enjoyed their efforts to avoid the Black Queen, as Mrs Hookham was nicknamed, and her matchmaking schemes. Danton recalls that on one occasion all three of them hid in a wardrobe while she tried in vain to find them, like naughty children playing sardines.

In Plaidy, Danton and Volkova threw caution aside and displayed their passion for one another freely. When Ian Gibson-Smith came to photograph Volkova for *Life* magazine, Danton appeared in the pictures too. The photographs (numbers 24 and 25) show a very different side to Volkova from the painted siren of Shanghai or the chic ballet mistress. Dressed in shorts, un-made-up and with loose hair, she dances uninhibitedly with her lover on the beach, looking infinitely more liberated than in any other image that has survived.

Ultimately, dance was at the centre of Volkova's life, and Danton was astounded by how she lived. She worked the whole time, and when classes were over she had to deal with pupils and observers of every type, who incessantly asked her questions and refused to release her, before continuing her day giving private lessons to Fonteyn or Violetta Elvin. She was in the theatre every evening and was seldom home before midnight: 'You had to take the underground to Putney', Danton continues:

and then you had to go across the river – there was a bridge across the river – to get to where her house was. Of course, she would come to performances and go back home late. I would also come back late, and sometimes we wouldn't come together. There was the blackout at that time, you know. I was concerned about her going across that bridge in the dark at 11 o'clock at night. So I said, why don't we make an arrangement to meet and go across together somehow? But she said, 'Don't worry, dear, I have very strong legs, and I know exactly where to kick!' Which I thought was wonderful, and it was so typical of her: I mean, she knew exactly how to meet any encounter.

In any case, with a programme like that she had no time to keep house, and there was hardly ever any food in the flat. If it had not been for plump little Gwen, who lived in the flat above and often brought her some food, she would have starved. Gwen's husband was also on active service, and we imagined that she was fascinated by the thought that Vera had taken a lover – fascinated and also a little envious.

We laughed all the time. Volkova called me her Slimkin and herself Mousekin. I remember a story she once told me. She had gone to the hairdresser's in Paris, and the lady sitting next to her, no longer quite young, had been given an all-embracing and prolonged facial treatment. When it was over, she studied herself in the mirror and sighed despondently, '*En avant, Caroline!*' We often used that expression.

Danton, a descendant of Scottish aristocrats, found the snobbery and pretension of the ballet world 'elite' distasteful, and he and Volkova never became part of it, or of Robert Helpmann's camp and affected arty circle, in which photographer Cecil Beaton and actors Laurence Olivier and Vivien Leigh massaged each others' egos and traded witticisms in put-on, cut-glass accents. 'Volkova was too serious to be a part of that', according to Danton. In spite of her popularity, he felt that she was really a lonely and isolated figure, and that her only real friends were probably Marie Rambert, Sophie Fedorovitch, Margot Fonteyn and David Arkell.

Volkova may well have been a woman of the world, but she had an innocence about her and was pure in heart. I'll never forget the day when we went for a walk in the woods – her delight about the beauty of the place, the clear spring light and the carpet of flowers. I don't think I have ever seen her happier, and I remember her speaking very pensively about the enormous contrast between nature and classical ballet, which is such a sophisticated art.

When the Sadler's Wells Ballet went on tour again in November 1945, he received a letter from Fonteyn, who had stayed in London: Volkova had been taken to hospital after a miscarriage. Fonteyn wrote that she had visited Volkova, and that she resembled 'a little girl with pigtails'.

Danton was shaken by the letter, and was convinced that Volkova must have provoked an abortion. When he got back to London, her only comment was, 'It's a good thing Hugh wasn't there'. He must have been shocked by her coldness, but she had never told him about her previous false pregnancy and the doctors' prognosis that she would never be able to have children. Perhaps Volkova had subdued her emotions into extinction; perhaps she was trying to protect the young and vulnerable Danton from her own feelings? And maybe it was easier for her to control her own emotions if she remained Danton's 'teacher' and kept them to herself?

Whether it was an abortion or a miscarriage, it signalled the end of the affair. Early in their relationship, Volkova had given Danton a copy of Flaubert's *Madame Bovary*. She cannot have believed that she resembled Madame Bovary, but perhaps the gift was a warning to Henry that, unlike the novel's heroine, she would not risk her marriage or her reputation for love. In spite of the gift, and in spite of his mother's attempt to make him see reason, Danton had believed it to be Volkova's intention to divorce Finch Williams, and he felt she had encouraged that belief.

Whatever the truth, Volkova ended the affair in a panic in the spring of 1946, when Hugh Finch Williams was demobbed and returned from India. After Danton had left for class, Volkova received a telegram saying that her husband would be coming back the next day, and she told Danton in West Street that he would have to move out.

'I had been very happy with her', Danton recalls. He was heartbroken, but still hoped to win her back.

In August, he invited her to join his family again on their annual holiday to Cornwall. Volkova accepted, but turned up with Finch Williams. 'I think she wanted to show me that our relationship really was over. I just couldn't understand how she could be with him! She could have had anybody she wanted', says Danton.

To this day Danton does not know if Hugh Finch Williams knew of the affair, but finds it hard to believe that he did not. In Cornwall, Danton courted Volkova shamelessly in front of her husband, dancing Fokine's ballet *Le Spectre de la rose* on the terrace, adoringly spinning and jumping, prostrating himself in front of Volkova, who was seated in a chair and didn't react.

Danton left Sadler's Wells shortly after and, ever the rebel, handed his resignation to Ninette de Valois with 'an outrageous letter' telling her what he thought of the way she treated people. Incredulous, de Valois carried the letter around in her handbag and showed it to everybody, including Ashton and Volkova, saying, 'What on earth does he mean?' She even asked Danton's mother to come to a meeting, asking her, 'Is there something wrong with the Boy's head?' Danton proudly reports that his mother put de Valois in her place and walked out, and that she continued to stand by him when he left England to resume his training with Gsovsky in France.

In 1953, after seven years' silence, Danton finally contacted Volkova. He addressed her bitterly as 'the famous, fashionable Mme Volkova' but insisted that he no longer harboured any grudge against her. She answered him with a letter that he understood, and which he has kept ever since. 'I can't tell you how happy I was to receive your letter, the kind of letter I always waited for', said Volkova:

I often feel nostalgic myself, it was such a short, beautiful page from the long, grey book of my life. I had to tear that page abruptly, hurting you and myself. Grey memories linger still.

She admitted her wrongdoing: 'I have a purity in my heart but it was bruised', asking him for forgiveness:

Leave a pure place in your heart for me as I do in regard to you, even if our roads don't cross anymore.

She continued, explaining:

I live for my work only, I believe in it. I am always ready to improve it. You know how sincere I am about it. I never was and never will be 'famous, fashionable Mme Volkova' in my own eyes. I am much too intelligent and humble for this. These are the trimmings that people supplied me with. It means nothing to me.[148]

She wrote about the irresistible power of her motivation, with which she knew Danton would identify:

I have a plastic purity in my own dancing with the steel-like bones underneath. The muscles everywhere, that nobody is aware of when I move. It was so wonderful to dance. The famous critic Volynsky wrote about one of my performances once. Part of it was written in the form of a poem. My mother kept this article for years. It was in a magazine called *Life of Art*. If only I could translate it to you ... The reason I am writing to you about it at all is that for years I wanted to make people feel the way I felt when I was dancing. I started to teach because I had to. It was a personal thing with me, not ambition and money et cetera.

Help me if you like, write to me all about the ballet, your thoughts, your discoveries, but never put cold water on me.

I am very fond of you, Henry, and I understand you much more than you think. I am grateful for everything ...[149]

What Volkova wanted Danton to know was probably that she had never been torn between her lover and her husband. The conflict that tormented her – and had done since her days of juggling training and family responsibilities in Revolutionary Russia – was between her private life and her work. Volkova would choose the dance over personal happiness every time, and perhaps the same was true of Danton himself. It was their overriding passion for dance that had brought them together and fuelled their relationship. Volkova had seen into her lover's 'fanatic eyes', and perhaps recognised part of herself in him when she foretold his future: 'I think you will finish up by being a teacher.'

She was not wrong. Danton's life turned out to be as rootless, but also as rich, as her own. He began to teach in France, partnered the ballerina Lycette Darsonval on tour, and danced with Roland Petit's Ballets des Champs-Élysées and the Ballets de Paris in the USA. After a year as a guest artist with the Australian National Ballet, he served briefly as the company's Artistic Director. He then taught in New York, at Carnegie Hall and the Julliard School, before moving to Venezuela, where he co-founded what was to become the country's National Ballet. Danton opened an organic restaurant in Caracas and bought a farm, before finally settling in the USA in 1982, where he has been teaching in Texas, Florida, Mississippi and Pennsylvania, still looking for the truth of classical dance. He never married.

Madame Volkova

When the war ended, London began to develop into an international centre for dance. American and European ballet companies came on tour, and dancers from all over the world flocked to train or to find jobs in British companies. Nearly all of them found their way to West Street for class with Volkova, who was now a much-admired and respected authority.

Danish dancers Erik Bruhn and Poul Gnatt had joined the Metropolitan Ballet and, with their partners Sonia Arova and Svetlana Beriosova, trained with Volkova between tours. All the ballerinas from the Original Ballet Russe came, as did Rosella Hightower on her way to join the Marquis de Cuevas's company.

Against choreographer Kurt Jooss's wishes, members of his modern dance company, including Hans Zullig, Peter Wright, Ulla Soderbaum and Noelle de Mosa, sneaked to Volkova's studio: the girls had to hide their blocked *pointe*-shoes from Jooss. What they learned from Volkova overcame Jooss's prejudice against classical dance, and eventually he asked her to work with him.

Roland Petit's Ballets des Champs-Élysées came over from Paris, bringing Renée Jeanmaire, Jean Babilée and Nathalie Philippart. Ballet Theatre's Nora Kaye and Melissa Hayden trained alongside Toni Pihl of the Royal Danish Ballet, whose ballet-master Harald Lander wanted her to develop 'better arms' to lift her into the ballerina category.

Barbara Walczak, a member of the New York City Ballet's corps de ballet, attended class with a number of colleagues. One day, as they were leaving, they met Balanchine and his stars Maria Tallchief and Tanaquil LeClercq in the doorway: 'He was astonished that we had beaten him to Volkova.'[150]

Madame Volkova was rapidly gaining an international reputation – and she really was 'Madame' now. At the end of her affair with Henry Danton, she had become middle-aged almost overnight. It was as if that passion had been her last moment of youth. Sexy, vivid, one-of-the-gang Vera had vanished, to be replaced by a respectable and respected pillar of the ballet world.

Volkova had been more or less invisible during the war, some thought because of Ninette de Valois's enmity. But now hardly a day passed without critics watching her class and writing enthusiastically of her mystique and charisma. 'Their gaze is fixed upon a little woman with a pale Russian skin, a face as beautiful as a Madonna in an Eastern church, who now gives the signal to commence. "*Mes enfants*, your *pliés*, please."

Pliés, to a dancer, are as scales to a singer', wrote a columnist from one of Britain's daily papers. He enthused:

> Look at the girl opposite whose skin is like a magnolia – do you recognise her? I could not believe for a moment that I did myself, for it is Margot Fonteyn.[151]

Critic Beryl de Zöete wrote more seriously about Volkova that her *énchainements* rose above technique and became choreography. She realised:

> with a pang of delight, that this expressive and sympathetic, but very unobtrusive personality was a creative artist, with a subtle and exquisite sense of life. I can see her now standing with her back to the class, frowning and with eyes shut, her lips moving as if reciting mantras, and her hands sketching steps and directions like an Indian guru. Then, unlike the guru, she would demonstrate a sequence with such perfection that one realised what a fine dancer is still alive in this teacher.[152]

In 1946 Agrippina Vaganova's book of Soviet training methods, *Fundamentals of the Classic Dance*, was published in New York and was a sensation. When Volkova had arrived in Britain, hardly anyone had heard of Vaganova, but now having been trained by Vaganova, and being the only teacher in the West to have had first-hand experience of the system, made Volkova a valuable commodity. Volkova's teaching did not directly follow the system delineated by Vaganova; it would be more precise to say that Volkova had been inspired by her teacher's original principles. Watching how she had worked, Volkova had seen how a system could be developed in an almost scientific way. Vaganova had shown the young Volkova the potential and the advantages of a method based on understanding the body as a coordinated and expressive whole, in contrast with the old Italian and French schools' standardised and far less flexible systems. Though her involvement in Vaganova's early experiments now proved invaluable, Volkova admitted to Henry Danton that 'she was already a fully trained dancer before she realised how it happened'. She had studied with Vaganova to become a dancer, not a teacher, and had not absorbed Vaganova's method with an eye for teaching herself.

During the 1940s, Volkova's London classes[153] always began with *pliés*, in the second, first, fifth and fourth positions, each position followed by a rise and balance. Volkova insisted on a soft and fluid *plié*, telling the dancers that this was a 'single movement'. *Battements tendus*, *jétés*, *ronds de jambe à terre*, *ports de bras* and *battements fondus* followed, with stretching exercises to ensure that all the small muscles of the foot were flexed, before the warming-up and precision training continued with *grands battements* and *ronds de jambe en l'air*.

'Lean back against a cloud and enjoy it', the professionals were told when practicing the *développé devant en effacé* in an adagio of *développés*. The barre usually lasted about half an hour, and Volkova's goal was to warm the body and its muscles, especially the legs. The last exercises included *battement frappé*, *petit battement* and, finally, *battement en balançoire (grand battement jeté balance)*, before the first part of the class concluded with *relevés* in first position facing the barre.

Volkova always began centre practice with an *adage* or a version of *temps lié*, which combined the transfer of weight with coordination of *port de bras* and the use of head and eyes.

She gave corrections throughout the whole class, with special focus on the details of *port de bras*. She paid particular attention to the rounded shapes and expression of the arms, and concentrated on developing the full expressive potential of the upper body. Her goal was to create a degree of co-ordination that would enable the dancer to use every necessary limb and muscle at the same time – from the feet to the fingers. Volkova regarded coordination as the dancer's most essential quality, and she often set an exercise using the head and shoulders in counterpoint to develop it.

Next came a combination of *battement tendu*, *battement glissé* and *pirouettes*: 'Imagine you have pink air between your arms, and you carry the air around with you', Volkova would suggest.

The *battement fondu* exercise was fundamental: the perfect preparation for jumps and allegro, and a logical development from the adagio section. Here the leg was held at an angle of 45 degrees, and the exercise was done both with and without a *relevé sur la demi-pointe*. The class also included *enchaînements*, which made use of *rond de jambe à terre* and *en l'air*, *battement frappé* and *petit battement à terre et sur la demi-pointe*, and throughout the class the use of *épaulement* and the directions *croisé*, *effacé* and *écarté* gave the steps light and shade.

Aplomb, balancing on *pointe* and *demi-pointe*, was a central part of Volkova's teaching. Each exercise at the barre ended in a balance. This particular exercise, some say, was what developed Margot Fonteyn's famous sense of balance, and gave her the strength and confidence to tackle one of the most challenging dances of the entire ballet canon, the Rose Adagio in *The Sleeping Beauty*.

Assemblé combinations preceded the allegro series, followed by *petite batterie* and *grand allegro*, the big jumps. The girls then changed into *pointe* shoes while the boys practiced *tour en l'air*, *sauté-pirouette* and *grand pirouette* and other bravura steps. For the girls, *pointe* work included

18. In Shanghai, Volkova met an English businessman, Hugh Finch Williams, who aspired to be an architect. Finch Williams helped Volkova when she was seriously ill and, in 1934, secured a visa for her to settle in the British Crown Colony of Hong Kong.

Photograph courtesy of the Royal Ballet School Archives, the Vera Volkova Collection.

19. When Volkova (right) arrived in Hong Kong, she immediately set up a ballet school. This photograph shows her with one of her students.

Photograph courtesy of the Royal Ballet School Archives, the Vera Volkova Collection.

20. After Volkova and Finch Williams were married in 1936 they settled in Putney, in a house called Swan Studios. Finch Williams felt that the first months of their life together as man and wife were, in many ways, their happiest.

Photograph courtesy of the Royal Ballet School Archives, the Vera Volkova Collection.

21. A wartime portrait of Volkova, taken while her husband was serving in India as a Major in the British Army.
   Photograph courtesy of the Royal Ballet School Archives, the Vera Volkova Collection.

22. At 40, Volkova was still attractive in her dramatic, feline way. Henry Danton, who was 15 years younger than her when he became her lover thinks: 'She had an oriental way of moving her head. She was exotic, elegant and mysterious; she was Mata Hari.'
 Private collection.

23. Volkova and Danton with Margot Fonteyn's mother, Mrs. Hilda Hookham, who was known throughout the British ballet community as 'the Black Queen'.

Private collection.

24. On holiday in Plaidy, with Danton's family, Fonteyn and Mrs Hookham, Danton and Volkova threw caution aside and displayed their passion freely. When Ian Gibson-Smith came to photograph Volkova for Life, Danton appeared in the pictures too.

Photographer: Ian Gibson-Smith.

25. Idem.

Photographer: Ian Gibson-Smith.

26. When the War ended and Hugh Finch Williams returned to London,
Volkova ended her affair with Henry Danton. She had become an
internationally recognised and established teacher and would not risk her
marriage or her reputation for love.
   Photographer: Felix Fonteyn.

27. Volkova in her West Street studio.
 Photograph courtesy of the Royal Ballet School Archives, the Vera Volkova
Collection.

28. During the War, dancers from all London's ballet companies started coming to West Street. Diana Gould said of Volkova's classes: 'under her tuition one became a conduit through which passed the rhythm and the melody, not just a muscular gymnast ...' Here Volkova instructs Violetta Elvin and Moira Shearer.

Photographer: Felix Fonteyn.

29. In Margot Fonteyn, Volkova found a dancer who had not only ability, but also the will to make every second of her training count: a kindred spirit who recognised the obligation that comes with talent and was prepared to give her all to fulfil it.

Photographer: Felix Fonteyn.

.30. When Volkova and Margot Fonteyn began working together in London
they developed an intense collaboration that was, in the best sense of the
word, an exchange: a working relationship, and a way of working, that was
both professional and personal.

Photograph courtesy of the Royal Ballet School Archives, the Vera Volkova
Collection.

31. As most people never saw them. Volkova and French choreographer
Roland Petit having fun.
   Photograph courtesy of the Royal Ballet School Archives, the Vera Volkova
Collection.

32. In 1950 Volkova took on the job of Director of the ballet at La Scala in Milan, one of Europe's biggest companies. Only the Sadler's Wells Ballet, the Paris Opéra Ballet and the Royal Danish Ballet in Copenhagen were of comparable size.

Photograph courtesy of the Royal Ballet School Archives, the Vera Volkova Collection.

33. The Director at La Scala, Dr Ghiringhelli, had wanted Volkova to produce quick results, expecting her to make the ballet one of the world's four best companies within five years, but when she tried to instigate reforms in the top-heavy organisation, he usually failed to back her up, and by April she was ready to throw in the towel.

   Photograph courtesy of the Royal Ballet School Archives, the Vera Volkova Collection.

34. In June 1950, the Soviet ballerina Galina Ulanova gave her first performance in the West at the Teatro Communale in Florence. Volkova was spellbound by Ulanova's performance and had a private reunion with her childhood friend that was her first contact with the Soviet ballet world since her emigration.

Photographer unknown.

échappé and *relevé* followed by virtuoso combinations with 32 *fouettés* and other *pirouettes*, before concluding with *grand battement sur les pointes*. The class always ended with a *port de bras* followed by 16 *petits changements de pieds*, 16 *grands changements* or a series of *entrechat six*.

Finally the *révérence*: the boys bowed and the girls curtsied. 'For them it was a sinking into relaxation after supreme effort, and a thanks, not to an audience for once, but to their great teacher', Richard Ingram remembers. 'For me it was my first witnessing of the master-class relationship between great artist teacher and artist pupils humble enough to always be learning', he adds:

> To this professional regard they also added love, because it was quite obvious none of them were there but from their own choice. She was an example which they emulated and they came for love of her personality.[154]

Volkova herself casually remarked to the dancer William Chappell after a class: 'It's a form of torture, isn't it? I wonder why we do it.'[155]

The critic Richard Buckle, who also watched classes in West Street, believed that it was her 'personality, her psychological insight and her devout, mystical understanding of the classical tradition' that made her 'the pre-eminent teacher of the Western world today'.[156]

Buckle first came to Volkova's studio because she had convinced him that it would be useful for him to gain a deeper understanding of the dance through dancing himself. When the students had left, she asked him to change into practice clothes. He remembered that:

> Vera, her dark eyes lit by a serious smile, looked tired and untidy but full of determination to do her best in educating a ballet critic, and exclaimed, to put me more at ease, 'What a back! What strong legs!'; then, lighting one cigarette from another, drew her fur-lined coat about her and led me to the *barre*.[157]
>
> Working with her I realised more than ever before why classical exercises were not only the most perfect physical training in the world but also the necessary daily ritual from which all ballets must spring. I did not have many lessons, but the few I had altered my outlook considerably.[158]

It was, of course, those who worked the hardest who were rewarded with Volkova's special attention. 'She didn't really give me a single correction for two months', Gilbert Vernon recalls, 'but one day she said: "Gilbert, would you stay behind after class?"'

> And I thought, oh no, what have I done? She made me stand in profile in front of the mirror and look at my image over my shoulder as she corrected my posture. Tuck in the pelvis, pull in the diaphragm. Eventually she was satisfied: 'Zat is how you have to dance!' I told her I didn't think I could walk like that,

never mind dance. She laughed and said: 'Till zat is right, nussing else will come right.' That's when I knew that she was interested and decided I was serious. From then on I didn't get away with anything.

Vernon continues:

I was having trouble with the *double tour en l'air*. She took me aside and said: 'Think you are holding a piece of paper between ze cheeks of your buttocks. Wiz you ze paper would fall out. Pinch ze paper!' Within weeks it was one of my most secure steps... Taught by a woman, not a man... that was interesting.

At the end of the 1940s the British actress Claire Bloom, who had made her début as the ballerina in Chaplin's film *Limelight*, was torn between acting and dance. Later on, when Bloom had given up ballet completely and was acting in *Ring Round the Moon*, she met Volkova on the bus: 'Ah, Claire,' said Volkova, 'I am so happy for you. I always knew you were an artiste – not a dancer, but an artiste.'

When Bloom was still dancing, she took classes only with Volkova, because of 'the openness of her interpretation of classical movement', which was new to Bloom. She later wrote in her memoirs that it was with Volkova that she first realised that 'movement was connected to the realm of feeling'.

'There was Volkova', Bloom wrote:

her every word wisdom to me. The boys were doing leaps, each straining to get higher than the other. 'No, no, no,' said Volkova. 'When you leave the ground, yes you leave the ground, but you go *back* to the ground, because there is your root. Not trying to jump up in the air, but to keep to the ground and then to show you can leave it – there is your power.'[159]

As well as explaining the spirit of the steps, Volkova offered practical advice in strikingly original terms, which would bring out a very precise quality in each step: 'Do *cabriole* like you're wearing a very tight skirt' was one of Volkova's metaphorical suggestions. 'Do *plié* like put your hand on hot iron' was another. On landing from a jump, Volkova would say: 'Drop egg, goes straight into floor, doesn't bounce.'

Maurice Béjart also came to London to dance and studied with Volkova in West Street. He, too, found in her an understanding of classical dance that he never experienced again:

I have had three or four great teachers in my life and Vera was among them with Asaf Messerer and Maya Plisetskaya, yet Vera was unlike any other Russian teacher I have seen before and after. Sometimes she would be English, sometimes Russian, but really she transcended nationality! I don't know where she drew her inspiration from, but it was often unexpected, original and new, what she did.

'She knew and understood ballet better than anyone else', Béjart remembers today,

and she was very special in that she could intuit people immediately and would behave in different ways with different people. She was not the same person to everybody. For instance, she could be very naughty with one person, very straightforward with somebody else and very, very gentle with others. And it was not about her liking people but because she knew what kind of teacher they needed to become better dancers. And people. Her gift for understanding the psychology of people was something very unique, something one rarely sees in a teacher.

Béjart was terrified when he first met her:

I remember I was very intimidated by her. Often when you meet great people you come with terror of them, but after you get to know them it's different, of course. I was happy to discover the person. In class she was Madame Volkova but outside the class she became a friend, and I felt we had a good communication ... She was a very intelligent person with a great mind, and this was one of the most important things about her. She was dynamic and full of life, she was never tired, she was driven, and she was a woman in the real sense of the word. She had character and strength. In fact, she was a goddess to me.

After class, Volkova always found herself surrounded by dancers looking for advice or career counselling. Richard Ingram remembers that 'Vera was the confidante of half the dancers in town ... She knew all the legends and all the tribulations of dancers in their totally unsubsidised and unprotected lives.'[160]

She used to have lunch every day in a cheap Greek restaurant in Soho called 'The Star', where the staff always had a table ready for her to the right of the entrance. Dancers who wanted advice followed her to the restaurant and would order lunch or just sit down at her table and pour out their hearts.

'She was better than the Delphic Oracle', Richard Ingram says:

because she actually gave positive advice. Usually it was a joint problem inextricably linked between the sufferer's sex life and their dancing career. Dancers of every variety of amatory persuasion trusted her opinion, and it was an unspoken legend that her own adventures gave her the confidence to suggest the best way out of entanglement for others.[161]

One day, Ingram asked Volkova why so many asked her advice: She replied with a Russian hum with the tongue moving on the roof of her mouth: 'I don't make any offering; I just light my lamp and they seem to come.'[162]

In 1948, amid all her professional success, disaster struck in Volkova's private life. She survived a life-threatening ectopic pregnancy and, shortly afterwards, received a letter from her sister Irina, the first in 9 years:

> I have attempted to write to you for more than a year ... How sad it is for me to tell you that I have been alone now since 1942, Mama is dead and Ljova [the Volkov sisters' elder brother, Lev] has disappeared without trace. It happened like this: I was called up for military-medical service. I studied for four months and was in the barracks the rest of the time until 1943, during which time Mama should have been evacuated, but it kept on being put off and it ended sadly. There was terrible hunger and she died of a coma, which she lapsed into because of malnutrition. Ljova said goodbye to us in 1941 and no one knows anything about him.[163]

Having conveyed the devastating news, the letter, written on the back of a torn piece of flowered wallpaper, became a desperate plea for help:

> We went through incredible times and as I was evacuated alone I could breathe freely. It was in Rybinsk, where you should write to me poste restante, because I lost the right to live in Leningrad ... My mother-in-law lives in Moscow, but Vladislav [Irina's husband] himself seems to have perished. Our flat was requisitioned and I was left alone and helpless and was at first at a loss.

Irina longed to leave the Soviet Union:

> The first thing I wanted to do was to leave everything and set off to meet you, first go to Estonia, then to Latvia and so on, but I have decided to wait at least for a letter from you. If you were to write while I was on my way, I wouldn't know. I decided to lay some money aside for the journey and await an answer ... I must see you. We have not seen one another for 19 years and you have probably changed during those years. ... Write to me about everything and think of something witty ...[164]

Volkova tried to contact Irina and send money via the Red Cross, but letters were never collected. No further news came from Irina. Volkova did not know whether she was dead or alive; her last contact with Russia was broken.

Again, she submerged her sadness in her work. When she was not in her studio in West Street, she attended the Sadler's Wells Ballet's seasons. 'At one time hardly a performance went by without Volkova being in the theatre to criticise every detail and to correct afterwards', wrote Pigeon Crowle in *Enter the Ballerina*.[165] This was an unusual situation, since Volkova was not officially working with the company, but she said her work was the only thing she still took seriously. In the words of Gilbert Vernon: 'She was only happy when the work was good. And very good things were happening in London with Margot and British ballet during the war and after it.'

British dancers were a challenge to Volkova because:

they were beautifully trained. But their legs were more developed than their upper bodies. And so I had to find just the right approach to add harmony of arms and shoulders and to release them a bit emotionally.

Volkova was critical of the way the company was being trained by Ninette de Valois and her assistant Peggy van Praagh, who taught the class. 'Frankly, I don't think the Cecchetti technique is especially good for British dancers', she said:

it is too precise and confining. It was more suited to the Russian dancers of the Diaghilev era because they needed to be toned down. The British dancers need just the reverse.[166]

She also believed the Cecchetti technique gave the dancers 'heavy legs'.

At this point, Volkova sensed that she would not be able to go on working in England for much longer, but continued to give Fonteyn private lessons every afternoon. For more than 6 years they had worked on her Aurora in *The Sleeping Beauty*, and, 6 months before the Sadler's Wells Ballet's historic tour of America, they began to review that interpretation.

The Russian *regisseur* Nicholas Sergeyev had brought the choreographic text for the ballet with him from Russia and staged it for the Sadler's Wells. But Sergeyev was not a coach. Together, Volkova and Fonteyn now went through every step, phrase and gesture to create Aurora's character. It was a journey of discovery and revelation, with both Fonteyn and Volkova experimenting and refining up to the last minute.

'A day or two before the Sadler's Wells Ballet left England for their first visit to America, I was watching Fonteyn in class', wrote William Chappell.

I sat next to Vera Volkova in her studio in the West End of London. Beside me on the wooden bench Vera's cigarette was busily burning a black mark into the surface of the seat; a half-empty cup of tepid tea was in danger of being flung to the floor every time the teacher leapt to her feet to demonstrate some movement or correct some fault. It was a mixed bag of dancers who were performing the exercises. Sweating and gasping, they gazed always a little upwards, their eyes set in so beady a look of concentration I felt the wall above my head should be pockmarked with neatly punctured holes drilled by the very intensity of their regard. The room was close and smelt of hot human bodies, the pale autumn sun slanted sideways through the windows. I was half-dazed as I watched Fonteyn, her gaze as concentrated, her brow as damp as any of the others', unfolding, like the tendril of a plant, her delicate leg.

Vera leapt up for the twentieth time; her tea-cup rattled, the cigarette rolled to the floor and started to burn the boards. 'No! No!' Vera cried. 'Not like that – control it in the hips – like this.' She pulled her skirt above her knees and demonstrated.[167]

Fonteyn made her sensational début as Aurora at the Metropolitan Opera on 9 October 1949. Back in England her friends and followers waited excitedly for reports from New York. Pacing around his Bloomsbury flat, Richard Buckle pictured the theatre in his mind's eye and imagined the dancers' racing hearts. 'He thinks', he wrote of himself:

especially of the great ballerina who has to face a sceptical new public in that most exacting of dances, the Rose Adagio. As she stands in open perfect *attitude*, her eyes raised modestly towards her upheld arm, she supports the honour and glory of our nation and empire on the point of one beautiful foot! The critic imagines the suspense, the gossip in the foyer, the mounting excitement, the flowers and the applause; and he can hardly bear not to be there.[168]

But Gilbert Vernon was there:

I was on stage during the Rose Adagio on the opening night in New York. Halfway through the audience began to applaud and didn't stop. We couldn't hear a note of music on stage. She [Fonteyn] glanced at Constant Lambert in the orchestra pit and he signalled, 'Keep going, I will follow you.' ... What followed was pure Disney. The entire company was whisked by a limousine, with police escort sirens screaming, to Mayor O'Dwyer's residence on the East River, where we were given a champagne supper in the garden ... Within a month she was on the cover of *Time* and *Newsweek*.[169]

'What a proud and glorious night for de Valois, for Lambert, and for Fonteyn', wrote Richard Buckle. 'And for Vera Volkova, Margot Fonteyn's beloved teacher, who, back here in London two days later, came to luncheon with me at the "Dog and Duck" to discuss the news of triumph which had been printed in the newspapers!'[170] Fonteyn sent a telegram to Volkova:

Whole performance tremendous success. We all feel you share in it, and we thank you and miss you terribly. Love, Margot and whole company.

Apart from this, there was no official recognition of Volkova's contribution. She had given six months' intense if clandestine work, coaching not only Fonteyn but also most of the production's principal dancers. 'My work is in the kitchen', she noted with a touch of resignation: 'That is where the sauces are prepared.'[171]

Her relationship with Ninette de Valois and the Sadler's Wells Ballet remained cool, with no prospect of it warming. Adding insult to de Valois's sense of injury, Richard Buckle, who was critical of her leadership, wrote an article in *The Observer* asking what would happen if de Valois and Ashton were replaced by, for example, Massine and Volkova. Understandably, de Valois took it very badly.

One of Volkova's young pupils, Brenda Last, later to become a ballerina with the company, went to the theatre with Volkova one evening:

> She took me backstage, once, after a performance of *Sleeping Beauty*, to Robert Helpmann's dressing room. But even at that age I could feel there was a strange atmosphere. She had worked with the company, but she was not working there anymore. Something was not quite right.

Ninette de Valois continued to use her influence to exclude any mention of Volkova from articles about Sadler's Wells. After the success in the USA, an interview with Fonteyn in the *Sunday Times* caused Beryl de Zöete to respond:

> I have been hoping that someone of greater weight than myself in the ballet world would draw attention to a surprising omission in your recent profile of Margot Fonteyn. Two teachers of her childhood and early youth were named, but there was no mention of the great *maîtresse de ballet* who, for the last six years, the period of Margot's most wonderful artistic development, has been her teacher. I refer, of course, to Vera Volkova ... I cannot help wondering whether, if she had been British instead of Russian, her services to British ballet would have been passed over in silence.[172]

'She had a greater vision than many of those who worked with the company', maintains Mavis Ray, who danced with Sadler's Wells Ballet. 'But she was kept in the background; there was not room enough for Volkova in England.'

'When I came back from the second American tour, she had gone', Gilbert Vernon remembers. 'She had gone to Italy, to Milan. The light sort of went out when she left, and I never got back into [the dance] again.'

Richard Buckle greatly deplored Volkova's departure, as did a number of other ballet critics, including Peter Williams of the magazine *Dance and Dancers*:

> We have a habit, in England, of letting people slip through our fingers. The loss of the great teacher Vera Volkova to Italy is one of the bitterest blows to English ballet ... She, more than anybody, has been responsible for finishing and polishing our dancers until they gained the respect of the world. But she was more than a teacher, for she watched almost every performance of ballet and corrected dancers on their work in the public theatre (a very different thing to their work in the private classroom). She was also one of the soundest critics ... The dancers in this country have suffered an irreparable loss.[173]

Intermezzo

Ninette de Valois had encouraged Volkova to accept an invitation to become head of the dormant ballet company at La Scala, pronouncing it 'an offer you can't refuse'. In 1950, the Milan ballet was, in fact, one of Europe's biggest companies, boasting 18 men and 41 women in the corps de ballet, as well as two male principals and two ballerinas. Only the Sadler's Wells Ballet, the Paris Opéra Ballet and the Royal Danish Ballet in Copenhagen were of comparable size.

In the end, what made Volkova take on the challenge was her frustration that her work in England had always confined her to her West Street studio; that she never had the chance to follow it through all the way to performance. This peripheral role of outsider and freelance seemed to be a pattern in her life. In Russia she had never succeeded in joining either of the great state companies; similarly, in England she had not been offered a teaching position at the Sadler's Wells Ballet, although she trained so many of its dancers at West Street. The job at La Scala would be her ticket into the fortress.

She arrived in Milan on 10 December 1950, and was met at the station by a representative of the British Council, who instantly advised her, for reasons she would soon understand, to find a 'cautious' lawyer. She was welcomed by Milanese society with open arms, and courted at every turn by the Director of La Scala, Antonio Ghiringhelli – *il dottore*. He failed to give her a contract, though, despite Volkova's 'patient but persistent' requests.

At the Opera House, she found the programming and organisation short-sighted, chaotic and absurd: 'Instead of *Coppélia* they are after all putting on the old version of *Giselle* (not Romanoff's, who is leaving by the way on the 1st of January)', she reported to Hugh Finch Williams, who had stayed behind in London.

> Mr. Romanoff is terribly upset about the rejection of his *Giselle* – he even threatened to commit suicide. But I am greatly relieved.[174]

When the French ballerina Yvette Chauviré danced the title role in the Romantic ballet, the stage manager would allow her only two curtain calls although the audience was stamping and shouting, and despite Volkova's pleading with him in the wings: 'No, Madame – never more than two curtains for the ballet – for the opera, yes.'[175]

The British critic Arnold Haskell had visited Milan a couple of years previously, and had remarked on the difference in style and sensibility between Italian and British dancers:

It was a technique so very different, yet so slick and competent that I felt I was watching something totally unfamiliar. The choreography was nothing but an exploitation of that staccato graceless acrobatic technique and the dancers' legs would have supported a concert-grand.[176]

Volkova also found the company's style hard and cold: the Italians' footwork was good, but their hands and arms were stiff and expressionless. They had energy, but no sense of plastique or quality. Their famous *fouettés* failed to impress her, though the dancers were good at pirouettes.

She became fond of her Italian pupils and could see their potential, but she despaired at their lack of ambition and discipline: 'They simply are not serious', she later recalled. 'All during class the girls keep an eye on the clock because their boyfriends are waiting downstairs with motorcycles to take them off to the country. And their dietary habits! Well, no dancer can keep fit on pasta.'[177]

Still, after a few months' work, she submitted a proposal for the reorganisation of the ballet department to Dr Ghiringhelli and the Board of the Opera House in the spring of 1951. Ghiringhelli was, as always, enthusiastic, but shortly afterwards she was summoned to a meeting with the theatre's powerful Secretary, Signore Oldani, whom she had nicknamed the Grey Eminence. 'He (the Eminence) outlined to me his plans for the future of the ballet, which seemed to be the contrary of the report on the future of the department I had just put up', she wrote to her husband.

'We want', he said, 'a good corps de ballet as a background only for foreign 'étoiles', just as for the orchestra we invite famous conductors from abroad. Then very little classical work because it is a bore for the Milanese public; but plenty of novelties and modern ballets.'[178]

In her diary she reported despondently on one of the novelties Oldani preferred:

The stage is in darkness as the curtain rises slowly. A spotlight picks up the central figure (the author of the ballet) in brilliant red. All around him, prone in the semi-gloom, grovelling on the floor, the unfortunate corps de ballet representing (it is explained in the programme notes that one cannot read in the dark) his Conscience.[179]

Volkova was met with an opposition that was largely rooted in national chauvinism. It was spearheaded by the principal dancer Ugo dell'Ara, who had ambitions as a choreographer in the Oldani mould, and as a teacher. Dell'Ara began to write newspaper articles questioning Volkova's competence and ability to foster the La Scala Ballet's national identity. He considered it more important to present new ballets by Italian choreographers than to invite people like Balanchine to work in Milan, as Volkova had just done.

Dr Ghiringhelli had wanted Volkova to produce quick results, expecting her to make La Scala's ballet one of the word's four best companies within five years. But when she tried to instigate reforms in the top-heavy organisation, he usually failed to back her up, and by April she was ready to throw in the towel.

'That afternoon I watched *Légende de Joseph* in costume', she noted in her diary.

> ...a dreadful effort. The costumes were a hideous egg-yolk yellow and lilac – I could not look at it. Choreography as stilted as an opera chorus that doesn't sing. A typical La Scala production. Even Toumanova's beauty was overwhelmed with long, heavy skirts. Frustrating to sit in the stalls and not be able to say what I want ... as I have resigned. Just as well – it would have caused a terrible scene and Benois and de Chirico would never agree, and it would be a scandal. Very depressed. Balanchine is not sure he is coming. At least, he would have been an ally. Don't know any more what to do. Feel more than ever I must leave ...[180]

She resigned as Choreographic Director after barely six months, and stood by her decision although Dr Ghiringhelli begged her to stay.

After the defeat at La Scala, her old colitis broke out again and, with nothing else to do and nowhere else to go, she spent the rest of the summer in Italy getting over the disappointment. She told her husband she felt like 'a soldier who has been stripped of his medals'.

In June the Soviet ballerina Galina Ulanova gave her first performance in the West at the Teatro Communale in Florence. Volkova travelled to Florence, where ballet lovers from all over Europe, including Fonteyn and her mother as well as Hugh Finch Williams, waited for days until the red tape was cut through and Ulanova, with her partner Yuri Kondratov, could dance *Giselle*. Volkova was spellbound by the performance and said to Hugh Finch Williams that Ulanova's dancing gave her back her faith: 'I had forgotten what good dancing was...'

As well as a professional revelation, it was a significant moment for Volkova personally – it was her first contact with the Soviet ballet world since her emigration, as well as a warm reunion with an old friend. Ulanova was the daughter of her old teacher, Maria Romanova. They had trained together at the School of Russian Ballet, both had appeared at the School's concerts, and Volkova had had an almost sisterly relationship with the five-years-younger Ulanova, now the Soviet Union's leading ballerina and a national icon. In the USSR, people said that Ulanova's art could make even a dictator cry.

After the performance, Volkova was waiting at the stage door with a crowd of fans when Ulanova finally emerged, escorted by KGB agents. Volkova and Ulanova caught sight of each other and, although Volkova had not expected it, Ulanova recognised her right away, tore herself away from her guards and quickly asked Volkova to come back the next morning and meet her in the same spot.

The following day Volkova found herself alone in the theatre's ballet studio with Ulanova, Kondratov and a pianist, whose crisp notes broke the crystal silence of the room. The morning sun streamed in through the windows, and the warm, still air was slowly set in motion by the dancers exercising at the barre.

After the class, Volkova and Ulanova took a tourist trip into the country in an open landau. Volkova never revealed what they talked about, but after the performance that evening Volkova gave Ulanova a letter at the stage door, under the suspicious eyes of the KGB minders. On her return to Moscow, Ulanova told the story of her meeting with Volkova to the magazine *Soviet Art*:

> They say that there are many similarities between the British ballerina Margot Fonteyn and myself, and perhaps that is not so strange when one remembers that Fonteyn's teacher, Vera Volkova, was a pupil of my mother, Maria Romanova.[181]

To *Pravda*, she described Volkova's exit from Russia as 'escaping from the famine'.[182] In those times, it was a brave act on Ulanova's part to mention Volkova's name in the Russian media.

After Ulanova's departure, Volkova visited Rome, which reminded her of St Petersburg, while she considered her next step. She had been offered work in New York and Copenhagen, and she chose Copenhagen. On 25 August she wrote to David Arkell:

> A few days ago we went by motor-boat to visit Massine and his family on his island. It is a complete kingdom, Massine the king. The court consists (apart from his wife and two children) of French governess, Italian cook, gardener, boatman (he also lights the lighthouse every night), ballet mistress (Russian, she teaches Massine's daughter Tania, aged ten). Then Mother-in-law, who mostly looks after the goats and chickens and pours the tea, two maids and 18 workmen, who build new harbour, as well as another floor to house, and flirt with the two Italian maids …
>
> I am feeling like a horse put out to grass. Have lost count of days and months. In the meantime the horse just chews the grass and reads H. de

Balzac, the only non-Italian book I have found in Vico ...

All I know is that on 1 October I have to be in Copenhagen.[183]

Marking time in Campania, Volkova was oblivious to the dramatic events taking place in Copenhagen that would eventually change the scope and nature of her role at the Royal Danish Ballet. The company's ballet-master, Harald Lander, was suspended in the afternoon of 15 August 1951, following accusations of what would now be called 'sexual harassment', having sexual relations with under-aged female dancers while they were in his care, and colluding in the cover-up of a rape in the company. The scandal divided the company and the Danish public into two camps and quickly became political, involving both ministers and Parliament.

Although the issue of his morals had been decisive, Lander's high-handed manner and rigidity had been at the heart of an organised campaign against him and contributed to his dismissal. For two decades, he had ruled the company like an absolute dictator in an increasingly ruthless and insensitive way. Lander had the power to make or break a career or a life, and seems to have been strangely oblivious to the fear he struck into many people.

At the start of his career, Lander had been regarded as the great innovator in Danish ballet. One of the few Danes who had lived abroad for any length of time, he had studied the Russian school with Fokine and Ivan Tarasov in the USA, and character dance in Mexico. When he returned to Denmark in 1929, he turned to choreography and came to dominate the repertoire at the Royal Danish Ballet with his own works and radical revisions of the Bournonville repertoire.

Lander created character ballets inspired by Serge Diaghilev's Ballets Russes: *Football*, *Bolero*, *The Denmark Ballet*, *The Little Mermaid* and others. All but one, *Études*, are now forgotten. Created for the Royal Danish Ballet in 1948 under the title *Étude*, this became his chief work, and the myth of Lander as the lost genius of Danish ballet is inextricably linked with its success.

Étude was based on an idea of the composer Knudåge Riisager, whose original outline for a plot resembled a character ballet similar to Lander's other works: he imagined the dancers as notes coming to life, a bit like the brooms and buckets in *The Sorcerer's Apprentice* in the Disney film *Fantasia*. At the premiere in 1948 its sets, costumes and choreography were unmistakably typical of Danish ballet aesthetics, with dancers in black tutus or long evening gowns, and influenced by Massine's ballets and the trends current in Lander's youth in the 1930s. What was new about *Étude* was the amount of actual dancing it contained. In a theatre traditionally focused on storytelling rather than academic dance, *Étude* was a cornucopia of technique and virtuosity.

Lander revised the ballet several times, influenced by the wave of neo-classicism that swept over Europe after the War. He pared it more and more down to the bone, renamed it *Études*, and developed it in the style of George Balanchine's *Palais de Cristal* (1947) and Serge Lifar's *Suite en Blanc* (1943). *Études* became a study in the classicism that had begun to interest Lander, who realised that the Royal Danish Ballet lacked it but knew that he himself had not yet mastered it.

Erik Bruhn, Poul Gnatt, Frank Schaufuss, Mona Vangsaae and Elsa Marianne von Rosen had earlier trained with Volkova in London, but Lander knew nothing of Volkova's methods until he and his new wife, ballerina Toni Lander, formerly Toni Pihl, travelled to Paris and took class with Henry Danton, in a studio Danton rented on the Place Blanche. Danton remembers that he gave Lander a good 'imitation class without understanding the depth of Vera's teaching', but his 'imitation' was the final spur to Lander, who opened negotiations with Volkova, whom he now recognised as one of the classical tradition's leading exponents in the West. Volkova was also an authority in what was then described as modern ballet, the European neo-classical strain that he had begun to explore in *Études*; but Lander and Volkova lost contact when Volkova went to Italy, and Lander tried to get an English guest teacher, Joan Lawson, to come to Copenhagen instead.

In the wake of Lander's suspension, Lawson dropped out of the picture and the Royal Danish Theatre's Director, Henning Brøndsted, contacted Volkova himself, writing to her in Italy.

On Saturday 6 October 1951 she arrived on the Italian express from Florence at Copenhagen's Central Station, where she was met by the principal dancer Niels Bjørn Larsen. He had taken over as interim leader of the Royal Danish Ballet and accompanied her to the Royal Theatre, where she met Brøndsted in his office, and then to the Palace Hotel on the Copenhagen Town Hall Square, where she was to live during her stay in Copenhagen.

Unknowingly, she had stepped into an artistic vacuum, and moved from a position of empty status into one of unacknowledged but real influence.

Breaking Amber

Brøndsted and Larsen presented Volkova to the company on Monday 8 October 1951. She watched company class in the morning and the apprentices later in the day. Henning Kronstam, who took the apprentice class, remembered:

> ...she sat in front of the class looking very serious, giving no sign of either approval or dissent. Just watching intently with an expression that said nothing, revealed nothing!

Volkova spent the first few days studying the company to determine precisely what the dancers needed and what she could add to the Danish School. She identified mature and fully trained artists such as the principal dancers Mona Vangsaae and Frank Schaufuss, whose talent she felt she could take further still. She also noted gifted young dancers such as Henning Kronstam, Kirsten Simone and Kirsten Petersen, whose potential she believed she could bring out. And she sensed right away that the Danes were not just passionate performers: they took on every role with a direct honesty that made her describe the Royal Danish Ballet as 'a company with a heart'.[184]

The Danish dancers sized up the Russian woman, and Inger Thøfner, who was a member of the corps de ballet in 1951, remembers how Volkova stood out from their other teachers: 'It was the way she looked. It was obvious that she wasn't Danish.' She also did not behave like a Dane. There was a difference in mentality, professionally, that both impressed and intimidated the home-grown company.

> She was totally different from everything we knew – there wasn't all that giggling... Today it is difficult to say how she differed. Perhaps she was more serious, more professional? We knew nothing but our own little world. The ballet was a closed art form at that time, both because of the war, but also because Lander had wanted to be in charge of everything himself.

Volkova, who never learnt to speak Danish apart from a few simple phrases, also taught in English, but fortunately many Danes had picked up basic English during the war from listening to BBC broadcasts. After the war, speaking English had become fashionable and, even if the dancers had never had an English-speaking teacher before, it was not a problem for Volkova to get her intentions across.

'Nowadays all dancers know about placement and how everything is connected', Thøfner says, 'but that was all new to us.'

She showed us a different way of dancing from the one we already knew – she gave us freedom. Our training had been very rigid ... Lander used to say something like, 'Clench your buttocks and turn outwards from your feet'. But that often meant you raised your shoulders and tensed your upper body from the effort. Volkova explained how we should turn out from the front and all the way to the back by simply opening the hips. We shouldn't clench our buttocks – but open our hips. When she asked us to dance, she would say: 'Don't break the air. You should hang in the air, and it should lift you. The torso is in the air, it is free, while the legs are working.' The upper part of the body should not tense up when we were too eager or the steps were too difficult.

Before Volkova arrived, the training at the Royal Theatre was still based on the French School and saw the body as 'divided' horizontally at the hip. This led to occasionally clunky co-ordination of the movements of the upper and lower parts of the body. As a rule, focus was so concentrated on the lower half of the body that the expressiveness of the upper body was diminished. In effect, the dancers were so busy staying in the air and showing off their fancy footwork that their arms, torsos and heads – the most expressive parts of the body – were not being used. Volkova had learned from Vaganova to view the crucial division of the body as vertical rather than horizontal, and also to see the torso as the crucible of all movement, rather than the legs as did the French School.

Volkova's calm leadership and inspired teaching challenged the divided company and united the dancers in focusing again on their art, rather than on the company's internal politics. This in turn led to a relative truce between the pro- and anti-Lander factions. Even though Volkova maintained a determined neutrality on the Lander question, she had to face its ramifications every day and deflect manoeuvrings for her partisanship.

She claimed that, on the evening she arrived in Copenhagen, the critic Allan Fridericia had approached her in the lobby of her hotel – it was like a scene in a political thriller. Speaking for Lander, he had tried to persuade her to stay away from the following day's morning class and to leave the company in the lurch. The theory was that, in its current state of paralysis, the company would have to recall Lander, who would in turn bring Volkova back and they would rebuild the company together. Volkova chose to fulfil her contract and in doing so made a lifelong enemy of Lander and alienated many of Copenhagen's critics, including Fridericia. In London Volkova had enjoyed a close and respectful relationship, as well as a fruitful dialogue, with many critics. In Copenhagen in the fifties she was more cautious, regarding the Danish critics as being more interested in politics than in art, and she could not understand their persistent wish to reinstate Lander.

A slick self-publicist and a skilled politician, Lander struck back at Volkova in his memoirs, *Thi Kendes for Ret – ?* (The Judgment of the Court Is – ?). Lander's book laid out the whole case from his point of view and gave him an opportunity to deny animosity towards Volkova. He even went so far as to take credit for her appointment and, implicitly, for the progress the company was now making. But he could not entirely mask the bitter outrage of a deposed despot: 'It was with some amusement – or possibly even schadenfreude – that I learnt, having been suspended, how she now went to work with an even firmer hand than the one people had wanted removed from the Ballet at all costs...'[185]

Lander was right in that Volkova was an authoritarian, a highly demanding and temperamental teacher. 'The rings round her eyes could go completely black with fury, and it was as if her nose became even more pointed', Arlette Weinreich, an apprentice with the company, remembers. 'She didn't really have to say anything: we just knew when she was angry', says Inger Thøfner. 'One thing she would not accept was people being late for class. She would lock the door! And she would have a fit if a dancer left before class was over', Kirsten Simone recalls. Simone worked intensely with Volkova and later became one of the company's leading ballerinas.

But, however infuriated she became, her criticism of the dancers was never insulting or personal. Unlike Lander, who viewed the dancers as unruly children, treated them with disdain and inspired fear in them, Volkova saw them as semi-divine creatures, treating them as artists, with a kind of reverence.

In many theatres the cheapest seats are known as 'the gods' because they are the closest to the allegorical frescoes on the ceiling of the auditorium. 'That may be', Volkova once said, 'but why would anyone want to be up there with the gods when the angels are on stage?'

Henning Kronstam, an apprentice who formed a particularly close relationship with Volkova, summed up the feelings of the company.

> She was very firm when she came, she was very Russian, very disciplined. But during those first three, four months she was here, everyone warmed to her and became very close to her.[186]

The Royal Theatre was a match for La Scala in terms of intrigue and power politics, but this time Volkova was not intimidated. On 12 October 1951 she shared her first happy impressions of Copenhagen in a letter to David Arkell: 'Copenhagen is a dignified town. All the clocks have a chime.'[187] Later she wrote about the Royal Theatre:

A distinguished building in the Palladian formula, it is a well-loved landmark in the capital city. To see it, as one may on the King's birthday or some other special occasion, when the beacons are lit in the classical urns high against the sky, is a remembered sight, for one feels that here is one of those citadels of art and civilised endeavour that have made Europe what it is.[188]

Volkova believed that the Royal Danish Ballet's unique heritage of ballets by August Bournonville from the nineteenth century had survived at the Royal Theatre because no other choreographer had replaced the great ballet-master since his death in 1879. Scandinavia was also, in many ways, a self-sufficient entity and there had been little artistic exchange with the rest of Europe. The Danes had imported only very few works by foreign choreographers, and their influence had not lasted; and the Royal Theatre had never exported its own art. The theatre on Kongens Nytorv still belonged to 'the King, his court and his people'.

Even the company's name, the Royal Danish Ballet, appealed to Volkova: it spoke of stability, continuity and tradition, and she told the Danish newspaper *Politiken*:

> In many ways, the city reminds me of Leningrad. As Copenhagen was being rebuilt after the big fire, St. Petersburg was being built. Both cities are to some extent products of the same time and it shows in the architecture.[189]

Copenhagen had been all but destroyed by a huge fire in 1728, much as London had been in 1666. The higgledy-piggledy medieval capital was rebuilt in the elegantly simple Danish Neo-Classicist style, its buildings painted in pastel shades that would have reminded Volkova of her home city. Unlike London, Copenhagen had not been damaged during the war and retained its historic beauty. And although it was the biggest city in Scandinavia, Copenhagen was much smaller than St Petersburg, Shanghai or London, and Denmark's was a more tolerant and egalitarian society than any Volkova had experienced before. In such a small city, however politically and morally tolerant, everyone is also more visible and therefore more vulnerable, as she would soon discover.

Privately, she admitted to Arkell that

> it was wonderful to live alone in an unknown city, not knowing anybody. Staying in the hotel, I felt even my name ought to be changed. At the theatre I was what people expect me to be, but outside I was free and it was exciting. I used to come back to the hotel about 4.30, have a bath and tea and then peer through the curtain at the Town Hall Square with all the lights on.
>
> There was a statue in the middle of the square, an enormous Viking blowing a strange instrument, and he was level with my third-floor window. I walked alone in the streets, went to the ballet alone in the evening, met very few

people and then only formally, like my Director, the Conductor, journalists. I felt so adventurous, as if at any moment anything might happen, like a big fire in the hotel and me having to jump on the Viking from my balcony.

I like this town because it reminds me of Russia and [the paintings of] Kustodiev: two-horse sledges in the woods, with the little bells tinkling in the frosty air. Everything white and children skiing. A lot of things that I forgot, but used to love in Russia. I love snow, and then waiting for the spring during the long, long months of winter.[190]

The message she sent to her husband was entirely pragmatic: 'There is work to be done here. You had better come over.'

In January 1952, Margot Fonteyn spent a fortnight in Copenhagen – a visit that added to Volkova's prestige. The great English ballerina had been injured for three months and trusted only her old teacher to get her back in shape. A reporter from *Politiken* wrote about a meeting with the two women. He described them as interacting like 'friends, not as teacher and pupil as in fact they are'.[191] In the interview, Fonteyn expressed her respect for Volkova the teacher, and Volkova took the opportunity to explain some of the problems she detected in the training of the Royal Danish Ballet's dancers. Her statements also hinted at the influence she would have on the company's repertoire:

> When Ashton comes here he will expect to find a company that is familiar with the modern style.[192]

Fonteyn brought the offer of a job with Sadler's Wells from Ninette de Valois, but Volkova had decided to stay. She had fallen in love with Copenhagen, was excited by the challenge her new job presented, and saw possibilities that past experience made her believe de Valois would not offer. She could make a much greater difference in Denmark than she would be allowed to do in England. When the question of extending her three-month contract came up, her eagerness to stay on in Copenhagen made her tell the Theatre's management: 'If it is a question of money, I don't mind a lower salary.'[193]

In April 1952, the broadsheet *Berlingske Tidende* reported that Volkova's contract had been extended and she had been engaged for the entire coming season. Responding to rumours of redundancies among the teachers, Henning Brøndsted soberly addressed the concerns of a partisan reporter in an interview with the same newspaper:

> The fact is that Madame Volkova has been re-engaged as a ballet teacher at the Royal Theatre, and I have had a number of detailed discussions with her about what possible changes in the school should be undertaken. But that takes time, since there are many aspects to consider, and one must naturally try to find a

solution that can stand the test of time... The three principal dancers – Hans Brenaa, Børge Ralov and Stanley Williams – have been relieved of their teaching positions at the school, so that we can operate freely.[194]

Brøndsted made it clear that Volkova had won his trust and that he would act according to her recommendations. She compared the company to an insect caught in a piece of amber, and Brøndsted had given her the mandate to break that amber and 'set the Danes free'. Shortly afterwards, as a further development of the Lander crisis and in protest against Volkova's growing influence, Brenaa and Ralov resigned from the Ballet Union. Stanley Williams, who remained a member, was re-hired as a teacher, while Erik Bruhn, a principal dancer, became the new children's teacher.

Volkova trained both Williams and Bruhn, teaching them the new curriculum she created for the school. 'Stanley snatched up everything Volkova could teach him', says Arlette Weinreich, who was a student in Williams's class at the time. 'He was like a sponge, and they spent night after night together at the Palace Hotel bar, smoking, creating schools, talking steps, steps, steps.' Henning Kronstam also remembered that Stanley Williams:

> would come in dead tired in the morning, because she had been teaching him all night how to teach. Showing him what was right and wrong... I think she danced for him. Because that's what she did for me when I started teaching – lifted up her skirt and showed me the position and how to do and what to do and which things to use in order to get what she wanted out of the company at that time.[195]

Stanley Williams, who was 24 years old, had begun to teach the year before and was not only inexperienced, but also untrained: 'In the old days in Denmark when somebody retired from the stage he would just start giving classes. They were never taught the skill of teaching. So they would just give the same old steps every day. There was no thought or imagination behind it all', he told American *Dance Magazine* many years later.

> She took a liking to me. She felt I had a talent for teaching... She would talk to me, until four in the morning... I would ask her questions about specific things, and she would answer... She made me consider in a very professional way what I knew and what I didn't understand. But mostly we would just talk about *ideas* about dancing and teaching... She made me start thinking about what I was doing. Volkova taught me – I owe her a great deal – to use my imagination.[196]

Volkova also gave masterclasses to Erik Bruhn. 'My happiest memories of Volkova are our many conversations', he said in John Gruen's *Danseur Noble*. 'We talked every day I wasn't dancing. We discussed every limb, ligament and muscle.'[197]

Volkova was everywhere at once. All initiative seemed to rest with her. 'She was at the theatre all day long', Weinreich remembers.

> She sat in on all the rehearsals, and all the classes that she didn't teach herself. She watched all the performances. She didn't come to the Bournonville rehearsals, because she knew there was nothing for her to do there. The Bournonville stagers probably didn't want her there anyway.

She was one of the judges of the Ballet School's exams in May 1952, alongside Niels Bjørn Larsen, Stanley Williams, the Ballet Union's chairman Svend Karlog, Henning Brøndsted and the Theatre Secretary Henning Rohde. When selecting the company's future dancers, she went for longer, more streamlined bodies than the short, frontally broad, old-fashioned look that some thought had been a unique instrument for Bournonville's choreography.

The Royal Danish Ballet was still profoundly homophobic, and two of the judges were against making the gay apprentice Henning Kronstam a member of the company. Brøndsted was inclined to agree with them, fearing more scandal in the wake of the Lander affair. Kronstam's superlative artistic potential counted for little, until Volkova, incensed, folded her newspaper and whacked Henning Rohde over the head with it, shouting: 'If you throw that boy out, I will leave too.' Niels Bjørn Larsen also defended Kronstam: '[His sexuality] didn't matter to me... Henning was a good dancer, and he should have gotten into the company.'[198] Volkova got her own way that day. She secured for the company one of the greatest Danish dancers of the century, and a future ballet-master; but by putting Rohde in his place she also further antagonised her most powerful enemy at the Royal Theatre.

Niels Bjørn Larsen, who had formally taken over the job of ballet-master, worked hard to bring things back to normal and smooth over the differences in the company, but he did not have Harald Lander's authority and experience. An exceptional character dancer, he was not a choreographer, a teacher or even a particularly accomplished stager. He also had very limited knowledge of the international ballet repertoire and little experience in programming, which meant that he and Brøndsted came to rely on Volkova. Her influence on the Royal Danish Ballet's repertoire in the fifties was immense, and she effectively opened the company's door to the world outside Denmark. She not only knew everything worth knowing about European, Russian and American ballet, but she also knew every*one* worth knowing and had their telephone numbers in a little black address book.

She first contacted the English choreographer, David Lichine, who was able to come to Copenhagen at short notice to stage his entertaining, lyrical character ballet *Graduation Ball* at the Royal Theatre – a story ballet about a ball for cadets and pupils from a girls' school. The flirtatious meeting of the boys and girls and the many character parts in the ballet suited the company exceptionally well.

In June 1952, Volkova travelled with Brøndsted to The Hague, in Holland, where George Balanchine's New York City Ballet was performing. Volkova wanted to get the choreographer's *Symphony in C* for Copenhagen, and the negotiations with Balanchine went smoothly. Later that summer she wrote to David Arkell:

> Balanchine is a wonderful choreographer and I had real joy in The Hague watching his company dance every night for a week. When he rehearses the company he is so elegant, so professional, partnering the girls, explaining points to the boys. So quiet, modest and sure.
>
> A long time ago, one summer evening in London, I told him the story of how I escaped from Russia, and he told me that if he were a rich man he would make a film out of it. This time he told me about his own escape. One day I will tell you about it, because it requires acting, which he did most convincingly.
>
> Why is the English press so cruel to this lovely and subtle company? It looks as if the English are doomed to be bored with *The Sleeping Princess* forever.[199]

In the end, Balanchine was not able to come to Copenhagen to stage *Symphony in C* but, after Brøndsted had returned to Denmark, Balanchine and Volkova agreed that the dancer Vida Brown could do the job. 'I have just received your letter No. 2', Brøndsted wrote to Volkova when he got the news.

> Thank you very much indeed for all the trouble you have taken... I can't really tell you how grateful I am... When I get to Copenhagen one of these first days in August I will talk with Mr Niels Bjørn Larsen and then write to Miss Vida Brown to come here on the 9th or 10th September and stay to the 4th October and then return by Dutch boat. You have settled the economic question excellently... I think we must take this ballet and I am sure I would be of the same opinion as you regarding *Serenade*.[200]

On her own initiative she also wrote to the American choreographer Jerome Robbins:

> I feel it would be a highly interesting idea if you could come and do a ballet for us. The question is when and how and indeed what? I have always admired

your choreography but I felt up till now our company which was passing from Bournonville to the present in style and technique was not ready for you. Now I think it is.

She added:

I wish to stress that this letter represents only a general inquiry and is not an official invitation from the theatre. I want first your reactions to the idea so that I can put it up to my Director.[201]

With Brøndsted and Niels Bjørn Larsen on her side, she proceeded to extend a formal invitation to Robbins, encouraging him to create a new work for the company. Robbins opted for a restaging of an older work, *Fanfare* – an abstract, playful introduction to classical ballet set to Benjamin Britten's *A Young Person's Guide to the Orchestra*. Volkova was not thrilled but accepted it, seeing that *Fanfare* would pave the way for more collaborations with Robbins. She wanted to tie him further to the Royal Danish Ballet.

Wanting to promote the company's young talent, Volkova advised Robbins that he would have to:

insist on having the dancers in our company you really want, irrespective of their rank or age. Because our guest choreographers do not always realise they have the privilege of free choice.[202]

Robbins, in turn, assured Volkova that he would:

count most heavily on your assistance and advice in the selection of dancers etc. I thought it might be helpful if you were to have a cast list of the ballet and what is needed for each role so you could tentatively look about for the selection of dancers.[203]

While Niels Bjørn Larsen lacked the weight and vision that the Royal Danish Ballet needed in the 1950s, Volkova, the Theatre's strange bird, had plenty of both. She was given semi-official status as 'artistic advisor': it was a title the Theatre was reticent about advertising in Denmark but liked to publicise when touring abroad, to give the company extra clout. When the Royal Danish Ballet performed at Covent Garden in London in October 1953, Volkova staged the *pas de deux* from *The Nutcracker* and acted as the company's spokeswoman, giving a number of interviews to the British press.

Volkova was not encouraged to promote herself in the Danish press, but in 1954 she wrote a remarkable feature article for *Politiken*. It was, in effect, her artistic manifesto. Volkova explained that she had come to Denmark because of her historical interest in the Bournonville heritage and the French School. She was curious to learn:

what the Danes through Bournonville had made of the French school. And what difference, if any, there was between theirs and the old French School we knew in Russia.[204]

After having analysed the training at the Royal Theatre, she decided the challenge she had been presented with 'could only be dealt with as a long-term project'. In the article, she called for reforms at the Theatre. To improve the company's artistic level and scope, the Ballet School's very foundation would have to be restructured: 'school and choreography always go hand in hand'.[205]

Volkova pointed out that the Bournonville Schools that form the base of the Danish teaching system had not been set by Bournonville himself but by one of his successors, Hans Beck. She had quickly become acutely aware of a series of interesting links between the type of dancer Bournonville himself had been and the way the Royal Danish Ballet danced when she first saw the company.

In his memoirs, *My Theatre Life*, Bournonville speaks proudly of his flexible back as one of his greatest qualities as a dancer, but he regrets that he never properly mastered adagio. To Volkova, one explained the other:

> Personally, I think [the flexible back] is a defect, as it is responsible for the very lack of steadiness he complains of in his slow movements and static positions. Here, again, the Italians gave us the anatomical approach to the correct 'placing' of the body. In other words, the dependence of one part of the body on another and how to control it.[206]

In 1951, all Danish dancers danced with 'broken' wrists. Volkova disapproved of this stylistic feature and had said so when it was pointed out to her as a special trait of the Bournonville School. Having done her research, she now made the point that both Bournonville and his teacher, Vestris, had in fact listed his 'broken wrists' as prominent among his own faults as a dancer.

The company's dancing was characterised by quick jumps and hard landings. According to Volkova, the hard landings could be traced to:

> an inadequacy in [Bournonville's] Achilles tendon. The whole of his choreography suggests he avoids long jumps involving soft, slow landings, where the Achilles tendon should act as a 'shock absorber' to save the full weight of the body on the knee. Obviously, quick bouncing jumps suited him better, hence the famous Bournonville allegro came to the fore.[207]

Harald Lander had introduced changes to the training at the Royal Danish Ballet during his tenure as ballet-master, but Volkova felt that they had not been extensive enough and that he was not essentially a teacher; in her opinion the School lacked a basic understanding of the body's potential as a sophisticated instrument for dance. 'The Danes paid a heavy price for this neglect of the Italian methods, for it retarded, in some respects, their development for over 100 years', she wrote, and concluded:

> Now, if the Danish ballet is to take its place in the world as a contemporary organism, it still has to close this gap. There is no other way, and so the sooner we start, the better.[208]

Pointe work technique was almost non-existent, and, like Bournonville himself, the Danish dancers had neglected the *plié*. Henning Kronstam remembers Volkova started 'from the beginning' with the whole company, old and young, meaning that it was back to basics.

> When she took over the class herself, she started as if we were children – to lay the foundations of a whole new approach. She started working even with our basic turn-out. She tried to broaden our movements and gestures and to explain what she called 'the pleasure of line'. Much of what she then explained should have been inculcated in the early classes of the School. Her methods were insinuating; and, even as she developed our technique, style and quality came through slow moulding. She gave us all a new awareness of what style was all about.

The freshness of Volkova's new training rekindled Kronstam's interest in dance at a critical time when he was thinking of giving up dancing to become an actor. 'It was when Vera came that I knew I wanted to be a dancer',[209] he said.

Even many of the mature members of the company experienced Volkova's training as a revelation. Principal dancer Mona Vangsaae said in an interview:

> It was only when I started working with Volkova that I really began to understand classical dancing. Before that I did what I was told, without really knowing why. I imitated the things I was shown, and danced instinctively, because I enjoyed it: but now I am able to understand exactly what I am working for.[210]

The introduction of Volkova's training methods was the most far-reaching reform the Royal Danish Ballet had seen since August Bournonville returned to Copenhagen from Paris in 1829, having completed his own training as a dancer with Vestris.

While she acknowledged that her presence was controversial, Volkova publicly declared that she had not encountered opposition.

I am happy to say I have been unusually well supported by my teaching colleagues in this respect. They have shown a loyalty and enthusiasm that comes only from the best kind of teamwork. Such a spirit indeed promises well for our future ballet. What has helped me beyond all else is the fact that I teach, within the company class, the teachers of the Ballet School. In this way my principles are disseminated down to all grades. This will save valuable time, for in years to come when these children graduate into the senior class, they will have already assimilated the groundwork.[211]

The truth is that her work had detractors, especially among the company's older dancers, who were set in their ways, and the Lander supporters, who were unhappy about her growing influence. Kirsten Simone thinks 'it was difficult for some of the mature dancers, men in their forties, to suddenly be taken to task. She was really a professional and they were not.'

In his memoirs, Niels Bjørn Larsen recalled that there were 'instantly forces at work to make Volkova resign her job, forces that realised that the Ballet might not go to pieces, and might even have good possibilities developing, and that should preferably not happen'.[212] The Danish critics, most of whom were nationalist traditionalists and Lander supporters, were also sceptical of Volkova's work. Some genuinely feared she would ruin the Bournonville style and attacked her blatantly and aggressively.

When Allan Fridericia, the critic who had first approached Volkova on Lander's behalf, reviewed Kirsten Simone's début in the role of Hilda in Bournonville's ballet *A Folk Tale*, his piece was as much about Volkova as about Simone.

> The fair, poetic and slender Nordic mountain girl performed as if she came from one of the Maryinsky Theatre's school examinations, directed by an effect-seeking but dull ballerina... Yesterday much of what Bournonville hated and despised was introduced into his own ballet. Soul, spirit and poetry were sacrificed. To a devastating degree, the young dancer suffered from the lack of correct instruction.[213]

Simone, who was crushed, got a lecture from Volkova, who put her straight: 'Never give up', said Volkova. 'Write that on a piece of paper and hang it on your mirror so that you see it every day.' Volkova had already decided that Kirsten Simone would be the Royal Theatre's next ballerina. Kirsten Petersen, another of Volkova's favourites, had a better line and her technique was as strong as Simone's, but Simone had one thing Petersen did not: Volkova later explained to the Danish critic Erik Aschengreen that when she first came to Copenhagen, she 'looked around. And there was no one! But then there was Kirsten Simone... And she *wanted* it. And so she became the one.'

Throughout her career, Volkova acknowledged talent and natural gifts, but she respected willpower and ambition almost even more. There was always potential in dancers who were willing to slog.

The nature of Volkova's relationship with the Danish Bournonville heritage remains a bone of contention to this day. Her critics claim she despised the style, but in her *Politiken* article she tried to reassure the traditionalists, explaining that:

> the blending of schools of any given nationality produces different results. But they are always interesting and add new vitality to even the strongest traditions. It is not my intention, were it possible, to turn the Danes into Russian dancers. This can never happen, for national character always overrides finally any effect of mere school.[214]

That Volkova did not intend to destroy or eradicate, but simply to refine the Bournonville style, is confirmed by private letters to her old London pupil, Audrey Harman:

> I am still here in Copenhagen, working with the Danish dancers. Some of the old ballets by Bournonville are most interesting from a historical point of view. Such lovely variations, especially for the men. Altogether the boys are better taught than the girls and I find it needs a lot of patience to make the girls put the heels well down after jumps, keep their elbows slightly curved and *épaulement*, of course. Still, they are very keen and work hard.[215]
>
> What is very interesting is to experiment how it would look by the time they will learn from me the *épaulement*, the round elbows, pirouettes et cetera. As you said, Mona Vangsaae (the blonde girl) already got it. Most of the young girls of 17 and 18 also got it. If only one could preserve the quality of their own, old school and add 'me' on top of it! Anyway, it is well worth trying ... I also noticed how well disciplined the company is and yet nobody is really squashed and they preserve their individuality. I am very happy working in this old theatre and everybody is most kind.[216]

Arlette Weinreich remembers that Volkova 'kept on saying that it was the stager's job to teach us what to do with Bournonville. And when the Bournonville ballets were in the repertoire, she included Bournonville steps in her classes and they were not foreign to her; she knew them from Johansson.'

In Copenhagen Volkova had 'expected to find a considerably calmer temperament than in Italy. And in fact the Danish Ballet had to be cooled down. It was bubbling over with temperament.'[217] What she meant was that the company lacked 'stylistic discipline and understanding'.

She was unhappy with the *port de bras* and torso. Their arms, she told them, resembled alternately 'boiled spaghetti' or 'Japanese chopsticks'.

The famous rounded arms of the Romantic era, known from historical lithographs, were nowhere to be seen. One of the first things Volkova did, Arlette Weinreich explains, was to 'turn the elbows... She told us how to carry our arms from the back. Everything used to be so graceful in a cute, coy way.' The Swedish-Canadian teacher Margaret Mercier, who worked with Volkova in the USA and later became a teacher at the Royal Theatre, is convinced that the now-famous Bournonville arms 'are *her* arms'. Henning Kronstam agreed that the company was enthusiastic but its style of dancing had become 'sloppy'. In his view, Volkova gave the Royal Danish Ballet awareness of the 'pleasure of line' and 'taught us how to dance Bournonville'[218]

In May 1954, the English critic P.W. Manchester reviewed a performance of *Les Sylphides* in *Dance News*. The ballet is not by Bournonville, but by Mikhail Fokine; however, to Manchester;

> this ballet shows very clearly the great changes that Volkova is gradually making in the style of the girls whose arms, once all elbows and broken wrists, are now becoming rounded and flowing.
>
> Three years ago I felt that Fokine's romantic-lyric style was quite unsuited to these dancers. Now – and this must be largely due to Vera Volkova, their teacher – the corps de ballet dances it beautifully with only an occasional reminiscence of the old, hard arms.[219]

The American critic and historian Lillian Moore, who later wrote a book about the Bournonville technique with Erik Bruhn, observed Volkova's work in the studio and wrote: 'She has a deep respect for correct placement, and works always for length and simplicity of line ... With complete concentration on what she is doing, she studies each individual pupil. In class she never relaxes for a moment. When she notices a fault, she knows exactly how to correct it.'[220]

The Swedish critic Bengt Häger thinks that Volkova gave the dancers more than just a purer and more defined Bournonville style. He had married Pipaluk, the daughter of the Danish polar explorer Peter Freuchen, and while he was living in Copenhagen in the fifties he often attended rehearsals.

> In her classes I saw how subtle ballet is, how refined. Her teaching was poetic in a way. She could change a movement in such a way that it came to mean something entirely different. She did this with Bournonville, she analysed his choreography in a way no one else could. She brought out things in Bournonville that were already there but that nobody was aware of, qualities that had been neglected. Yes, she was a poet.

Henning Kronstam, who himself became an extremely style-conscious and sensitive director and coach under Volkova's guidance, believed it was Volkova who put '*La Sylphide* on *pointe*'. In Bournonville's day the *pointe* shoe had not really been developed, and many Bournonville steps were still performed on *demi-pointe* when Volkova first came to Copenhagen. Volkova worked to bring out the dramatic and aesthetic meaning of *pointe*-work, transforming it from a small trick or momentary vehicle for virtuosity into a subtle form of expression.

'She loved *La Sylphide* and really understood the ballet's lyrical qualities and the character of James', says Bengt Häger.

> She worked with several of the dancers in order to find the physical expressions that could correspond to the register of emotions. Kirsten Simone was of course one of them, but one could also see her influence on Margrethe Schanne, even though they didn't get on very well and only worked together rarely. But she naturally worked with Erik Bruhn and Henning Kronstam on the role of James in *La Sylphide*, which interested her so much. This was perhaps her greatest talent – that she could improve the existing choreography.

While she obviously found some of Bournonville's work old-fashioned, Volkova also found much to admire in his ballets and wrote respectfully of the Danish choreographer's integrity.

> His French logic requires attention to the structure of both the story and the way in which the dances fit in, and, unlike Petipa, he seldom permits a pause in the action in order, for example, to insert a *ballabile*.[221]

Bournonville's greatest works were not dated – on the contrary:

> No one unfolds a story with more clarity than Bournonville and programme notes are hardly necessary, however involved the plot. He created always memorable characters, clear cut and unequivocal that are as convincing today as they were then.[222]

But she remained implacable about the necessity of developing the repertoire at the Royal Theatre. She explained in her *Politiken* article that Bournonville could not be its sole mainstay.

> The repertoire must therefore take its course as a supplement to my own work. When the previous season ended, we thought the time was ripe to make the first attempt with the Petipa choreography. I felt that after two years of intensive work we had made such good progress that the dancers should be strong enough to manage it. I am happy to say that the management immediately saw the necessity and initiated the series of *Pas de deux* –

technically demanding dances in Petipa style – which we hope will pave the way for full-length ballets by this master in the not too distant future. However, Petipa must only be regarded as a halfway house on the way to our goal: Contemporary ballet.[223]

To Volkova, contemporary ballet meant not only Balanchine but also Frederick Ashton. In the summer of 1954 she travelled to England as Henning Brøndsted's delegate to negotiate with Ashton. She met him in his home in Yeoman's Row, and they discussed the possibilities until well into the night. Glazunov's unknown ballet score *The Seasons* was one option, but in the end they agreed that Ashton should create a full-length ballet for the Danish company: *Romeo and Juliet* to Prokofiev's score written in the 1930s.

Ashton was the first choreographer in the West to create a ballet based on Shakespeare's tragedy, and the piece was an instant hit in Copenhagen. It received a record number of curtain calls at the premiere in May 1955, and when the company took the ballet to America the following year people said that it could have played to full houses at the Metropolitan Opera House for months.

Volkova was delighted with Ashton's work. She thought it suited the Danish company perfectly: 'An old oak sprouting new green leaves', she said. In an article in the English publication *Ballet Annual* she wrote about Ashton's new ballet:

> Well within the Ashton compass was the balcony scene and other such tender moods; yet the theatrical sense with which he developed the action showed a new aspect of his talent from the dramatic point of view and revealed how well he had felt the pulse of the Company. Remarkable was the combat between Mercutio and Tybalt and later between Tybalt and Romeo. Also remarkable was the way he used the mass movement of the on-looking partisans to heighten the tension, moving them with a fine sense of timing from one side of the stage to the other and up and down the stairs, as the fight developed. Throughout, the choreography was infused with the broad flowing movement, subtle phrasing and sense of line so essentially Ashton's hallmark and it was interesting to see how responsive, under his guidance, the Danish dancers proved in the event to be.
>
> This, one felt, was production as it should be: an entity. Choreography, music, décor and dancing in mutual support. And even if, as some felt, the score was not quite vintage Prokofiev, the overall reaction was highly enthusiastic, the première being, according to the Danes themselves, one of the most notable in their ballet's long history. Not only did Ashton present us with a new ballet; he gave us a new star dancer. He picked as his Romeo the

young Henning Kronstam from the corps de ballet, and he brought out in Mona Vangsaa, the Juliet, a new lyrical quality.[224]

Casting was crucial to Volkova. In her *Politiken* article of 1954 she had written that 'with such an ensemble [one should] be extremely careful with the casting, so that everyone is given the role that suits him or her in particular'.[225] To her, Kronstam was the obvious choice for Romeo, but although the critics, the public and the ballerina herself thought that Margrethe Schanne should create the role of Juliet, Volkova thought her simply too old for the part. The cool relationship between the two women was notorious.

Volkova looked to the future, spotting and nurturing new talent with unfailing confidence. She could smell it. 'A trained eye never fails', she insisted in an interview, and explained that a ballerina:

> should be naturally musical, but technique can come later. Appearance and movements play a part. She doesn't need to be beautiful so long as she has an expressive face. Her neck must be long, otherwise she will look from the auditorium as if she were shrugging her shoulders. Her waist must be small, and she must have strong thigh muscles and a high instep. Her movements must be flowing, never jerky, and her face while dancing must not look strained. All that is seldom combined in one person – great dancers don't grow on trees.[226]

Niels Kehlet, who later became a principal dancer but was then at the Ballet School, realised early on that:

> she had a very clear eye. She saw and she understood. She could correct the smallest things, invent ways for you to discover how to do them right. But it was more than that. She had figured out, and she showed you, where the movement came from – where the impulse lay, and how it felt as it travelled through your body.[227]

The Russian teacher saw lines and found inspiration everywhere: with people she met in the street or at parties, in paintings by Modigliani, in modern sculpture, in buildings or even in a smile. She still made use of the metaphors that had characterised her teaching in London to get her ideas across, but in Copenhagen she was less poetic and more practical. 'Imagine you are carrying a ten-øre piece [a tiny, glittering coin] on the breastbone', she could say. Or 'Use the neck like a horse – bend it and move it up, bend it and move it up – suddenly so stallion-like, the nostrils might be flaring.' To one dancer she suggested, 'Hold your hand as if three fingers have been shot off in the war.' 'Open your arms as if you are leaning back in a sofa', was one dictum; and another, 'Turn as if every time your chin comes to rest on a shelf.'

Erik Bruhn, who was already a star in Denmark and had danced in London, completely changed his style after meeting Volkova, which was almost unprecedented for a dancer of his stature. He transformed his technique and his *emploi* from a *demi-caractère* dancer to *danseur noble* – the equivalent of a singer retraining his voice from baritone to tenor. Without this transformation he could have never developed into the international star he became, and he acknowledged that: 'The fact is, Volkova was my primary influence – the biggest and the best!'[228] he said.

Bruhn appreciated her common sense and the clarity with which she conveyed her instructions:

> For example, when she didn't want you to move your shoulders she would put a matchbox on one of them. If the matchbox fell off, you were doing something wrong. If she wanted you to clench your buttocks, she would place a handkerchief between the cheeks. If you lost it, it meant you were relaxing your ass. She had little tricks like that. They were simple things, nothing you couldn't understand. Except that you realised that you never thought – how simple it *could* be ... She would make me visualise a button at the centre of my chest and she would want me to raise that button, and the only way I could do that was to inhale very deeply. When I achieved this chest expansion, I had to learn how to breathe properly so as not to lose it. She helped me correct the position of my neck. She made it sit in the right position. She was absolutely marvellous![229]

The foreign critics who came to Copenhagen for the annual ballet and music festivals recognised the progress the company was making, but most of the Danish critics still had reservations. One or two were decidedly hostile. The death sentence was passed on the company more than once: it was often said that it had now reached rock bottom. Although Lander had moved to Paris and was working at the Opéra, he was still very much a presence in Copenhagen and never stopped dreaming up ways to regain his old position.

The leading Danish critic, Svend Kragh-Jacobsen of *Berlingske Tidende*, acknowledged the time as 'a new and international epoch for the Danish ballet and its artists', but 'regretted that the national choreography remains in the shadows – and that the best contemporary Danish choreographer is now at work in Paris'. He did concede, however, that:

> it is a comfort that the international repertoire and international choreographers, plus Vera Volkova's important daily work at the Ballet School, have succeeded in maintaining the high level of performances of the Royal Danish Ballet so that it also attracts the attention of the public outside Denmark's boundaries.[230]

But international attention and recognition were, in fact, real indicators of success. For Volkova, that meant job offers from abroad, which in turn strengthened her reputation in Copenhagen. The Royal Swedish Ballet and Ballet Theatre (later American Ballet Theatre) repeatedly put out feelers to her, and in September 1954 Lincoln Kirstein and George Balanchine invited her to teach the New York City Ballet. But Volkova, who was a long-term strategist, still had ambitions for the Royal Theatre and was not tempted. She thought the Royal Danish Ballet was a unique company with unique resources, and that it should become one of the best ballet companies in the world: not a curiosity cabinet with an inheritance of nineteenth-century ballets, but a modern, living organism.

The Danish Divide

In December 1955 Volkova delivered *A Confidential Report On The Subject of the Ballet Department and Its Future* to Henning Brøndsted, pointing out in her introduction that the ballet-master Niels Bjørn Larsen had not read it, 'although most of the matter has in fact been discussed with him at various times'.[231]

Brøndsted had commissioned the report from her, 'based on four years' work at the Theatre', and the document explains Volkova's vision for the Royal Danish Ballet. Some feel it has not been surpassed in clarity and scope to this day.

Volkova first made clear the need for a balance between classical ballets and character ballets in the repertoire, i.e. a balance between ballets solely based on steps from the classical *danse d'école* and ballets with a more modern element or with an emphasis on pantomime and steps from various folk-dances. According to Volkova, there were too many character ballets, while the classical ballets tended to be sidelined.

She substantiated her claims with statistics showing that, of the previous season's 161 performances, 51 had been classical ballets and 110 character ballets. Volkova defined *The Whims of Cupid and The Ballet Master*, *Dream Pictures*, *Graduation Ball* and *La Sonnambula* as character ballets, and *Romeo and Juliet*, *La Sylphide* and *Giselle* and most of Balanchine's works as classical ballets.

She reminded the Director that Sadler's Wells Ballet had developed from nothing into one of the world's leading companies in only 20 years, thanks to a policy of emphasis on classical ballet. In the same period, famous old companies such as the La Scala Ballet and the Royal Swedish Ballet had degenerated: 'All history shows you neglect the classical repertoire at your peril',[232] she argued.

She stressed that she was not prejudiced against character ballets, but believed that, when programming any ballet, one had to consider its appeal to the public, the historical importance of its choreography and the company's technical and artistic development. For instance, in Volkova's opinion, Fokine's *Les Sylphides* fulfilled all three criteria, whereas *Graduation Ball*, although popular, did not challenge or develop the company artistically. *The Whims of Cupid and The Ballet Master* was a work of mostly historical interest.

> To preserve we have the old masters like Bournonville and Galeotti. To develop we have established modern masters like Balanchine and Ashton. To experiment we have the coming talent from either abroad or at home.[233]

The most glaring omission in the Danish repertoire was still Marius Petipa's great Russian ballets. Watching performances of Balanchine's neo-classical *Symphony in C,* Volkova said, one could see how the company had not gained the relevant experience through dancing *The Sleeping Beauty, Swan Lake* or *La Bayadère,* even though the training system she had introduced four years previously had helped raise the company's technical standards and produced a new type of dancer 'whose aspirations the Theatre has been slow to understand'.[234]

In Volkova's opinion, 'we have no great choreographer in our midst at the present', and she could not endorse a policy of allowing untried choreographers to create works for the company to be performed on the Theatre's main stage, Gamle Scene. Ballets such as Birger Bartholin's *Parisiana* and Fredbjørn Bjørnsson's *Behind the Scenes* were examples of 'some of the transparent errors that have been made in this sense during the past few years'. They should have been invited to create smaller works for the Theatre's secondary New Stage, and young international 'names' should be approached before they were too much in demand and too expensive.

Harshly critical of Niels Bjørn Larsen's casting policies, she wrote: 'It is not given to everybody to be able to cast accurately and a second and even third opinion is often wise.' For Volkova this was especially important in the case of the Royal Danish Ballet, where 'a role is frequently held for life'. She would 'almost rather see a second rate ballet well cast, than a good ballet wrongly cast'.[235]

Many of Volkova's statements are clearly made from a teacher's point of view. Still, her vision has proved itself with time. To this day, the greatest successes of the Royal Danish Ballet are those that are correctly cast. Volkova regretted the nepotism she felt was rampant in the Theatre, and insisted that roles should be assigned 'strictly on merit'.

Her thoughts on casting led directly to the difficult question of the age of retirement. Volkova thought it useless 'to argue as to the relative importance of the classical or character artist'. The important thing to make clear was that:

> the working span of the classical dancer is much shorter. Therefore, logically, they should start sooner. Once they have their technique it can hardly be too soon. Failure to do so is the background for the increasing demand by our young *classical* dancers to go abroad. Be it noted it is not our character dancers who wish to do so.
>
> Nothing enriches a ballet performance more than a fine piece of characterisation by a mature artist; nothing more lowers the tone than an

over age classical dancer still desperately clinging to his roles. You cannot blame them. It is our responsibility.[236]

Volkova appreciated that young dancers are often unreasonably impatient, but explained that this was due to an awareness of how short their careers would be. However, she advised moderation with regard to promotion.

> Young talents are apt to make premature claims to the title of soloist. But *we* have to decide when the moment is ripe, remembering always that justice in this matter maintains the morale of the company ... We have a number of soloists who are so rather by title than qualification. It is a situation we have to accept for the present, but we must not repeat the mistake.[237]

Equally important to correct casting was the choice of stager.

> It is not sufficient that a producer 'knows' a ballet and merely takes his dancers through the basic steps. He himself must be truly aware of the *style* of a work ... Bournonville calls for one kind of experience, Fokine another, Balanchine still another. Failure in this respect leads only to mediocrity.[238]

Volkova again drew attention to the need for better planning, 'so as to avoid the error of last year when something like eighteen ballets were rehearsed in the space of ten days!' She recommended further reforms in the Ballet School and objected to a recent practice in which a ballet critic was invited to be a member of the panel that judged the Ballet School's exams.

> I do not find it a sound principle, and this opinion is shared by the whole company and most of the staff, to have, as these past two years, a professional critic sitting on the examination board. I am strongly against it because his technical knowledge is not sufficient to form a sound judgement. Also, it is unfair that our young dancers should have their weaknesses exposed before one who is, in future, to write of them as artists.[239]

Erik Bruhn and Poul Gnatt had been the first Danish dancers to make careers for themselves abroad after World War II and the desire to travel had spread: Flemming Flindt had gone to London shortly after graduating from the School.
'I would be the last to recommend we should prevent, in all contingencies, our dancers faring abroad', she admitted. 'At a certain moment in their artistic development it is probably good for them and if they are reasonably mature it advances the prestige of the Royal Danish Ballet.' On the other hand, young artists should be advised not to travel.

What should be discouraged is the immature artist so doing. After all the Royal Theatre both in general education and ballet tuition have given them of their best, for at least 10 years, and dancers must be made to feel they owe something to the Theatre that reared them.

Is it not time that entrance into the School was made conditional on dancers serving at least a prescribed number of years with the company so as to 'work their passage' as it were? Then, more mature as artists and having been of some practical use to us, they might accept, *for a limited period*, a contract abroad. Clearly, as things are at present we have trained ballet dancer Flemming Flindt, at state expense, for the convenience of the Director of the Festival Ballet, London.[240]

Volkova concluded her report with an uncompromising lecture on artistic justice and on consistency in the company's management.

One thing above all sustains company morale and that is justice. Particularly artistic justice. After all, our dancers are artists first and this is something they are ready to understand. Justice, artistic or otherwise, is not found by lending an ear to the merely disgruntled. Too often in the past the noisily articulate have gained at the expense of the better behaved yet often more talented. Dancers are slow to see their own limitations so it is not possible to please everyone. But even an initially unpopular decision comes to be accepted by them so long as they feel it truly disinterested. There has been evidence of 'peace' being bought. This never works in the long run in any walk of life and certainly not in the ballet.

A strong line should I think be taken against preferment by flirtation, flattery, press connections, or other subversive means and although it may not be possible to guarantee it is never attempted, our constant vigilance must ensure that it does not succeed. In the small, closed circle of a ballet company nothing of this kind goes un-remarked and it has a very bad effect indeed. Surely our policy should be, talent being equal, to reward the hard working and indeed the well behaved.

She then finished her report by tempering her comments with praise for the dancers and an acknowledgement that Rome was not built in a day.

We have a most talented company enjoying material conditions in many ways unique in the world. We ought therefore to be at the top. We can be. But our house wants putting in order. Times have changed and new conditions demand new methods.

It is not suggested that the recommendations here made should be carried out simultaneously. First things first. There may be objections. Let us scrutinise them with care before we accept them as valid.

> We all, I trust, have the same objective in view: to maintain and further the great traditions of the Royal Danish Ballet. But we have come to a turning point in its history and I must emphasise that it is upon the decisions we take now its future pattern depends.[241]

Volkova's grand designs and recommendations for the company effectively came to nothing and she would spend decades fighting, little by little, for their implementation. Just weeks after Volkova submitted her report to Brøndsted, Henning Rohde was promoted to Assistant Director of the Royal Theatre. Rohde was one of Harald Lander's strongest supporters and he immediately began plotting his friend's return to the Theatre from his new position of power.

In March 1956, Frank Schaufuss, originally anti-Lander, secretly travelled to Paris and met with the dethroned leader. Meanwhile Rohde slowly undermined Niels Bjørn Larsen's authority as ballet-master and ultimately succeeded in removing him from his job, which was offered to Schaufuss in July.

To Henning Rohde, Schaufuss was merely a stopgap before Lander was reinstated, but Schaufuss himself was ambitious and determined to make the most of this opportunity. He made it clear to Volkova that her star was on the wane, and she should not expect to have his ear or any influence on his decisions. 'He worked against her to an incredible extent', Arlette Weinreich remembers. 'He was a proletarian and she was so refined. He felt inferior in front of her and that made him even more of the hard man.'

Volkova's daily work at the Theatre rapidly became a form of hell. Schaufuss seized every opportunity to put her in her place publicly, and tormented her with petty rudeness and intentional 'forgetfulness'. The teaching schedules would be changed but no one would notify Volkova; pianists would fail to turn up for her classes because they had not been told to go; and she stopped receiving invitations to receptions or meetings she had attended as a matter of course in the past.

Jurij Moskvitin, a young pianist and budding philosopher and writer with a Russian mother and a Danish father, regarded Volkova and Hugh Finch Williams as his surrogate parents. He remembered the pinpricks and their cause.

> The main point of attack was that she had acted treacherously towards Harald Lander... Actually she really didn't get involved in that game, but personally she regarded him as a kind of Mafioso crook – and naturally all the accusations against him were true ... But the Lander clique's line of attack in support of Lander was that, without him, the ballet was doomed to wilt. That was precisely what the ballet under Volkova didn't do – on the contrary. And

thereby crumbled the myth that Denmark had sent one of her great sons packing. So one had to try another way – and that was by demonstrating that Volkova was not as brilliant and indispensable as she was made out to be. And by taking her down a peg or two.

In September and October 1956, the Royal Danish Ballet embarked on an extensive tour of the USA, visiting twelve cities and dancing forty-four performances, most of them at the Metropolitan Opera in New York. Volkova was pushed far into the background on opening night and she was not feeling very well.

Before leaving for America she had suffered chest pains that she had ascribed to stress. The pains worsened, and an American consultant diagnosed breast cancer. On 25 September she returned to Copenhagen, where she was admitted to a private clinic near Kongens Have, the Royal Park not far from the Royal Theatre.

> I am feeling better and am allowed to leave my bed for a few hours, and even go for 10 minutes' walk in the park. A treat! I am not strong enough yet to start the radium treatment, but the word radium makes me think of Mme Curie, and Mme Curie of the word cure.[242]

Jurij Moskvitin thought that 'in her religious and philosophical beliefs [Volkova] was like most educated, Orthodox Russians'.

> They were firmly convinced that there was more between Heaven and Earth than we are conscious of in our daily life, but that strange and incalculable elements can play a part in our lives. Like all Russians in that category, Vera was a little superstitious. She would dream about someone and meet them by chance the next day. A man would be walking along carrying an empty bucket, and she would know immediately that trouble was brewing at the Theatre. She was certainly not afraid of death but was also extremely glad to be alive, and it was rather for that reason that she didn't like the thought of dying.

Moskvitin's father, Arthur Hansen, sent Volkova a bouquet of red roses while she was in the clinic. 'This was the first thing she caught sight of when she woke up from the anaesthetic', Moskvitin said:

> and later she would always say that those roses had had overwhelming significance. She had felt that the things that had made her ill were all kinds of petty irritations and worries that had closed her eyes to the beauty of life itself. The roses had made her determined never to forget this truth, and she seriously thought that it was her experience with these roses that kept her alive for many more years than the doctors had predicted at the time.

In December, while she was still at the clinic, she was made a 'Knight of Dannebrog' – equivalent to a Dame of the British Empire – in recognition of her work at the Royal Danish Theatre. But for the first time Volkova lost faith in her future in Denmark. Her convalescence gave her time to read and think, and she went alone on a cruise of the Nordic fjords.

When she went back to work, she was welcomed warmly by the dancers and members of the administration. But she knew then that she would never really be accepted as part of the Royal Danish Ballet. 'The Director doesn't care one way or the other if I stay and the ballet-master would rather see me go', [243] she wrote to Colette Clark, whom she had first met in London the previous year, and who was to become one of her closest friends.

Bengt Häger confirms that she was 'isolated', but thinks it is 'important to remember that she had no ambition to become Artistic Director in Copenhagen'.

> I think she realised right from the start that it would never be possible: she was a woman, and she was not Danish, and she stood for an artistic renewal that was naturally controversial in such an old house as the Royal Theatre.
>
> But she was a threat to many people, you see... What irritated them, I think, was her tremendous self-confidence... She had integrity, and she knew what she was talking about!

The entire situation was so inflamed that 'she couldn't really trust anyone', Häger remembers. 'Since I, too, was an outsider, she could discuss things with me ... She didn't know what people were saying about her. It made her suspicious, and she had reason to be ... the only reason they couldn't get rid of her was because of her enormous talent. And the person who best understood what she was worth was Brøndsted, but he had now lost out to Rohde.'

According to Häger, who describes her as 'an aristocratic woman with an expressive face that could never hide her feelings', she was too frank.

> She resembled a borzoi – she had the same nervous alertness. Her nervousness controlled her...
>
> If she was asked to give her opinion, she did so. She was often accused of being biased, and this she naturally was. That was her job. Perhaps she didn't make sufficient compromises, but one could tell that she hated having to compromise in artistic questions, when she knew she was right.

Volkova slowly recovered her physical strength and her spirits and concentrated on her work with the dancers. Even though life at the Theatre became increasingly complicated, she continued the struggle to maintain her impartial stance in the political intrigues generated by the

Lander issue. Eske Holm, who was on the Board of the Ballet Union at the time, confirms that she 'chose to remain neutral even though she was inclined towards the majority who didn't want Lander back'.

She was afraid to say too much in front of the company, but admitted privately that she did not want Lander back. 'One should never reheat an old soup', she told Hugh Finch Williams, and she could not understand why Rohde and his political supporters failed to see that Lander represented a retrograde step in the company's development.

When the London Festival Ballet performed at Copenhagen's Tivoli Concert Hall in April 1957, the French version of Harald Lander's *Études* was on the bill, and the timing, which was probably not a coincidence, could not have been better. *Études* was an enormous success and effectively vindicated Lander in the eyes of the public. More importantly, the Labour Prime Minister H.C. Hansen had been invited to an after-performance reception, where he gave a speech in which he deplored how Lander had been treated.

> There are many here tonight who are ashamed of the way Harald Lander left us. Tonight we are thrilled about the way he and Toni Lander have come back to us. And we are proud to see how Harald and Toni Lander have represented Denmark abroad.

The Prime Minister's speech was the final endorsement Rohde needed for the Machiavellian plot he had conceived. Brøndsted and Rohde recommended to the Theatre's politically appointed Board that the Theatre should approach Lander with a formal invitation to return to Copenhagen to stage *Études*. Throughout the summer and autumn of 1957, Rohde corresponded extensively with Lander, who demanded 'full rehabilitation'; he wanted his pension back and wished to stage a whole evening of works, including a world premiere.

When news of Rohde's and Schaufuss's machinations leaked, the company was thrown into turmoil and the Second Lander Scandal erupted.

Schaufuss's wife, Mona Vangsaae, a principal dancer and a fervent member of the anti-Lander camp, confronted him in his office with the rumours. When he confirmed he had been working to bring Lander back, she had a nervous breakdown and had to be taken away in an ambulance. The outraged Ballet Union demanded Schaufuss's dismissal and he resigned on 13 December 1958.

But Henning Rohde, the Theatre's Assistant Director, again had the upper hand and appointed himself de facto ballet-master, taking the title of Administrative Director. He had been using Schaufuss as his puppet; but now, although he was a civil servant and not a dancer and had no real experience or understanding of ballet, he had manoeuvred himself into a position of even greater power.

Following negotiations between Henning Rohde and representatives of the Ballet Union, a council consisting of Niels Bjørn Larsen, Erik Bruhn, Vera Volkova and Hans Brenaa was created to advise Rohde on artistic matters. An unreconstructed Lander man, Hans Brenaa hated (and was hated by) the others so much that he had separate meetings with Rohde.

The Danish ballet critics had always backed Lander. Now, *Berlingske Tidende*'s ballet critic Svend Kragh-Jacobsen reported from his entrenchment that

> among the best omens for the future is the fact that the Royal Theatre and Harald Lander are at last carrying on negotiations for his return to Copenhagen, to begin with as guest choreographer.[244]

Like most of the company – 47 dancers were against Lander, 16 in favour – Volkova was disgusted with Rohde's dishonesty. She found his plans irresponsible and fumed about his indifference and insensitivity towards the theatre's artists. 'They are like butterflies, and he is pulling their wings off', she said to Hugh Finch Williams. She also reported on the crisis to Colette Clark:

> The company failed in their last appeal to stop the return of Harald Lander. It is officially announced that he is coming to stage three ballets this spring: *Etudes*, *Victoires d'amour* and something else ... The company is really devastated! One good thing is that as a result of this disappointment all the soloists are more united than they ever were before. They look grim and resolute. The first shock is beginning to wear off and they are thinking what else is left for them to do but protect their interests.
>
> I am trying to cheer them up, continue to give classes as usual because it is so very important at a time like this to keep their morale up ... It could be such a good company – all they need is peace of mind and a good repertoire, in fact leadership![245]

As it happened, the negotiations with Lander dragged on interminably. The plans were delayed by the Ballet Union's staunch opposition, and Lander did not return until March 1962, following a dramatic confrontation during which the Director of the Theatre announced he would fire all dancers who refused to collaborate with Lander and finally handed in his own letter of resignation.

Meanwhile, Volkova explained in the letter to Colette Clark that she hoped to remain in Copenhagen for the rest of the season and possibly also for the following one: 'There are many young talents coming up, and I haven't finished with Henning and Kirsten.'[246]

She continued to fight for her reforms and for her young dancers, and gave an interview to *Dance Magazine* in July 1958 in which she completely avoided mention of the political intrigues and glossed over the Schaufuss period entirely, focussing on pertinent artistic issues:

> We're progressing. We are broadening the technique. There's potential among the young people, and some of that talent is already blossoming. The talent is there.[247]

Yet again she drew attention to the fact that any further steps forward were hobbled by issues of casting and repertoire:

> It is my firm belief from experience that you can't develop talent in the classroom – only on stage. I would like to see double casts for each ballet – one composed of older, mature stars, and one with the young, growing dancers. The older group will feel some competition, which is good, and the young ones would have a chance to learn about the responsibility of a performing artist. Audiences would enjoy comparing the two casts.[248]

She commented that Balanchine's *Symphony in C*, which the company added to its repertoire in 1952:

> is a wonderful ballet for developing a company's technique. But at that time, only the established stars were ready for this ballet – Margrethe Schanne, Mona Vangsaae, Inge Sand and Kirsten Ralov. It was my intention that a second cast would eventually alternate with these four. And now I have four girls in their early twenties – Kirsten Petersen, Kirsten Simone, Solveig Østergaard and Hanne Marie Ravn – who can dance this ballet beautifully, but they rarely get a chance.[249]

Volkova pointed out how Kirsten Petersen had had great personal success as Juliet on the American tour but only Vangsaae was allowed to dance the role in Denmark. She also mentioned the young Niels Kehlet, who occasionally danced the *pas de deux* from *Don Quixote*, 'but not consistently enough'.

She defended Marius Petipa's *The Sleeping Beauty*, which she had finally managed to add to the repertoire in 1957, but which had been scrapped – and, Volkova thought, misunderstood:

> That's the value of *The Sleeping Beauty*. A girl has been progressing nicely, so she's given Bluebird as something to get her teeth into. A little later she becomes ready for Aurora. Maybe she'll be good in only one of the three acts, but after a few performances she'll improve the other two...
>
> Young talent is a rare thing. It must be nursed gently and intelligently, or it's lost.[250]

Volkova, who was still worried that young, talented dancers might leave the company, was not without a sense of intrigue herself and was determined both to develop her dancers and to make her own vision a reality. In 1956 and 1957 she again secretly corresponded with Jerome Robbins, trying to persuade him to come back to Copenhagen to create a new work for her company. Robbins was interested. On his first visit, he had had 'such a really marvellous time working there, and as much as I enjoyed it while in Copenhagen it was only after returning here, thinking about it, I feel the amount of joy and happiness of it all.'[251] Robbins suggested a production of his latest work, *Afternoon of a Faun*: 'I think Henning or little Niels would be marvellous in it', but also asked: 'what do you think the chances are of doing one of the large Stravinsky works like *Sacre?*'[252]

Robbins's idea for a new version of Stravinsky's seminal ballet *The Rite of Spring* surpassed everything Volkova had dreamed of, and she insisted he stick to his original idea when he suggested a three-act ballet based on *Peter Pan* as a possible alternative.[253]

The plans for *Rite of Spring* went ahead. Having presented them with a *fait accompli*, Volkova convinced Henning Brøndsted and Frank Schaufuss to underwrite the project, for which Robbins now wanted Picasso to create sets and costumes. 'I am very excited about doing *Rite of Spring* for the company', he wrote to her.

> I feel I'm ready to do a large and important work at this time, however I must have a certain freedom in the creation of the work, to be able to change, throw out, experiment and shift material and people if necessary.
>
> At this point my idea is to make the sacrificial dance for Henning [Kronstam] rather than for a girl. Even this idea may change by the time I come to Copenhagen, but all I can assure you is of some inner creative voice which says it's right and it's the right time and something good will happen. Do let me know what my manoeuvres must be in terms of Brøndsted and Schaufuss et cetera.[254]

In mid-November 1957, only a few weeks before rehearsals were to about to begin, the project collapsed: someone suddenly found out that the Royal Theatre's old orchestra pit was not big enough to accommodate the more than one hundred musicians Stravinsky's score demanded.

Volkova was flabbergasted that she had not been warned earlier, and Robbins – a volatile man – was so shocked and disappointed that he did not think he would ever come to Denmark again. But Volkova did not give up hope:

You MUST wait for us. Do, please, Jerry. Believe me there is not even a whiff of intrigue in this affair. One and all want you... I will be so grateful if you will be patient and keep *Sacre* for us.[255]

Volkova wrote to Stravinsky, whom she had met in London after World War II, and tried to persuade him to accept a performance of his music with a smaller orchestra. Stravinsky, who knew he would be coming to Copenhagen in 1959 to receive the Léonie Sonning Music Prize, suggested they discuss it then.

When the day came, however, the Theatre had forgotten to forward Volkova her tickets for the award ceremony. Jurij Moskvitin claims it was simply another example of chicanery. Henning Rohde was behind it and it was still part of his policy 'that Vera shouldn't shine too much – she had to be kept out of the limelight'.

> When Hugh complained to me on behalf of Vera that Léonie Sonning had not sent them tickets for the award ceremony, and when I phoned Mrs Sonning (she was almost a fixture in my parents' home), she said that she had in fact expressly asked the festival committee to send tickets to Vera Volkova and her husband. The festival committee assured her that they had scrupulously carried out her wishes and sent the tickets to the Royal Theatre – and from there they had got no further. So Volkova and Hugh's meetings with Stravinsky and his wife turned into a private dinner with Mrs Sonning, and a dinner at the Hotel d´Angleterre as Stravinsky's guests.

In the end, Volkova's efforts were in vain. Stravinsky was adamant: 'When the Ballets Russes performed the ballet, there was not enough room in the orchestra pit either, so we put extra musicians in the boxes.' Robbins's new work for the Royal Danish Ballet never came to anything, but Volkova kept on lobbying on his behalf for years, as well as for her other favourites Ashton and Balanchine. 'Before Robbins left for Europe, I watched some of his rehearsals', she wrote to Henning Kronstam from New York when she taught the Joffrey Ballet in 1959.

> He asked me how you were and told me that he is still waiting for an 'official' invitation to come to us and stage a ballet. It was very tempting for me to sign him just then with the date and all. But I was relieved to learn that he is not angry after all this mess with Frank Schaufuss and Henning Rohde. Tonight I am going to dinner with George Balanchine.
>
> I also have seen Fred Ashton in London. He is free to revive Romeo for us, anytime between January and June.
>
> Kenneth MacMillan is free from April to June and is also willing to come.
>
> Everybody is expecting us here in 1960. It is so important to have a good season this year and at least one good ballet, preferably by an American

choreographer. So Robbins is just the man. But as neither Erik [Bruhn] nor I are given the authority to act, I was unable to make definite arrangements.[256]

Ten years later, the Royal Danish Ballet did get *Afternoon of a Faun* for Henning Kronstam, but the new ballet-master Flemming Flindt turned Volkova down, when, on behalf of Robbins, she offered the company his latest ballet, *Dances at a Gathering*.

'One is responsible for training students, and one is responsible for them as people',[257] Volkova said. Love was an element in a strong relationship between teacher and pupil, and many of her students, male and female, gay and straight, experienced falling in love with her. 'I love you as my pupil', she reassured one when he revealed his feelings to her.

Her solicitude for Henning Kronstam was legendary and is well described in Alexandra Tomalonis's biography, *Henning Kronstam – Portrait of a Danish Dancer*. A letter to Colette Clark speaks of her continued concern for Margot Fonteyn and Erik Bruhn, who were both standing at crossroads in the spring of 1961.

> Erik Bruhn came back from the gala a bit sad. He told me he danced badly and fell over in all his pirouettes. At first I thought he was trying to be modest but having received your letter I am sorry to hear that he really did dance better in rehearsals ... I am just as worried about him as I am about Margot. They have both reached the top of their careers and still both are in danger but for different reasons.[258]

According to Volkova, Bruhn was 'neurotic', and his psychological problems were closely bound up in his career.

> It is a hard illness to cure unless it is detected and checked from the start. He has reached the point of being a really great dancer. He knows it, he feels it and people tell him so all the time. He now finds it hard to live up to his own immense reputation and is consumed by fears. His greatest fear is disappointing his public; that people will one day shrug after a performance and say, "So, that is the great Erik Bruhn?"
>
> I was told once that it happens inevitably to all great bullfighters. At the height of their fame and powers they develop tremendous fears they will disappoint the crowds; that they will fail to live up to their expectations. And so they do something desperate, trying deliberately to repeat a previous successful feat that came spontaneously to them before. In the end some of them get themselves killed. Luckily our dear friends do not put their life at stake, but it's the same thing when nerves get in the way ...[259]

'Erik is a sick boy. This far, physical exercises have saved him from most of it', Volkova thought. She was equally convinced that it was the daily training that had saved Henning Kronstam in times when his manic depression threatened to overwhelm him.

His [Erik's] appearance is very misleading: he looks so composed and cool with this granite-like profile and blue eyes. But actually he is wearing himself out with worries, complexes, imaginary conversations, self-doubts et cetera.

Most sensitive people know about that, of course, but they scramble their way out of it and come to terms with life. But Danes are so different. They appear so lost when confronted with problems, they seem unable to solve them and don't even try to nine times out of ten. They just wallow in it.[260]

Volkova had vested interests in Bruhn's career as a dancer, but on a personal level she was more concerned about his welfare. She considered suggesting to him that he devote himself more to teaching than to dance.

He is a good teacher and I am sure he will be a much happier man when he stops dancing. But it is tragic. He is only 31 or 32 but I feel it will be a short career.

Everybody told me he danced beautifully in Moscow and Leningrad, and Erik told me he was himself amazed: 'I really enjoyed dancing and everything "came off". It was wonderful. Nobody knew about me... '[261]

'Another problem is Margot', Volkova continued in her letter to Colette Clark, touching upon Fonteyn's problematic marriage to the Panamanian diplomat Tito Arias:

I have been worried about her for some time ... I think she is too proud to admit that she knows about Tito's unfaithfulness and instinctively feels that if she stops dancing, she will lose him altogether, as it is the glamour that comes with Margot's stage career that really attracts him. And because she loves him deeply she will do anything to keep him. The other reason is money. She is the highest paid dancer in the world today but their daily expenses are huge and Tito's earnings erratic.

She knows herself, I am sure, that she is dead tired, that she does not rest enough between performances as a dancer her age should do. But she is caught in a web. Even if she is aware of the fact that her dancing is not always up to standard, it is difficult for her to say goodbye to it all in one gesture. Personally, I think she should stop dancing. Dancers have nothing to leave behind but their legend. She will gradually kill hers.

Even if all was well in her private life it would of course still be difficult not to go down hill after the age of 40. Let's hope she will have a good rest during February, let's hope she will dance well in Moscow and then she really should reconsider the situation. Perhaps Tito will, in fact, be just as proud of her as a successful Ambassadress, the former great Margot Fonteyn, still beautiful, wonderful hostess, still a public figure, useful to him with all her social savoir faire (which by now she has perfected). The only difference being that a great load will have been taken off her shoulders. I really feel that her married life with Tito means to her more than anything else. After all she worked hard as a dancer all her life, she gave pleasure to thousands of people and she is entitled to rest on her laurels. Why not now? Before she collapses with a nervous breakdown. Nobody can stand such a strain for so long. If not for her marriage she could have drifted for a few more years on a moonlit stage in long flowing dresses, like Markova.[262]

By an incredible coincidence, the Russian dancer Rudolf Nureyev laid to rest all Volkova's worries about both Fonteyn and Bruhn when, on 17 June 1961 at Le Bourget Airport in Paris, he sought political asylum in France. With 'a single handsome gesture', Nureyev made ballet history and altered life and career for the two dancers: both of them fell in love with him and both their careers were hugely boosted by the dancing Tartar, who became the twentieth century's most photographed and talked-about dancer.

Just under a month after he had defected, Nureyev travelled to Copenhagen to train with Volkova. Officially, it was because he needed to work with a genuine Russian-trained teacher, but he really went to Copenhagen to meet Erik Bruhn: 'the only dancer who has anything to show me I don't already know'.[263]

He had seen film footage of the Danish dancer in Russia, and admired his dancing. 'I wanted to go to Denmark because I wanted to study with his teachers – Volkova', Nureyev recalled years later. 'I didn't know it was Volkova, but I wanted to go to study with his teachers. As a friend, lover or enemy, I had to go to that camp!' Nureyev's Leningrad teacher Alexander Pushkin had told him, 'Go and attack!', but Nureyev was amazed to discover that his old and new Russian teachers had been dancing partners 35 years before.

Like other professionals, Volkova quickly recognised the twenty-three-year-old Nureyev's exceptional talent, but she was sceptical about his temperament, high-handedness, poor discipline and bad manners. According to Peter Martins, then a young dancer in the company, Nureyev's behaviour towards the Danes:

> was just plain obnoxious ... I was taking the adult classes when he first came to Copenhagen, and my first impression of him was that he was rude, enormously rude to everybody – to the other dancers, to the pianists, to every single one of the teachers with the exception of Volkova.[264]

It was Nureyev's dream to become as pure a classical dancer as Erik Bruhn, and that made him treat Volkova with respect. Even so, when Nureyev and Bruhn took joint classes with Volkova there was a marked tension between the two Russians. Volkova felt Nureyev was too closed-minded and stubborn to really learn anything from her. Nureyev accepted the quality of Volkova's teaching but regretted that it was not identical to Pushkin's.

> I admired and liked Vera Volkova as much as I had expected. But it was clear that she had worked with Vaganova when that teacher was still working out the vocabulary of her system. Since then she had introduced many refinements and improvements. And these of course were lacking.[265]

David Arkell, who had read Nureyev's comments about Volkova's teaching, wrote to her: 'I thought that Nureyev's remark that Vaganova had developed her methods since you were with her was a little naive – because you too, obviously, have developed them just as much.'[266] Volkova agreed. She thought it was self-evident that 'even Vaganova's work must breathe', and that she had developed a system that suited both the aesthetics and the temperaments of European dancers.

'When Rudi first came to Copenhagen', Volkova later wrote, 'he was still in his early youth and unsure of the ways of the West.' She conceded that 'as a pupil he was highly professional, beautifully trained, and I enjoyed teaching him'.

Her public assessment of Nureyev was far more gracious than his of her, but also hints at their differences and what she regarded as his immaturity.

> He took correction seriously and always gave of his best. He has matured as an artist and as a person. He is always well organised, and he plans his career with forethought. It is always a pleasure for a teacher to instruct a great talent, and I feel that we spoke the same language in more ways than one.[267]

In private, however, she was never afraid to stand up to him. The Danish critic Erik Aschengreen remembers watching the performance with Volkova when Nureyev came to Copenhagen to dance Albrecht in *Giselle* in 1968. 'His costume was low-necked right down to here', Aschengreen remembers, pointing roughly at his navel,

> and during the performance he shouted at the conductor Poul Jørgensen in the orchestra pit. In the studio, Nureyev had insisted on a particularly slow tempo – because he thought it would make him look good, probably. On stage, he realised it didn't work after all, and shouted, 'Quicker, quicker'. He was throwing Merle Park around. The whole thing was most unfortunate.

Volkova did not comment, but after the performance she asked Aschengreen if he would like to come backstage to meet the star. They found Nureyev surrounded by the ballet-master Flemming Flindt, the Theatre Director and other admirers, looking pretty smug. 'He asked her what she thought of the performance', Aschengreen remembers, 'and she said,

> 'Do you really want to know?' Then she spoke Russian! And he got such a dressing-down, because in her opinion it was so unartistic what he had done. She had given him a lot, so she had carte blanche to speak out. He went completely pale. And then she turned and strode out of the room.

Volkova and Nureyev continued to train for two hours every afternoon to polish the young man's raw dancing, and gradually a warm friendship developed, strengthened by Volkova's unprejudiced acceptance of Nureyev's love affair with Erik Bruhn. The relationship between the two star dancers had rapidly become romantic, and they spent their evenings, and sometimes nights, in Volkova's home.

One evening the telephone rang at Volkova's home. It was Colette Clark who, with Margot Fonteyn, was busy arranging a London benefit for the Royal Academy of Dancing. With Volkova as interpreter and go-between, Fonteyn and Clark asked Nureyev whether he would perform. Nureyev said he would, but only on condition that he danced with Fonteyn, whom Volkova had told him about. Fonteyn was unconvinced, but Clark told the ballerina: 'Well, Vera thinks he's a genius. She says he has "the nostrils", you know what I mean? People of genius have "nostrils".'[268] Clark dilated hers to illustrate the point. The conversation ended in Nureyev's agreeing to go to London, even if he were not to dance with Fonteyn, and Volkova sent him off, saying to Clark and Fonteyn: 'Now I hand you the baby.'

'Nureyev is in London', Volkova wrote to Hugh Finch Williams in Paris:

> he left Friday morning by plane. He had another telephone call from Leningrad, this time from his teacher A. Pushkin begging him to return. But Nureyev said he does not want to go back. I rang up Margot from Mr Brøndsted's office and told her that, finally, Nureyev is on the way.[269]

In the end, Nureyev made his début in London with a solo created for him by Frederick Ashton to Scriabin's *Poème Tragique*. Cecil Beaton, who was electrified by Nureyev's performance, wrote:

> The huge stage was empty except for the scarlet-shrouded object standing centre. Suddenly the cloak moved more swiftly than the eye could follow and was violently whisked away to reveal a savage young creature, half naked, with wild eyes on an ecstatic, gaunt face, and a long mop of flying, silk hair, rushing towards the footlights.[270]

It is impossible not to speculate that Ashton had known of, or perhaps even seen, Volkova's performance to the same piece of music in Gunter's

Grove in 1938. The title was the same, and the costuming and the theme were similar for both Russian's débuts in London.

In 1961 Henning Rohde left the Royal Theatre to become Permanent Undersecretary at the newly-established Ministry of Culture. Niels Bjørn Larsen was re-appointed as ballet-master and Harald Lander finally returned to the Royal Theatre to stage *Études* and create a new ballet for the Danes.

'Harald Lander left Copenhagen this afternoon', Volkova reported in a letter to Hugh Finch Williams:

> for two days he was sitting watching the classes and making lists. Hans Brenaa, Vessel and Lis Barfoed at his elbow. On the whole, in spite of the strain, all went well. He is going to post his casting list from Paris. He was very polite to me the first day. The second day he tried to be friendly and had a little conversation. His policy is to charm everybody, I feel. But on the whole he looks tired and worried. He refused any interviews to the newspapers, or perhaps he was ordered to do so? ... Anyway, that was that! I was very calm ... and in a way it was an anti-climax, everybody is bored! Of course Larsen had mostly to deal with Lander and got so exhausted at the end of the two days.[271]

'Muscles don't understand politics', she said, and she 'gave the classes as usual', while noting people's reactions to Lander with detached indulgence.

> Niels Bjørn is so worried about Lander returning in January, so he also leans towards me as he always does when he thinks his position is in danger. [Paul] Vessel [the Ballet's *régisseur* and a close personal friend of Harald Lander] is particularly nice, I think he was relieved that all went so peacefully when Lander was here and I gave classes without a fuss.[272]

'Lander's *Les Victoires de l'amour* is the joke of the moment', she told her husband when Lander started rehearsals at the Theatre. Lander, who was under incredible strain, had not created a successful work since *Études*, and the dancers intensely disliked his stuffy new ballet, inspired by one of the Sun King's court ballets, with music by Lully. It was titled *Les Victoires de l'amour* but was quickly nicknamed Victor's Mor [Victor's Mum], and the atmosphere during rehearsals was tense. At one point, Lander staged a grand entrance for the ballerina Kirsten Simone, who was wearing a large headdress. 'It would be good if Miss Simone could smile a little', Lander hissed from the auditorium. Simone shot right back at him: 'There's nothing to smile about.'[273]

'I have not seen it', Volkova wrote:

I am waiting till rehearsals will be held on stage so I can watch it unobtrusively... I am very devoted to my work now that I have peace of mind, with all this Lander nonsense over with and the muddler Hr. Rohde out of the way.[274]

During Lander's last weeks at the Royal Theatre, Volkova was 'lent' to the Royal Swedish Ballet. According to Bengt Häger, the timing was 'naturally no coincidence. It was arranged in that manner in order to avoid problems, and [Lander] wanted preferably to avoid her.'

Volkova herself was happy to be teaching the Swedish dancers. She found them hard-working and 'much more humble and eager than the Danes', but less well-trained:

Mary [Skeaping, the Artistic Director] has done quite a lot for the company. Her mistake was, not being a pedagogue at heart, she should have delegated this department to somebody else. The mingy Italian technique does not really suit the tall Nordic people.[275]

Ironically, Volkova had landed in the middle of yet another intrigue. Having learned from her experience in Copenhagen, she kept well out of it – but she could not help becoming a witness to it.

It is amazing how unpopular poor Mary Skeaping is with everybody. With critics, society, the dancers. I have a feeling that the Director rather likes her and defends her and that's what really saved her. Still, she feels it is time for her to resign so she has written a letter to the directors about it, asking them for one more year to liquidate all her commitments and pass the reins to her successor. Now she is waiting for their reply. All this was said to me in the greatest confidence by Mary so of course I didn't breathe a word to Bengt, whom many consider to be her greatest enemy. Mary, of course, appreciates that I cannot avoid meeting her enemies socially but I assured her that I am very discreet in regard to theatre politics as I had such an excellent training in that respect in Copenhagen.[276]

During the 1950s the Opera in Stockholm had made overtures to Volkova, offering her the job of Director of the ballet company. Now she thought they might do so again, but:

I have a feeling that it is 'too late' for me to embark on this new and complicated kind of job but I have to be prepared that they might offer it to me ... I still feel that I was right choosing Copenhagen instead of Stockholm, in spite of all the difficulties and the Lander scandal, and I did deliver the goods, as Bill Manchester put it. The scandals, the intrigues and the local gossip failed to affect my reputation in the long run, thank goodness. And it is a better company and that is the general opinion. It is very difficult to speculate what could have happened with the Swedish Ballet if I had worked there for 10 years instead. I would have needed at least two Stanley Williamses to help me. There would have been a very strong opera tradition to overcome (not existent in Denmark) and a strong 'modern' influence right inside the theatre: Mme Cullberg, Mrs. Åkesson, Ivo Cramér, all heavily backed by the critics (Anne-Greta Ståhle, Bengt Häger et cetera) ... I don't discuss the subject with anybody, I just listen to them all (Mary, Bengt, Kozlovsky, Anna-Greta S.) and have my own thoughts.[277]

While Volkova was working in Stockholm, the Russian choreographer Yuri Grigorovitch staged his ballet *The Stone Flower* at the theatre. She thought it was 'a success because it was very well-cast and rehearsed but I was disappointed (I did not tell anybody, of course). So much stomping in boots, the worst kind of Russian folklore, endless Ivans doing the same kind of showy steps. But some lovely passages when the lovers come and dance their *pas de deux* with lifts and big broad movements, very lyrical and musical.'

Grigorovitch is definitely a talented man. But Prokofiev's music thunders on in a dreary way and the whole ballet seems so long. I would never have recommended this ballet to the Danes! But Virsaladze (the designer) told me that he had made another ballet called *Legende d'amour* based on a poem by a famous Turkish poet, Nasim Hikmet, and it is much better. Nureyev told me the same, actually ...

I got on very well with all three Russians. Especially with the artist, who has such good manners and is definitely from a good pre-revolutionary family (and he did not even try to hide the fact from me). Kissed my hand, got up when I got up and so on.

The management and the company gave a big farewell party to the Russians. Grigorovitch told me that he would love to come to Copenhagen to do *Legende d'amour* for the Danes so I am keeping that in mind. Virsaladze told me that Grigorovitch also came from a 'good family'. His mother's name was Rosai. I said: 'I wonder if she is related to a girl dancer called Klavdia Rosai, that I knew in my youth?' He said 'This is my mother' and it made his evening.[278]

Towards the end of Volkova's stay in Stockholm, the intrigue reached new heights of absurdity when one of the Opera ballet-masters and his wife offered Volkova a lift back to her hotel:

Mary S. said, 'You can trust them'. Bengt said they particularly loathe Mary!! I am afraid I cannot take the theatre seriously anymore, I only take dancing seriously.[279]

Dancing and dancers! Volkova was still deeply involved with Henning Kronstam, and many people think that, in the end, he was the reason she stayed in Copenhagen. Volkova would turn to him when her position at the theatre was insecure. 'In Henning I find all the moral support and help I need',[280] she confided in her husband.

> We trust each other and love each other and are helping each other. He always keeps me well informed and we like to discuss daily problems, dancers, classes and so on. Also he has a formality that appeals to me. It is very important to have one person in the theatre who is 100% behind me. Also, he is respected by the company and his opinion has weight.[281]

Arlette Weinreich thinks that 'She had lost her heart to Henning, we could all see that.' Rumour had it that Kronstam resembled a man Volkova had been in love with in Russia, but who had been executed. No one knew the man's name but it must have been Serge Toropov, with whom she had escaped to China.

In turn, Volkova supported Kronstam in every way she could, and he used to go to her when he had problems with his partner Franz von Gerstenberg, or with his family.

They also discussed the repertoire and casting, and Volkova taught Kronstam always to keep an eye on the School. She put all her hopes in him and envisaged that he would one day become Artistic Director of the company, and trained him not only as a dancer but also as a teacher and ballet-master.

Kronstam said later that he learned from Volkova how to develop a state company: in her 1956 report to Henning Brøndsted, she had laid out the artistic guidelines that Kronstam would try to follow when he became ballet-master for the Royal Danish Ballet in 1979.

When Kronstam danced with Marquis de Cuevas's company in France at the beginning of the 1960s, he took class with Maria Fay, as she relates:

> I was giving the class on stage under very odd circumstances, with dancers hanging on to the sets and wings and piano because there was no barre, when I caught a glimpse of somebody working in the wings and looking very concentrated. I didn't recognise the face, but I immediately knew this was a great dancer. After the class I went to compliment him; you have to when you see such elegance and such style! It was the first time I had met him and when I did compliment him, he looked at me and said, 'This has nothing to do with me, this is because of my teacher, Vera Volkova.' I nearly cried; Henning was one of the gods of dance of his time, and the way he so humbly gave credit to his teacher was such a noble thing.

And later I found that, of all her pupils, the ones that were the most special and unique artistically and morally spoke of her with the same veneration. Teaching at the Royal Swedish Ballet, I spoke with Erik Bruhn who said almost the same thing: 'You know, I owe almost everything to Vera.'

At the start of the sixties there was an up-and-coming generation of dancers who had been trained by Stanley Williams. Volkova called them the 'juice generation', because they were much taller and stronger than preceding generations, and liked one girl in particular. 'I got interested in a girl called Mette Hønningen, she is a first year apprentice and has a quality and style.'[282]

'She was my path-clearer', says Mette Hønningen, who fulfilled all Volkova's hopes and became the Royal Danish Ballet's leading ballerina during the sixties and seventies.

> She took hold of me even before I became an apprentice, and I don't know what would have happened if she hadn't been there. That's what it's like in a place where everything depends on the management, and where it isn't always a matter of talent, but sometimes of what colour hair or what colour eyes one has. To dance was my only wish, but I don't think there was anyone else other than Volkova who would have noticed me at the time. She saw something in me that nobody else did.

Volkova wrote to Finch Williams about her gentle prodding of the dancer.

> What pleased me particularly is that Mette Hønningen came and worked with Benny [another dancer who was doing National Service and attended weekend classes to stay in shape] on Saturday evening, just the two of them. She is lovely, has a real feeling for dancing and works really hard. I am so happy that you have spotted her and liked her too. It is so gratifying to work with a real talent.[283]

It had become fashionable for dancers to take yoga classes but Volkova was strongly against the trend. She had already had problems with Kirsten Simone, who had secretly been doing 'relaxation exercises', and immediately took measures to prevent Hønningen following suit.

> Benny assured me that she is not interested in yoga, but I coached him and asked him to speak to her just in case. They are friends. He promised to do it. I like the boy, he is very serious and polite, has will power too. I don't know if he has talent or how much talent.[284]

Volkova's interest in and solicitude for Hønningen was overwhelming. 'She was almost like a ballet mother', Hønningen recalls. 'She fussed about me as if I were her daughter. She became wrapped up in all aspects

of my life, and that surprised me, because I already had a mother.'
Hønningen sensed that Volkova's interest was perhaps a result of her
unfulfilled desire to have children, and the two women developed a close,
personal relationship.

> She was a didact in many ways, and there were things she tried to tell me, but
> I was so young… Things like having talent, and the responsibility that went
> with it. Maybe I wasn't as hard-working as I should have been, and she tried to
> make me understand that if I had this talent, I had to work for it. Once she
> explained to me what ambition was and gave me some examples.
>
> She taught us common courtesy – to say 'good morning' to people properly.
> That was important to her. Good manners. To make sure to thank the pianist,
> who had been playing gratis at our private lessons. One should buy a man like
> that a cup of coffee, she taught me. She herself wouldn't have anything! But
> she taught the rest of us that we shouldn't just be takers, but also givers.

Artistically speaking, it soon became clear to Hønningen that Volkova
didn't care for dancers who could merely do pirouettes:

> Art for her was a melding together of many elements. She naturally
> appreciated outstanding technique, but it was the aesthetic aspect, beauty,
> that meant something to her, and she worked uncompromisingly to achieve it.
> She fought stoutly for those she trusted and believed in. She cushioned me, and
> I have no doubt that I can thank her for the things I got in my time. She fought
> so hard to get some classics for her classical dancers. I should have done *The
> Sleeping Beauty* when I was young. She never got that, and that grieved her.
>
> She never told me that she was badly treated, but she gave me to understand
> that it was not all roses, that she didn't get on with all the different ballet-
> masters. She had to weave her way in and out of difficulties, and she hinted
> that that was how she had to go about it, without being dishonest.

As Mette Hønningen put it, a lot of Volkova's work was 'underground'.
She had to be careful, because her situation at the Theatre 'was not too
stable'.

Stanley Williams had started going to New York as guest teacher at
Balanchine's School of American Ballet, and Volkova was worried that
her main teaching protégé would eventually leave the Royal Danish
Ballet. (He moved to New York in 1964 and his departure was a great loss
to her.) In 1961, the Theatre hired a new teacher for the School, the
Latvian Edite Feifere Frandsen. She had had a private ballet school in
Copenhagen and had trained several talented dancers who later joined
both the Royal Danish Ballet and the ballet at the Pantomime Theatre at
the Tivoli Gardens.

Frandsen, who had danced with the ballet in Riga, also 'followed' Vaganova's Russian system – she had studied with Helen Tangieva-Birzniece, a pupil of Vaganova's from Leningrad. The relationship between Volkova and Frandsen was strained from the outset, partly owing to a clash of personalities and partly because of a fundamental disagreement about the training of the Ballet School pupils. Volkova thought Frandsen put inhuman and unnecessary pressure on the children, physically and mentally, where she should really be helping them to unfold.

They also disagreed artistically. Arlette Weinreich says that, with Volkova:

> you were not supposed to raise your leg as high as possible. You should lift it as high as your turnout at the hip would allow. Here Edite Frandsen differed, and the generation that was trained by her raised their legs higher. It looked mighty impressive – and BOOM, it said, when the leg went down again.

The leg would *fall* down because the dancer didn't have the strength and placement to control its descent.

Mette Hønningen, who also took classes with Frandsen, remembers that Volkova could be jealous. 'She thought at one point that I tended too much in the other direction, and so she flattened me. She said silly things like, I should start right from the beginning again. Frandsen wasn't quite as bad as all that, but they were clearly competitors.'

On the other hand, Volkova liked and accepted one of her rival's more single-minded protégées, the ballerina Anna Lærkesen. 'Of course I am very, very fond of Anna, as a person and as a dancer', she openly admitted in a letter to her husband.

> We have a good understanding. After morning class the pianist Ib Martin stayed for an extra ten minutes and Anna and I worked on *pointe* work and jumps ... She looked so happy. I was thinking today how musical she is, she really phrases. Also she dances with such good taste, like people who have good table manners. Of course she is very young and uneven but here and there she just surprises me with real subtleties. She works really hard and is as devoted and dedicated to dancing as Ulanova or Nureyev ... Real Russian fanaticism![285]

Volkova nevertheless watched developments carefully, making sure that her own plans were not jeopardised.

> Erik Bruhn is rehearsing *Nutcracker pas de deux* with Anna Lærkesen, they are going to dance it at this Festival. My feelings are mixed about this new couple. Psychologically people will think that Anna is the ballerina of the company

and more important than Kirsten. On the other hand Henning Kronstam has just as big success abroad but is not as big a name yet as Erik ... Henning is more reliable as a person and is younger, as far as long-term policy is concerned it is a good partnership. As you know I am very fond of both – Erik and Anna – and I will do my best not to upset our relationship. But it is a delicate situation. There will be a lot of competition between those two couples. But Kirsten, more than anybody, needs the competition and we need good girl dancers. Then we can wait quietly for Mette Hønningen to be ready.[286]

In the autumn of 1962 both Stanley Williams and Anna Lærkesen spotted Hønningen and the progress she had made. Volkova wrote to Hugh Finch Williams that she had not commented upon their discovery.

They like to feel that they have spotted new talent themselves. Henning, who was also present, simply smiled. We have been working with Mette for such a long time.

Volkova contacted Henning Brøndsted directly to draw attention to Hønningen's talent and to make sure of his backing in paving the way for a great career. 'We must do everything to help her, if she is a real talent', he promised Volkova, who concluded that there were still moments when she thought the Royal Theatre was 'a wonderful theatre to work in'.[287]

Fundamental Rules Apply

The British Royal Ballet Touring Company's season in Copenhagen in October 1962 became a reunion with some of the dancers Volkova had worked with in London more than a decade before. After the last performance, there had been a reception backstage with speeches by Brøndsted and the Director of the Touring Company, John Field, who made a point of thanking Volkova: 'What made our stay in Copenhagen memorable is the fact that we have met dear Vera Volkova again. She is a jewel, and we English dancers just want to kidnap her.'

'Everybody applauded. It's really extraordinary how they never forgot me',[288] Volkova wrote to Hugh Finch Williams. She was bowled over by the young Canadian-born ballerina Lynn Seymour's performances, and went on to say how wonderful it was to see Petipa's and Ashton's classical ballets on stage at the Royal Theatre; but also said:

> It made me almost ill with sadness at the thought that by now Kirsten Simone would have out-danced all these dancers if we really had kept the classical ballets in the repertoire all these years! Anna Lærkesen would have been a wonderful Lilac Fairy, and Solveig Østergaard and Niels Kehlet such exciting Blue Birds ... But I have done my fighting for the Danes... I have no official power to plan their repertoire but I still keep on giving my advice, which is usually ignored.[289]

She reflected on the career path she had chosen, leaving one Royal Ballet for another, comparing the two companies, which were rivals on the international stage of the 1960s.

> I was sitting in the canteen having my lunch, thinking about the Danes and the English and my own destiny, when Stanley Williams came and joined me. He was deeply impressed with the way the English dancers had treated me, he became very emotional and told me he had been thinking about me these five days. He feels I have put up with a lot of things in the past, to help the company, and that nobody really appreciates it.[290]

'Anyway, it is all for the best', she concluded. 'I don't want to leave this theatre, but the Danes need a little shaking-up sometimes, as it is so easy to take me for granted now that I have been here 11 years.'[291]

Without any direct influence on the direction the company was taking, Volkova devoted herself entirely to teaching and to refining her craft. Bengt Häger, who watched her work with the 'juice generation', remembers:

the afternoon classes when she was working with four or five dancers. The warm atmosphere, the strong wish to cooperate, the common search for understanding and a language. Watching one of her classes was like witnessing the creation of a work of art. It was an act of devotion. What made it so exceptional was the intensity and depth of the corrections she gave her pupils. Her movements had an inherent logic and expressiveness that one found nowhere else – the way in which she could alter things just a tiny bit and completely change the effect.

When she injured her knee and was admitted to hospital in Århus for an operation in the autumn of 1964, she began to define her method. She had once said, 'It takes seven years to become a good teacher.' She had now taught for almost 24 years, had studied and assimilated practically all the existing schools of training, and was acclaimed by many as the world's greatest ballet teacher.

In Copenhagen she had conducted a great historical experiment: she had created a new School, blending the Danish and Russian Schools, just as Vaganova had merged the old French School with the Italian and created the Vaganova method. Even if the Danes were not aware of what they were part of, Volkova was, and she was torn about whether to formulate it or not, whether actually to write it down and put it in the public domain.

Confined by her injury, she finally did begin to record it; but in the end she never finished, characteristically denying herself a permanent place in history, entrusting the fragile legacy of her teaching only to her students. Although it was passed on from dancer to dancer for a while, today that legacy is, for the most part, lost.

'Firstly, I think it is not stressed enough, the fact that one never at any time stands on two feet', she wrote in the notes that survive, 'even in the fifth position.'

One's weight is always on one or the other foot, already in preparation for the step that is to follow.

After all, this is a basic principle in that allegro should be a test of a good and accurate dancer and the allegro is the transference of weight from one foot to the other, from one position to another as quickly and as accurately and therefore as economically as possible. Such a lot of time is wasted by dancing on two feet – one has to readjust the body for the new step, so time and effort are wasted. With this idea in mind practically every passage through the fifth position becomes like a *coupé*.

Out of this grows the conception of always being on top of the leg, which one is supposed to be standing or working on. Not only does this make for more accurate positioning of the body, but it is also the only way that one can get a true *plié* out of the leg.[292]

Her philosophy of dance was based on the intense study of the torso, an approach she had inherited from Vaganova but which diverges sharply from that of her contemporary George Balanchine and many teachers today.

'Another fundamental, if not missed altogether then not sufficiently appreciated, is the fact of working from the centre of the body out towards the extremities rather than from the extremities inwards', she explained.

> This applies to arms as well as legs. Whereas the first fundamental applies most to the supporting leg, the second one applies to the working leg.
>
> If one works with a hard foot, over pointed, then one conditions the whole of the rest of the leg from that foot. The calf, the knee, the thigh and the hip, in that order, they have to go where that hard foot dictates – which is just the reverse of what it should be.
>
> The leg should be placed from the centre of the back — through the hip and groin down the thigh through the knee, thence the calf and foot, and the whole leg then goes where the back dictates and not where the foot dictates.
>
> Like this you have a centring of the seat of all power in the small of the back. Which makes for a bigger concentration of strength and an economy of whatever movement one makes, if the movement comes from the back and involves the leg simply because it is attached to the body.
>
> Thus the foot becomes the farthest and most unimportant part of the leg.
>
> So many teachers are saying all the while, 'Point your working foot.' Vladimiroff says the opposite: 'Don't point your feet too hard, don't dance with the feet only.'
>
> The same thing applies exactly to the arms and hands, which should be quite relaxed. They are held and placed from the back and go where the back tells them to go. Thus one can educate the top part of the back as well as the lower. Any tensions in the extremities of either arms or working leg tends to remove the centre of power from the back and to displace the body from its true positioning over the supporting foot.
>
> I think a good comparison is the use of a long bamboo pole by a tightrope walker. The ends of the pole are quite relaxed and flexible, so to speak, whereas the centre of the pole – the section between the two hands – is almost rigid, at least held firm. The very fact that the ends of the pole are moveable and loose gives the tightrope walker balance. If the ends of the pole were to be held tight or moved in a rigid way, he would easily be pushed off balance by the pole itself.
>
> Thus also tight arms and a tight working leg in the air can throw the body out of balance and so create unnecessary muscles to compensate the lack of

balance. 'Relax your hands and arms and hold them from the back' then becomes another important cry in the desert. This applies of course to the way one works on the barre. The fact of hanging tightly to the barre is the same as in life if one clings to anything too tightly; when one doesn't have it, one is unable to stand alone without it. 'Don't hang on the barre, stand on your own leg' should be another maxim of every dancing school.[293]

Volkova often used the phrase 'a back that speaks'. What she meant was that, in theory, a dancer should be able to dance a full-length ballet such as *Swan Lake* and convey its every emotional nuance without even moving his or her arms and legs. The importance she placed on the expressiveness of the back reveals Volkova's awareness of *plastique*. It was irrelevant how high a dancer could jump; she did not care how much effort the dancer put into it. What mattered were the perfect shapes the dance created in response to the music, and which all originated from the centre of the body and radiated from it.

Henning Kronstam and Kirsten Simone knew that she did not want them to stretch movements, for instance an *arabesque*, to extremes. The dancer should keep something back, a mystery, a feeling that the arm could reach further, that the leg could be raised higher. The power of suggestion was extremely important to her. 'When you go beyond the balance, that is when it almost takes flight', she advised, but above all she insisted on the use of the eyes, 'following through, letting the audience know the person within the step, the *arabesque*'.

'She was aware of the form as a whole, eye to toe, following through with your eyes, following to the fullest', says Mimi Paul, who came to Copenhagen from New York City Ballet to train with her.

> She stressed the importance of incorporating your entire self within any role that you were doing, using any kind of rich fantasy or sense of imagination to make it become something more than just the steps to the music.

Volkova encouraged Erik Aschengreen not to look at the legs when assessing the talent of a young dancer.

> She suggested I look at hands. 'The legs', said Volkova, 'they can all do that. That's not where the talent is.' Svend Kragh-Jacobsen [Danish critic and Aschengreen's mentor] never spoke about things like that; I don't think it had ever occurred to him. She was the one who taught me that ballet is an art form, and that it's all about expression.

Maina Gielgud, who briefly served as Artistic Director of the Royal Danish Ballet in the nineties, took private lessons with Volkova in the sixties. It was her impression that Volkova:

never wanted anything forced, but all done in a very natural way, which was particularly emphasised for me in the use of very relaxed hands and fingers, and an organic way of moving from one's centre out – rather than focusing on the extremities, which can tend to be a misunderstanding of classical dance by even some very good dancers.

Anne Woolliams, another dancer who became a teacher (as well as Artistic Director of the Australian Ballet) and often quoted Volkova as an important influence, remembered that:

> she used to correct my arms a lot, my head, and *épaulement* ... I think she despaired of my feet, which were never good, and my lack of turn-out. But she was a teacher who understood the possibilities of the body and didn't keep harping on something that wasn't going to be possible. And she always encouraged when she saw improvement.[294]

David Moroni, a Canadian who later became Director of the Royal Winnipeg Ballet's school, and who considers Volkova his mentor, sees her teaching as the very essence of classical dance as it had developed over the centuries. According to Moroni, Volkova's training was neither neo-classical nor an idiosyncratic personal interpretation, but encompassed 'the truth about classical training'. It was the distillation of a lifetime's thoughts on Vaganova and the other Russian teachers, Cecchetti, Blasis, the Italian School and the French School. Bengt Häger thinks she was 'the only teacher who understood Blasis. For her his nineteenth-century system was not dead, but lodged in her backbone, and she used elements of his work when she needed it.'

Volkova's Russian temperament had softened over the years, and Moroni recalls that he never saw Volkova angry – except once:

> She was teaching in Banff when she same into the rehearsal room one day and saw a dancer doing warm-up exercises. 'How dare you!' she exclaimed. 'Everything you need you will get in class, but if you start stretching now you'll injure yourself. Dancers do not get injuries in my classes, it just doesn't happen! All the exercises you need as a classical dancer you will get in class, and you will get them in the correct order.'

She explained to him that it was a 'great responsibility to teach dancers', and that she took it very seriously.

Volkova's classes[295] were logically composed and fantastically well structured. She herself compared a class to a menu: 'We start with the soup, then fish, meat, dessert and coffee – and perhaps even a brandy to finish with.'

As a rule, the barre would occupy a third or even half of the lesson. Volkova emphasised a subtle foot and correct placement. Holding oneself

35. Volkova had been invited to teach the Royal Danish Ballet for three months in 1951 but found the company in deep crisis when she arrived. Her calm leadership and inspired teaching challenged the divided company and united the dancers in focusing again on their art, rather than on the company's internal politics.

Photograph courtesy of the Royal Ballet School Archives, the Vera Volkova Collection.

36. Volkova and Frank Schaufuss, Director of the Royal Danish Ballet, welcome British ballerina Moira Shearer and her husband Ludovic Kennedy to the Royal Theatre.

Photograph courtesy of the Royal Ballet School Archives, the Vera Volkova Collection.

37. Volkova-trained dancers acquired an understanding of plasticity that distinguished them from all others. Kirsten Simone and Erik Bruhn, pictured here, were typical products of this aspect of Volkova's teaching.

Photographer unknown.

38. When Nureyev came to Copenhagen after his defection in 1961, he
trained for two hours every afternoon with Volkova. A warm friendship
developed between them, strengthened by Volkova's unprejudiced acceptance
of Nureyev's love affair with Erik Bruhn.

Photographer: Costa

39. Volkova quickly recognised the 23-year-old Nureyev's exceptional talent, but she was sceptical about his temperament, high-handedness, poor discipline and bad manners.

Photographer: Costa

40. In the autumn of 1964, Volkova started writing down the curriculum she had developed over 24 years of teaching. In the end she never finished, characteristically denying herself a permanent place in history, entrusting the fragile legacy of her work only to her students. Although it was passed on from dancer to dancer for a while, today that legacy is, for the most part, lost.

Photographer unknown.

41. Henning Kronstam and Kirsten Simone knew that she did not want them to stretch movements to extremes, but to suggest possibilities of infinite movement: 'When you go beyond the balance,' she said, 'that is when it almost takes flight'.

Photographer unknown.

42. Volkova put all her hopes in Henning Kronstam, to whom she was very close. She envisaged that he would one day become Artistic Director of the Royal Danish Ballet, and trained him not only as a dancer but also as a teacher and ballet-master.

Private collection.

43. When Volkova finally came to America to teach in 1959 it was a young, eager, proud Robert Joffrey who secured her for his company.

Photograph courtesy of the Royal Ballet School Archives, the Vera Volkova Collection.

44. Hermien Dommisse receives Volkova and Hugh Finch Williams in Johannesburg. Volkova had wanted to stage *La Sylphide* for the PACT Ballet, but the Royal Theatre would not give its permission. Instead she produced *Swan Lake* with sets and costumes by her husband.

Photograph courtesy of the Royal Ballet School Archives, the Vera Volkova Collection.

45. Towards the end of her life Volkova again started travelling, teaching new companies in Australia, New Zealand, the US and Canada. Here she is seen with members of the Royal Winnipeg Ballet. Left to right: Winthrop Corey, Alexandra Nadel, Maria Lang, Eugene Slavin, Artistic Director Arnold Spohr and Vera Volkova.

Photograph courtesy of the Royal Ballet School Archives, the Vera Volkova Collection.

46. Many of Volkova's ambitions for the Royal Danish Ballet were finally thwarted when Flemming Flindt took over the direction of the company in 1966, and privately she felt lonely and isolated in Copenhagen.

Photograph courtesy of the Royal Ballet School Archives, the Vera Volkova Collection.

47. Among the company at this 1970 class in Copenhagen are Peter
Schaufuss and Peter Martins, both of whom would become international
stars having been nurtured by Volkova.
  Photographer: Karsten Bundgaard.

48. Volkova and Finch Williams were a couple for almost 40 years, but their marriage remained a source of wonder to people who knew them.
   Private collection.

49. In 1975, Volkova started planning a celebration of her 25 years with the Royal Danish Ballet. She had been deeply touched when awarded the Carlsberg Memorial Award in the autumn of 1974, the year of the Royal Theatre's centenary.

Photographer unknown.

50. Volkova, sketch by Hugh Finch Williams

straight meant maintaining the proper distance between hip joint and ribcage. Volkova started centre practice with various *port de bras* before moving on to strenuous movements, and placed great emphasis on *fondu* sequences.

> Now for the *fondu*. Completely ignored in all European schools – and I can't understand why, as it is the perfect preparation for jumps and allegro and the logical development from adagio. The essence of the *fondu* is not only the accurate transference of weight from one foot to the other, but also the accurate working of the supporting leg from the *plié* to the half toe.
>
> So one now has movement in two planes – the maximum movement short of actually jumping: forward and back, or side to side, or corner to corner, and up and down.
>
> I cannot imagine how one can hope to jump satisfactorily without this preparation. Without it the jump just becomes animated adagio without fluidity or softness at all, because the adagio is not preparation for jumping only, but also deals with placement.
>
> Once again, in *fondu* the secret seems to be never a fifth position of two feet but always more of a *coupé* through fifth position, and of course from this develops the idea of jumping from foot to foot.[296]

Volkova had her dancers start with jumps on both feet. Again, she said: 'I will not have injuries in my class, it is a great responsibility.' Only then would she allow small jumps with landings on one foot and big leaps across the room.

Many jumps fell on the downbeat of the music, not on the upbeat, which is more commonly the case. 'I have always been interested in landings, it is easier to jump than to land', she explained.

As always, Volkova expressed the special sensitivity and quality of movement she wanted with idiosyncratic imagery. David Moroni recalls that, 'when one stood at the barre and had to open one's arms from first to second position, she used to say, "Open your arms as if you are in water. It's as if you have dropped a pebble in the middle and the pebble creates rings that grow outwards: that's how you move your arms from first to second."'

'It's not positive enough', Volkova would tell a dancer. 'You must be more positive.' If a male variation demanded it, she could tell the dancer to do the steps 'like a sprint'.

In 1963 Volkova staged a Bournonville *Divertissement* for the Harkness Ballet in the USA, and that same autumn the leader of Johannesburg's PACT Ballet, Hermien Dommisse, came to Copenhagen to offer her the job of Director of the company. They talked about the possibility of Volkova staging a full-length ballet. Volkova was keen to produce *La Sylphide* and suggested that Hugh Finch Williams should create the sets and costumes. When Henning Brøndsted vetoed the idea, Volkova decided to put on *Swan Lake* instead. 'It was a challenge and a great experience', she wrote to Colette Clark.

> Everybody was most helpful. Hugh was asked to do the costumes and the décor. The premiere was scheduled for the 14th of November but I could stay only to the middle of August, which is when we start the season in Copenhagen. I was heartbroken not to have the final rehearsals on the stage with light and orchestra and not to be able to see Hugh's décor and costumes from the audience. To my surprise the Performing Arts Council of Transvaal (PACT) sent for me again and Mr Brøndsted gave me permission to leave for one week!
>
> Finally Hugh and I arrived in Johannesburg. What a week it was! We were so busy we hardly spoke to each other. During the day I had all the rehearsals on stage with the company and at night with the technical staff, lighting the scenery ... I seldom went to bed before 2 o'clock in the morning, and Hugh often came at 4 o'clock.
>
> Anyway, I can say that the success of the first night was chiefly contributed to by a beautiful décor Hugh has designed. Each time the curtain went up, the audience applauded ... I wish you could have been there with us to see it. I was sitting in the audience with Hugh on one side and the Danish consul on the other. It was one of the proudest moments of my life. The costumes were also beautiful. He has good taste. Beryl Grey danced beautifully. She also liked the décor. For her it was a personal success. I created some new choreography: a waltz in the first act, a solo for the fool and a solo for the prince in the second act ... Please forgive me for boasting but I have enjoyed it all so much. Such a change from my daily routine and teaching.[297]

In the end, Volkova turned down the Director job, but wondered if a new start might have been good for her husband:

> Sometimes I think he needs a new and younger wife and then he can go and live there. This is just a passing thought, he would be horrified if he read it ... He loves me and misses me et cetera. But sometimes I feel the limitations of life, there is so little of it left and so much one wants to do still. But is there enough time, and does one have the energy?[298]

Volkova and Finch Williams had now been a couple for 30 years and their marriage remained a source of wonder to people who knew them. Outwardly it was a typical middle-class union, but, unusually for the time, Hugh was not the breadwinner – he was not even his wife's equal in earning power. He was clearly marked by his jealousy of Volkova's achievements as much as by his own failure as an artist. Several friends of the couple knew that, to spare him embarrassment, Volkova would leave cash in books around the house for him to 'find' – neither of them could bear for her to hand him 'pocket money'.

According to Colette Clark, Finch Williams's need for attention and recognition led him to undermine Volkova's self-confidence and correct her at every opportunity: 'No, Vera, do shut up! You talk too much. Be quiet', Clark remembers as the kind of thing he would say all the time.

Clark says, 'On her own and relaxed, Vera was very, very funny and could talk at a stretch of two or three hours, four, five, in full flight – perhaps in compensation for when she was with Hugh, when she couldn't.' She recalls that Volkova's friends dreaded Williams's presence at their meetings, and regarded him as 'a millstone' around Volkova's neck.

> She was handicapped by Hugh. She had to completely support him, he never let her out of sight, he followed her everywhere. If Hugh came along, I would consider it a waste of time. Everybody had to take him on... However much he pushed himself forward, he must have known in his heart that people only wanted to be with her.

But Volkova explained that she needed a 'solid' husband, and 'I must say that she was very devoted to him. They really enjoyed their travels together', Clark adds.

Mette Hønningen also knew the couple well. She believes:

> there was mutual trust and respect between them ... I think the relationship must have grown into something indispensable for her. They were very loving with each other, but they were also critical of each other. He protected her – he didn't want anyone to harm her. He admired her, but in an almost fanatical way.
>
> They came to visit me for a cup of coffee one day. I had a reasonably big apartment at the time, and he thought it wasn't warm enough for her because she had been ill, and nearly broke a plate in his fury. She tried to calm him down ... They could really only trust each other.

Volkova clearly felt guilty that she had never been the standard 'little woman'. Paula Hostrup-Jessen – David Arkell's cousin who had married a Dane and moved to Denmark in the early sixties – remembers her asking several times: 'I am being a good wife, aren't I?' And as well as doing her utmost to talk her husband up and to further his career when she could, she was keen for him to realise how important he was to her. When he was living in Paris in the early sixties pursuing his career as an artist, Volkova wrote to him:

Please don't blame yourself that you have not done enough to support me. You have done everything that is really important from every point of view. Everybody who meets me thinks I am a happy person. Compared to my poor compatriots who got stuck in Russia for good I live in great luxury. I am very grateful for everything.[299]

I really feel I am loved! It makes me feel so warm inside, like a little lamp is lit in my heart. Perhaps people feel that little light. Now that I am no longer young, I am happy you love me just the same. You are such a wonderful boy, all the goodness comes out of me thanks to you. I never felt once since I have met you disillusioned, embittered or dissatisfied in some way.

On the contrary, I am feeling full of purpose, my life is rich, varied and everything is shared. I have a wonderful life, full of surprises. I particularly appreciate the fact that my work brings me into contact with young people. I am very grateful to dear old Provy [Providence]! Even my separation from you I don't really resent, it is only temporary.

I am feeling so peaceful and serene these days. My mind and my being is absorbed by two things – my work and Hughnia [Volkova's pet name for her husband], the rest is by the way.

I am sorry for people like Antony Tudor who wants to become a Tibetan monk in order to find peace inside himself ... but then he is lonely ... and he feels the only salvation for his tortured, complicated soul is to be on the top of a mountain. I am too simple for that, thank goodness.

The snow is still falling and the town looks poetic and unreal. It is so quiet in my little flat and of course beautifully warm. I am sitting at the dining room table, with my elbows well spread, writing to you and thinking what are you doing right now at 10 in the evening on Monday?[300]

Jurij Moskvitin believed Volkova's and Williams's marriage was 'based, on Vera's part, on a mixture of awe-inspiring devotion and the desire to nurse a spoilt child'. It is not unusual in childless couples for the wife to develop motherly feelings towards her husband, and that was the case with this marriage.

'Hugh was loyal enough to her', Moskvitin said, 'but had a succession of mistresses. I had ample opportunity to see this when he and I lived in Paris at the same time. But he also had his admirers in Copenhagen. Vera was "a lonely rider". Vera was naïve in her own way', Moskvitin thought. 'She felt a little outside *wie die Andern es treiben* ["the way other people do things"]. She lived in a world in which most people did terrible things that they managed to conceal, but which she, after a lifetime's experience, had learnt to make allowances for... Nothing human was foreign to her.'

In 1965 the Royal Danish Ballet returned to the United States for another punishing tour – eighty-two performances in eighteen cities in barely three months. The tour was a success, and Volkova thought that in many ways the company had never danced better – that her work had finally borne fruit and resulted in a uniformly well-schooled company.

'The school started changing as soon as she arrived in 1951', says Arlette Weinreich. 'And by the mid-sixties you could see how many fantastic dancers the company now had. You had never before seen twelve boys walk to the front of the stage with Henning Kronstam in a ballet like *Cyrano de Bergerac*, all of them doing double *tour*, boom, double *tour*, boom, double *tour*. You'd never seen that before. Not in any company.'

When it arrived back in Denmark, the company was fêted on 20 January 1966 with a gala performance attended by the entire Royal family.

The performance also marked a farewell to Niels Bjørn Larsen as ballet-master and a welcome to Flemming Flindt, who was to take over the company. Flindt's *The Lesson*, Roland Petit's *Carmen* and the third act of Bournonville's *Napoli* were on the programme and the entire company came on stage at the end, where they were given a laurel wreath from King Frederik IX, were praised in speeches and received a standing ovation from the audience.

'Finally the Theatre's incomparable teacher, Vera Volkova, came on stage from the King's side [the left side of the stage]', the critic Svend Kragh-Jacobsen wrote in *Berlingske Tidende*.

Despite this unusual public recognition of Volkova, who, uniquely, appeared on stage during the event, the Russian teacher's prospects at the Danish theatre were dismal. She confided in Colette Clark:

> I am very worried about Flindt taking charge of the company. The first thing he did was to appoint Henning Kronstam Director of the Ballet School! I have a heavy heart about the whole thing. I have an offer to be the Director of a ballet school in New York. Mrs Harkness invited me. It is also a chance for Hugh to have a job there as a consultant and a director of an art gallery attached to the ballet school. They just bought a new building. We both are tempted. But this season I am still with the Danes.[301]

Historically, the ballet-master had been responsible for the Ballet School. Though Volkova had been the School's de facto leader since 1951 and had set its curriculum, she had never been given the position of Director. It was a slap in the face for Volkova that Flindt never offered her the job but gave it to her pupil, Kronstam, who was still active as a principal dancer at the Theatre. Kronstam later told the American author Alexandra Tomalonis that he accepted the position to protect Volkova. She wrote to Colette Clark:

In a way I am relieved. It gives me freedom. I can do what I like and I don't owe the Danes anything. I have done my work. I gave them a new generation of dancers and I don't feel like going on playing safe, hoping for a pension as a final reward. I am not even sure I will get one.[302]

Erik Aschengreen remembers that Volkova invited him to watch an apprentice class, and that Flemming Flindt reprimanded her in a most humiliating way when he found out. 'I did not go again, but was invited to dinner instead'.

Another prominent critic, Ebbe Mørk, with whom Volkova also became friendly at the end of the sixties, went to the cinema and enjoyed cooking with her. He remembers that Flemming Flindt did not invite Volkova to accompany them when the Royal Danish Ballet performed in Paris:

> She was very bitter about it – quite rightly so. She considered paying her own way, but, sad to say, she could not afford it. I often had the impression that she was hard up. Hugh had his own studio, and the rent was probably more than he made on the sale of his paintings.

In 1966 Volkova was sixty-one years old. She had been at the Theatre for 15 years but had never been guaranteed a pension, despite her repeated enquiries.

> Everybody is very vague about my pension. I went twice to the Ministry of Culture and was told that, 'when the time comes, then the matter will be taken up.' I was not satisfied with this reply. And now Flindt. Also, I feel that Hugh must be given a chance to support me as was always his dream and ambition. He really suffers and hates the idea of living off my earnings.[303]

The Harkness Ballet was still interested in engaging Volkova; and after Harald Lander had left the Paris Opéra, the French national company also offered her a job, which she wrote to Colette Clark about in 1966.

> M. Auric asked me if I would come as a guest teacher for three months and look at their school. I can't go for three months but I would like to go for one month after the American tour if I can get permission from Mr Flindt. Perhaps in March? But to be honest I don't feel like working with the French for a longer period of time. There are even more intrigues than here and on the whole my style would not suit them ... But for a change and out of curiosity I would not mind working there for a month's time. Flindt is very keen for me to have 'stars' from other theatres as it adds to the 'prestige' of the Royal Theatre. For me it is a change but I don't really encourage it. It adds to my daily work.[304]

Flindt would not give her permission to go to Paris, but whenever she had time off she would travel to work with other companies. It fed her need for appreciation, inspiration and money. Since the Danes would not give her a pension and she was notoriously underpaid at the Royal Theatre, she had to bolster her salary herself. Apart from teaching in the USA, during the sixties and seventies Volkova taught in all her holidays in South Africa, Australia, New Zealand, Germany and Canada, and she was received like a star with great press coverage, receptions and honours.

In Copenhagen, Volkova still had no contract; she simply continued her work year after year without ever being sure that she had a continuing job. The Theatre paid her salary automatically, irrespective of what her field of responsibility in a given season would be, and she was never compensated for the rising cost of living or given a pay rise. So her real earnings actually decreased, and after 15 years she had become the Royal Danish Ballet's lowest-paid employee, on the same salary scale as an apprentice dancer.

'Hugh was bitter on Vera's behalf, but she was not bitter herself', Mette Hønningen recalls, but:

> she held her peace when she was hidden away in Copenhagen. She was not allowed to be anybody; there were so many others who wanted to be 'somebody'. We didn't know at the time how badly she was treated.

'She was a creative woman', says Ib Andersen, one of Volkova's last students, who later had a great career with Balanchine in New York.

> I'm sure they wanted to slap her down. In that place, if you're different ... And she was a very powerful woman. It's impressive that she stuck it out... I don't understand... Why did she stay?

With her strong belief in Providence, Volkova probably accepted the card dealt to her by fate. To Colette Clark she said, 'You have always got your work. The only thing that never lets you down is your work.' She never forgot the Kantian ethical imperative that Volynsky had impressed on her: of one's own volition to make the most of every second of every day and fulfil the obligations of an innate talent.

Besides, there was really nowhere else for her to go – except back.

Memento Mori

> If only I could actually see you and talk to you about my pilgrimage. How can I explain what I felt, standing in front of my house on the Kutuzov Embankment?

In 1967 Volkova finally returned to Leningrad, and now she finally started answering the questions Arkell had been asking her for years, for herself as well as for him.

During a visit to Copenhagen in 1963 he had noticed that she had a photo album of Leningrad lying on the table. It had looked as if something in Volkova was thawing, and Arkell was convinced that the political reforms Khrushchev had set in motion in the Soviet Union would make it possible for her to revisit her native country one day.

Volkova's replies to Arkell's gentle questioning about her life in Russia came irregularly, if at all. 'VV is a woman of mystery. She has not replied to any of my letters this year. So I won't ask anything (it's too frustrating), I'll just tell you what I have been doing',[305] he wrote to her indulgently before he got a reaction. 'I know I have not sent you the picture of me as a Smolny girl', was Volkova's reply.

> It is difficult to explain why. It was something to do with Leningrad. My heart got heavy. I got disturbed in a strange way ... Memories flood my mind, and I did not know how to cope with them. Something deep down in me resents the fact that none of my family met a natural death. I thought I had got over it. I tried so hard to forget it. I did in a way, but it lurks somewhere in the subconscious. I could not find the words to write what I really felt, so I have not written.[306]

Though he may have suspected it, Arkell never knew the whole truth about her family's fate. He did not understand the extent of the tragedy, Volkova's role in her family's misfortune, or the guilt she felt. Not only was she her family's sole survivor, but her sister had hinted that she had been the cause of its persecution during the Great Terror.

Volkova had started opening up but, intentionally or not, she continued to confuse dates, names and places. One reason could have been that she had taken two years off her age when she had first met Hugh Finch Williams in Shanghai, and the inquisitive Arkell had caught her out on that. She did not want people to know about her first marriage in Russia, and Arkell also had the impression that she was embarrassed by her failure to make a career as a dancer – although she insisted to the end of her life that she had been a good one. Amid all the uncertainty, one thing was for sure: Volkova was like a bubble about to burst, and strong forces were drawing her back to the city that she said she had 'loved with bitter love'.

As it happened, Arkell was the first of them to go to Leningrad; and when he visited the Soviet Union for the first time in September 1965, he saw the country through Volkova's eyes.

> Dear Vera, I am writing this in my room on the corner of Isaakievskaya Place facing the cathedral. It is nearly seven and the sun is setting over the houses in the direction of the Gulf of Finland. Twelve hours ago I got up and I have been walking ever since. I think Leningrad is the most romantic city I have ever seen.[307]

He continued, enchanted: 'the Canaletto river-scapes alternating with the dark, still canals. In the pale Northern sunlight the colours of the palaces are extremely subtle – they are already very delicate but they are softened by an autumn mistiness.' He exclaimed, delightedly: 'the Winter Palace truly *is* eau de nil. The buildings on the Strelka are turquoise, light brown, terra cotta, pale emerald, ochre and so on. Always with the windows and panels and pilasters picked out in white.'[308]

But more important to him than the Winter Palace was the building on Kutuzov Embankment, which Volkova had described in detail and which he visited on the first day of his stay. Early in the morning he walked from the Winter Palace along the embankment beside the Neva, then past the Summer Garden to the Liteiny Bridge:

> I saw the house where that friend of mine used to live years ago. It is like a dilapidated palace, two stories high with a basement – three stories the Russians would call it. Painted terra cotta with the Corinthian pilasters and windows picked out in coffee colour. With its twin across the road it makes a rather splendid beginning to the street but it is definitely shabby now, especially at the back where there is a courtyard with a little garden in the middle. Here the plaster has peeled off in many places, leaving the bricks exposed. In spite of that the building as a whole is rather grand – in other cities it would stand out, but Leningrad is so full of fine buildings it hasn't the chance.[309]

Volkova rejoiced to hear that her childhood home had survived. 'So you have fallen in love with Leningrad, my city', she replied, full of nervous excitement, from the USA where she was on tour with the Royal Danish Ballet.

> Imagine your looking at the actual house where I lived! I spent hours sitting on the windowsill, watching the Neva and all the goings-on. Barges moving to

and fro full of wood. Listening to fog horns in the autumn. And the rush of ice
when it breaks in the spring and sparkles in the sun.

Now you know where my childhood and youth were spent. An urchin from
a dilapidated palace, wandering, dreaming, along the canals. I don't often
allow myself the luxury of opening that secret door, but I would love to have
you here, right now in Boston, and just listen to you talking about my poor,
beautiful city.[310]

But even after Arkell's visit to Leningrad, Volkova remained
determined to guard her secrets. Arkell had written to her after she had
sent him a copy of an article about her in *Dance Magazine*:

I would still like to write a book about you (and with you) but your answer is
given at the end of the article: 'Dance historians are preoccupied with
yesterday. I care about the future.' And what you care about is to extend the
frontiers of ballet in little notebooks that will be read one day by the happy few
– and not sell your life's story to a wider public.[311]

At that time, Volkova did not seriously think she would ever see
Leningrad again, but when the Kirov Ballet danced at Covent Garden in
London in 1965 she went to England. Unexpectedly, she was introduced
to the company's Director, Konstantin Sergeyev, at a reception. Without
any warning, he invited her to Russia to see the company rehearse and
perform but it was obviously not a spur-of-the-moment invitation:
although she was a 'non-person', Volkova could serve as an intermediary
between the Royal Danish Ballet and the Russian Kirov and Bolshoi
companies. Sergeyev's overture to Volkova initiated an exchange that
would make it possible for the Royal Danish Ballet to visit Russia. That
was instantly understood at the Royal Theatre in Copenhagen, whose
administration gave Volkova leave and a grant for the trip. The Danish
Ministry of Culture extracted the guarantee of Volkova's safe return from
the Soviets.

'In two hours I will be in a plane that will take me to Leningrad',
Volkova wrote to Arkell in June 1967, from the airport in Stockholm. 'My
feelings are mixed but I am very excited. For the last three months I was
in my own monastery.'[312]

Volkova was terrified about crossing the Soviet border. She was
constantly afraid that she would never get out again. But her desire to go
back to Leningrad was stronger than her fears. The journey was, in her
own words, 'a pilgrimage'.

Her reunion with the Russian ballet also proved to be a form of
rehabilitation for Volkova, who had left the country 37 years previously
and had felt like an outcast ever since. Now she was received with
enormous ceremony and respect and saw many of the dancers she had

known as a young woman: 'What made me happy was the reception I was given by the ballet people', Volkova wrote to Arkell.

> Nina Ponomarova was there to greet us – and, as I walked into the classroom, the teacher narrowed his eyes and cried 'Verotchka!' and kissed me. It was Alexander Pushkin (Nureyev's teacher). Then he said: 'Do you remember, Verotchka, we danced [Mendelssohn's] *Romances sans paroles* together? Ulanova's mother arranged the choreography.' I was then seventeen. It was all very touching.
>
> They knew all about me professionally, chiefly as the teacher of Erik Bruhn, whom they all greatly admire. They made three films of him dancing, when he was there with Ballet Theatre four years ago. The films are shown to students and members of the company. M. Sergeyev was so pleased that I came. He had suggested that I should visit them and I must say he kept his word and looked after me. The best tickets in the parterre for all performances at the Kirov Theatre. I was allowed to see all the rehearsals, all the classes.
>
> The *régisseur* (Misha Georgievsky) also recognised me. He and Nina took us everywhere. We visited Pavlovsk together, and Tsarskoye Selo as well, where A. Pushkin (the other one, the poet) composed most of his poems as a young man ...
>
> One thing impressed me deeply: how kind everybody is and what good manners they all have. I loved meeting them all. They are proud, intelligent, uncomplaining. I felt that their life is hard by ordinary standards, although ballet people enjoy certain privileges, like foreign travel.
>
> I loved walking from the Kirov to the Astoria, late at night, after the performances – white nights, glittering canals, like a stage set for an old Italian opera, with deep shadows and a complete silence.[313]

In her free time from her professional world, Volkova took a personal journey back into the world of her childhood and youth. Osip Mandelstam, who had lived in the House of Arts with Akim Volynsky, had written: 'I have returned to my city, which I know so well that it makes me weep.' Volkova shed her own tears in front of her childhood home and in front of her mother's last address, which Maria Volkova had scribbled on a postcard. She knocked on the door, and the woman who answered told her that when she had taken over the flat in 1943 it had been empty. She had neither met nor heard of a Maria Volkova. As with so many victims of war, no one would ever know where Maria was buried.

An old acquaintance told Volkova that in all probability her brother had died not at the front, as Irina had suggested, but during the bombardment of a hospital. And that he too had been buried in an unmarked grave. Volkova finally gave up hope that Irina might still be alive. 'I prayed for a miracle', she wrote to David Arkell, that she might be one of the museum-keepers, and I looked so carefully at their faces, just in case. I only hope that she died peacefully somewhere and that somebody kind looked after her, so she was not too lonely.[314]

Volkova saw Volynsky everywhere: in the museums through which they had wandered together; at the House of Arts; and at the School of Russian Ballet, which was round the corner from her hotel.

> Misha G. said he 'disappeared' – was arrested and died, nobody knows under exactly what circumstances. His books are banned and nobody is allowed to mention his name – only in a whisper as one looks over one's shoulder. Pushkin confirmed this ... So as not to embarrass people, I asked no more questions.
>
> Misha took us to the Alexander Nevsky Lavra, where as a child my glove was frozen to the jug of soup, to show us the monuments to Russian composers, and the grave of Marius Petipa. We saw three cemeteries altogether, I wonder why? They seem to live in the past, they are so proud of it. The present is a struggle, and the future a five-year-plan. I am just the opposite. I am so interested in the present (and the future) that I hate raking up the past.
>
> The city is beautiful. You described it to me so well. So happy I saw it again, and I don't regret going there, despite a deep sorrow that memories evoked.[315]

Volkova had another opportunity to visit the Soviet Union the following year, when Flemming Flindt and Kirsten Simone danced *Giselle* at the Bolshoi Theatre in Moscow. Volkova's second journey to Russia was shrouded in more mystery than the first, since she had never admitted to having lived in Moscow and still insisted that this was her first visit to the Soviet capital. To David Arkell she wrote:

> I spent an hour in a General Post Office with an old friend of mine whose first husband was Director of the Hermitage Museum. She is a wonderful person ... she has lovely, trusting blue eyes. She was the last person to my knowledge who saw my mother and my sister Ira. (Why the Post Office? She did not want to come to my hotel.)[316]

When the Royal Danish Ballet finally visited the Soviet Union in February and March 1973, Volkova was as anxious as she had been on her previous trips, and in Copenhagen Airport she nervously displayed her British passport to the Danish dancers, insisting: 'I am a British subject. They can't keep me.'

The tour opened in Moscow, where the company danced alternately with the Bolshoi Ballet on the Bolshoi's big stage. One of the Russian company's performances was the star dancer Alexander Godunov's début in Petipa's bravura ballet, *Don Quixote*. Godunov had just won the gold medal in Moscow's International Ballet Competition and the house was buzzing with anticipation. Shortly before the lights were dimmed in the enormous red and gold auditorium, Volkova stepped into the theatre's big box on the left side, the equivalent of a Royal box, quite alone. The Bolshoi's ballet-master, Yuri Grigorovich, was sitting in the opposite box with his wife, the ballerina Natalia Bessmertnova. At the curtain calls, the performers moved downstage and bowed first to Volkova and then to the rest of the audience.

The next day Volkova watched the famous Russian men's teacher Asaf Messerer give a class, and the Director of the school, Sofia Golovkina, arranged a special concert by her pupils.

Mette Hønningen danced the ballerina parts in *Études* and *The Nutcracker*, and in the auditorium Volkova sat next to the Russian ballerina Maya Plisetskaya, who praised her student. Volkova wrote to Hugh Finch Williams: 'Hønningen was radiant in *Études*, and I was very happy to see her dance on such a big stage.'[317]

She took special care of Hønningen, whose dancing she hoped and prayed would save the company's reputation after the embarrassment Flemming Flindt's version of *The Nutcracker* had been to her in Moscow:

> The audience accepted the *Moor's Pavane* but *Napoli* was met with a cool reception. *The Nutcracker* was an artistic disaster and I was very upset. The Russians found the production absurd, tasteless and un-musical. It was madness to bring it to Russia. I cringe at the thought of seeing it in Leningrad.[318]

After the performance Hønningen had stomach trouble, and Volkova brought her the Russian household remedy: a glass of vodka with a tablespoon of salt. A tumbler full of vodka! 'I liked Russian blocked shoes so much', Hønningen remembers, 'that she ran round and bought some for me. When I got back to the hotel in the evening, there was a little note lying under my door ... she was like that with me.'

Volkova was also welcomed as an honoured guest at the Kirov Ballet in Leningrad and invited to watch the performances from the Tsar's box, usually reserved for Party leaders. Henning Kronstam recalled that she felt embarrassed about sitting there alone and asked him to join her. When they stepped into the box, the audience stood up respectfully, thinking Volkova and Kronstam were important politicians or dignitaries. During the curtain calls, the Kirov paid homage to Volkova just as the Bolshoi had done: bowing first to her, and then to the rest of the audience.

Mette Hønningen was astonished to see Volkova in the place of honour:

We all were! Is that our Vera? people asked themselves. Our Madame? The Royal Theatre's management should have taken note of the respect shown her by people in other countries. We in Copenhagen did not appreciate her in the same way – it was a crime! But in Russia, we could all see it. They knew what she was worth.

David Arkell was curious to learn more about Volkova's feelings during her tour:

Do you still love the city of your birth? And is what you like about it the same as what you liked about it before – or does it seem different to you now, and do you like it for different reasons? ... You must please tell me about the things you still like about your city. Don't bother so much about the things you don't like, I can imagine those ... Of course your feelings must be so mixed.[319]

With her usual modesty, Volkova did not tell him about her wonderful, semi-official reception, but she did tell him about the genuine warmth and interest she was welcomed with:

I was invited home by most of my friends, which would have been unthinkable a few years ago. It made such a difference. Both lots of directors – Yuri Grigorovich and his wife N. Bessmertnova from the Bolshoi in Moscow and Sergeyev and Dudinskaya from the Kirov in Leningrad – were so excited to see me, and in some ways I felt they were proud of me.

In Leningrad there was also a party arranged by the dancers who remembered me, though some were out of town (and some had died!). We drank Russian champagne (not bad!). It was a real *Carnet de Bal* atmosphere, of warmth and reunion. And just to be able to speak Russian, it meant so much to me![320]

On that tour, Volkova visited her childhood home for the last time:

One day I went to see my own house again. The front door was locked and I had to go through the courtyard at the back. I tried to peep through some holes in the doors of the stables, where my father kept his horses. The old wood was painted *sang de boeuf* and, as I fingered the lock, hoping to find perhaps a saddle or a lost ornament, a window opened and a woman cried out: what was I doing there? She came down and was very suspicious. I tried to explain that I lived in the house long ago and what she called 'storage space' had once been stables. After that she was very kind and sympathetic. She invited me to have tea in the basement. She was a kind of concierge, but quite well educated, and she told me a lot of interesting things.[321]

As usual, Volkova made new friends. This time a young Russian conductor, Janis Kallyn, accompanied her on her walks:

As my companion I found a young conductor about to sit his final exams, who loves wandering, and we walked miles, over the bridges, by the Neva and canals. I hardly slept and just had enough energy to give company class in the morning! I found a house on the way to the Kirov (45 Ulitsa Gertsena), which I just loved. Today it is occupied by the Union of Composers, but it was built by a famous French architect for himself. Small, elegant, mysterious, it was called 'My House'.

Late one evening, Janis accompanied me back to the Astoria after the performance and offered to play me some Sibelius. I wasn't sure the Astoria had a piano, but we finally found one in the bar. To the astonishment of the tourists with their Scotches in front of them, a concert was improvised. The Russian waiter was deeply moved. All this happened about 1 a.m. ...

I am quite intoxicated by my visit to Leningrad. I felt at times that I had never left it. I love the city and I love the people, everybody I met was so kind to me. Of course, Leningrad is almost an architectural museum, and the setting hardly suits the way people dress and live and struggle today. But even so, in Leningrad they have more interesting faces than in Moscow (a very generalised statement, of course!). Grave faces, strong eyebrows, straighter noses, better manners. One young girl was so disappointed when she learned in a bookshop that they hadn't got Camus in translation, her eyebrows just quivered in disappointment.

When I was in Moscow, Y. Grigorovich offered me a job, to teach at the Bolshoi any time I want. I also spent an evening with Ulanova and promised her to look at the house in Leningrad (north-east corner of Gogol–Gorohovaya crossing) where she lived with her parents and where I often went. So I did as I promised, I stood in front of it. Everything is still simmering in me. I was so terribly happy there. Perhaps after all it is my country.[322]

'I Remembered Every Step'

Volkova's journeys to the Soviet Union were turning points in her life. They strengthened her spiritual resources and her belief in the art she created every day – an art whose influence she had been instrumental in developing and spreading in the Western world.

Through her passion, talent and almost evangelical zeal, as well as through the artistic heritage she brought with her to Europe, Volkova was indisputably one of the most important people in ballet in the twentieth century.

She had been a kind of midwife for classical ballet. In London at a time when it was very much a nascent art form, she had nurtured what would become Great Britain's national ballet company – as well as many international dancers. She revived the moribund Royal Danish Ballet and, when she felt that it no longer needed her, she began to travel the world as a guest teacher.

She worked in New York with the Harkness Ballet and the Joffrey Ballet, in Canada with the Royal Winnipeg Ballet, and in South Africa with the PACT Ballet. She gave classes to the Australian Ballet, the Royal New Zealand Ballet and the Royal Swedish Ballet. She taught the Kurt Jooss company in Essen, and Béjart invited her to work with his Ballet du XXe Siècle. She attended ballet seminars and competitions all over Europe and gave private lessons to students from around the world who came to her in Copenhagen.

Towards the end of her life, she came to see her travels as an expression of her rootlessness – an endless search she found difficult to define, but sensed was motivated by a need to belong. Though she was very involved with a number of dancers in Copenhagen, she knew that she was still, essentially, an outsider – just as she had been in London and, before that, as a young dancer in Leningrad. Loneliness had been her life-long condition.

Palle Jacobsen, a principal dancer in the company, thinks that 'she was in love with the Royal Danish Ballet, for good and ill', but Volkova's relationship with the company was ambivalent to the end.

She felt that the atmosphere at the Theatre had become less fraught over the years, and she was deeply touched when she was awarded the Carlsberg Memorial Award in the autumn of 1974 – the year of the Royal Theatre's centenary. The award was given in recognition of her contribution to the Royal Danish Ballet, and she spoke warmly about her nearly 25 years in Copenhagen. Volkova even began to make plans for her approaching jubilee instead of sweeping it under the carpet.

On the other hand, she remained angry that the Theatre had still not guaranteed her a pension, despite all her insistence and patience, and her verdict over Flemming Flindt as ballet-master was uncompromising. He was a 'disaster', she thought, and she regarded his period at the head of the company as one of the most 'traumatic'[323] in the history of Danish ballet. She found it agonising to see her dancers wilt because Flindt either would not or could not give them the repertoire they needed, and because he often favoured a different type of dancer from Volkova.

What was the point of her training classical dancers to express spiritual ideals and symbolise a search for universal truth and perfection, if all Flindt asked them to do was wriggle their bare bottoms in gold cages in nude ballets like *Triumph of Death* and *Felix Luna?*

Volynsky had fought his battles in Petrograd 50 years previously, Volkova herself had countered similar artistic strains in London and Milan, and she was surprised that anybody could think now that Flindt had done other than re-invent the wheel. 'Give the ballet a pretentious title, throw in some disturbing musical background and some dramatic lighting effects, and you can be sure to have the serious attention of the press',[324] she said.

'Ballet is a science as well as an art, because it has rules', she once explained to the English dancer David Blair. She continued:

> It is a science, also, because if any of the rules which are propounded in the classroom are broken, not only the experts can see it is wrong but the audience too can see it is wrong. It is our job as teachers to see that the rules are maintained and that the dancers understand the rules. It is the job of the choreographer then to break all the rules, to use distortions from the basic classroom technique.

For Volkova, classical dance was governed by an inherent logic, like the periodic table. A sensitive choreographer could explore the mystery of the dance, and mould, or even bend, its elements to create transcendent works of art; but Flindt was not such a man.

The fundamental lack of understanding between Volkova and Flindt filtered down to all levels of the company.

Towards the end of her life, Volkova was in some ways more isolated than ever. Arlette Weinreich thinks that 'she was not appreciated at all, in the end'. Eske Holm had left the Royal Theatre to become a modern dancer in the 1960s. When he was invited back to the Theatre a decade later as a choreographer, he found it:

> poignant that she had been sidelined. Where did she fit into the picture? It was clear that she now played a very modest role, and she bore the marks of

someone who had lost confidence. She was nervily apologetic, and quietly looked after her apprentices up under the roof. It was a sad fate, one might say.

Volkova, who had grown up in Tsarist St Petersburg, who had seen the Imperial Ballet dance at the Maryinsky Theatre, and had lived in her youth among the cream of the old capital's intellectuals, was nicknamed 'Mother Moustache' among Copenhagen's young dancers. People laughed at Hugh Finch Williams behind his back and called him 'the Toiler', because everyone knew he never did a day's work. The classical style she had brought to the Royal Danish Ballet over 20 years ago had now become so ingrained that many dancers felt she could no longer teach them anything. And, inevitably, Volkova's style was no longer fashionable. Like Ashton in London, she was 'old hat', a state David Arkell understood and regretted. He wrote to her: 'I have now paid homage to the modern deities (Kenneth MacMillan and Peter Wright) but it doesn't seem to have quite the old glamour.'[325]

Volkova was still an important influence on some dancers, however. Arne Villumsen's most vivid image of her is her 'squinting eyes':

> You had the feeling she penetrated you with that look. That she could see things other people couldn't.

In Villumsen, Volkova had spotted the *danseur noble* the company would come to need ten years later. 'One day she told me stay on after class', Villumsen remembers. 'Then she fetched Henning Kronstam and they asked me to show them various steps and positions.' Villumsen was eleven years old when Volkova instructed Kronstam to work with Villumsen privately for half an hour every day, which he did. Later, when Peter Martins left the Royal Danish Ballet to join New York City Ballet in 1970, Volkova and Kronstam intensified their efforts with Villumsen.

Eva Sømoed, another apprentice, remembers how Volkova always had a little hanky with her, which she fiddled with incessantly and used to dab the drips off her nose and eyes. 'She was small and thin', Sømoed says, but 'she was not fragile. She had stamina!'

Among the company's young women, Mette-Ida Kirk, who became an apprentice in 1971, was particularly receptive to Volkova's teaching:

> As a person I remember her as a kind woman; she had great understanding for her pupils. If anyone had any problems, she would encourage them not to give up: 'You will succeed, you yourself will find the key, a better coordination.' She made one believe that. There was no doubt about it.

'She was unconventional', Kirk continues, 'because of the dialogue with the pupil.' For Kirk, Volkova's was a kind of teaching:

that was based on trust, responsibility and respect. Very different from toeing the line. The afternoon classes lasted from four o'clock to six o'clock, but we often used to work on until seven o'clock. She encouraged us to do this if we were interested in the possibility of intensive collaboration. Volkova was not keen on working with dancers who did not wish to make that extra effort that makes all the difference. Her way of getting around that was to say, 'If you're tired or your toes hurt, just say so.' In that way some would leave when time was up, while others would remain and go on working.

Kirk recalls that there was a natural distance between them – 'because she was such an authority and I was a young girl, full of respect'. But while Kirk experienced Volkova as a 'wise old woman', she also felt that their relationship was close and sympathetic. 'It was my impression that she had a wide knowledge of music, art and literature. She also had a broader outlook, wider knowledge and a deeper understanding of dance than most people.'

In 1974 John Neumeier staged his version of *Romeo and Juliet* at the Royal Theatre. Neumeier, who had studied with Volkova as a private pupil at the beginning of the 1960s, was 'honoured' to be asked to stage the ballet in Copenhagen, 'but in reality I was mostly pleased at the thought of having the opportunity to show Volkova my work ... In many ways I created the ballet for her.'

When he arrived in Copenhagen, he requested Volkova as ballet-mistress for the production and was surprised to find that the Theatre's management opposed the idea. Neumeier insisted, and got his way. He also involved his old teacher in the casting of his ballet, giving Volkova the opportunity to launch her last ballerina, Mette-Ida Kirk, as Juliet. Kirk remembers Flindt, Kronstam, Neumeier and Volkova watching her from the wings one night, dancing a small solo in a ballet called *Dreamland*, and she knew then that something was in the air.

Neumeier saw how hard Volkova worked with Kirk: she took part in all the rehearsals until the premiere in December 1974, but it was also clear to him how Volkova had aged and how tired she was, often falling asleep in her chair.

Frederick Ashton had written to her in October, saying, 'I hope your pension will soon be forthcoming, so that you can leave the Danes to stew in their own butter!'[326] But Volkova had already decided that the coming season would be her last in Copenhagen, pension or no pension, and she and Finch Williams planned to build a house in the south of France, in the hills around Grasse, in Provence.

'I am tired of packing and unpacking my suitcases', Volkova complained crossly to Hugh Finch Williams one morning in February 1975, as they were about to leave for London. 'Just tired of it.'[327] He thought the outburst very uncharacteristic, but over Volkova's objections the couple travelled to England, where they spent a few days with Colette Clark and her son Samuel in their house near Battersea Park. Volkova and Clark – who was now on the Board of the Royal Opera House – gossiped over the kitchen table, and Finch Williams remembered how Volkova perked up. The next day Volkova, Finch Williams, Clark and her son went to Kent to visit Clark's parents, the art historian Sir Kenneth Clark and his wife Elizabeth Jane, at their home, Saltwood Castle.

According to Volkova's diary, Thursday 13 February was one of the busiest days of her life. In the morning she visited her old friend Marie Rambert at her house in Notting Hill. Rambert, who had once pronounced Volkova a Victorian at heart, now remarked on how 'spiritual' she looked. From Notting Hill, Volkova went to Covent Garden for lunch with John Tooley, Director of the Royal Opera House, who asked her to give classes to the Royal Ballet once the question of her pension from the Royal Theatre in Copenhagen had been settled. Next, she briefly met Maina Gielgud, who had sought her out for career advice.

In the evening Volkova and Finch Williams had dinner with Margot Fonteyn and her husband Tito at their home in Knightsbridge. Fonteyn's mother, Mrs Hookham, now in her eighties, also came to say hello. Finally, around midnight, Colette Clark drove Volkova and Finch Williams over to Rudolf Nureyev's home in Sheen, just south of London.

Everybody sat down to eat at one o'clock in the morning, but according to Clark 'it was a wonderful evening!' Nureyev and Volkova were very 'sweet and warm together, and they laughed and laughed'. Volkova entertained the party by doing her famous impersonations of Jerome Robbins and Balanchine, and was amused by Nureyev's new home – a little piece of Russia, which reminded her of a badly lit set for the opera *Boris Godunov.* They ate caviar and drank champagne into the dawn.

The following morning Volkova and Finch Williams got up early to have lunch outside London with two old friends, Nancy Harding and Ethel Jeffs, who saw right away how exhausted Volkova was. They made her have a rest and arranged for a taxi to take her and her husband to Banbury for their next appointment, with the former British Ambassador to Denmark, John Henniker-Major. At his house, Volkova's condition worsened. She complained of violent stomach pains. Finch Williams took her to see a local doctor who, realising the situation might be critical, advised them to return to Copenhagen immediately. An ambulance met them at Copenhagen Airport.

Volkova was admitted to St Lukas Hospital on Friday 15 February, and in the evening she noted in her diary:

So happy to be back here in my little room in this fine hospital where I am well cared for. Weight 45 kilos.[328]

Professor Thygesen, who had operated on Volkova's gallbladder the previous year, examined her. He decided to operate the next day, and found that Volkova had cancer of the liver. He did not think she would live very long, perhaps only a few days, maybe a couple of weeks, but in the end she spent two-and-a-half months in hospital.

'Although our dear Vera is doomed, she is presently in no pain and enjoying the post-operative respite predicted by the surgeon. She has perked up remarkably and is receiving visitors from the intimate circle here', Finch Williams wrote to Colette Clark, who wanted to fly to Copenhagen. But, Finch Williams continued, discouraging Clark,

> she has no knowledge of her fate and I see no reason to spoil her last days by disabusing her. That is why a visit from England by even her so dear Celly might prove a mistake. Vera's mind is alert as ever and I think she might guess.[329]

Although Finch Williams and Volkova had a long-standing agreement that they would tell each other the truth if one of them were dying, Finch Williams lost his nerve and sheltered her behind a wall of pretence.

In spite of her husband's attempts to protect her, Volkova knew her time was running out and, though neither of them mentioned the inevitable, she shared her thoughts with her husband, speaking in riddles and parables that Finch Williams perhaps did not fully understand but which he noted down. Her thoughts often returned to Russia and her childhood. One day, when it was snowing outside, she quoted Pushkin:

> Evil spirits, I see, have gathered
> amidst whitening valleys ...
> So many! Where are they being swept?
> What is their pitiful song?
> Are they burying a gnome?
> Are they marrying off the witch?

After a walk in the hospital's garden one morning, she stopped in front of a big tree and said, 'I would like to be a tiger, stretching myself on that big branch.' For Williams this was a typically cryptic Volkova remark, but later in the day she told him that the image came from the Prologue to Pushkin's *Ruslán and Ludmíla*:

> By the shores of a bay there is a green oak-tree; there is a golden chain on that oak; and day and night a learned cat ceaselessly walks round on the chain; as it moves to the right, it strikes up a song, as it moves to the left, it tells a story.

> There are marvels there: the wood-sprite roams, a mermaid sits in the
> branches; there are tracks of strange animals on mysterious paths ... [330]

The poem is the same one that haunts Masha in Chekhov's *Three Sisters*: 'Why do I keep on saying that? Those lines have been worrying me all day long!'[331] Volkova asked herself what she had achieved during her time on earth. For her, the old oak represented the dance. She had believed in it fervently and, like her mentor Volynsky, had dedicated her life to it with the conviction of a true Symbolist.

Her answer came later, in the form of another poem. Hugh Finch Williams heard Volkova recite the words under her breath, and he knew then she was talking about beauty as the ultimate truth of life:

> Do you know the place where everything breathes prosperity, where rivers
> flow clearer than silver, where light little breezes sweep over the grassland?
> Where little white houses lie buried in cherry blossom orchards? Young
> Marissa is making flower wreaths.

Before being taken to hospital, Volkova had been preparing for the apprentices' examination, but she had not finished teaching Eva Søemod her solo from the Russian ballet *The Little Humpbacked Horse*. Volkova suggested that the Theatre should send the dancer to her at the hospital, and Søemod came to take notes in Volkova's sick room. 'She was very small', Sømoed remembers:

> and she was lying in bed with her dark hair spread out on her pillow; her face
> was yellow. She made some corrections to my solo as well as to the music,
> which she asked me to give the pianist. And then she gave me a training plan
> and asked me to give it to Toni Lander, who had taken over rehearsals. Ulrik
> Trojaborg was with me, and as we were about to leave she said: 'Now I'll say
> goodbye, and my husband will probably tell you what is really the matter with
> me.' Yes, she knew she was dying.

John Neumeier flew to Copenhagen to visit Volkova, but Hugh Finch Williams insisted that he should pretend he happened to be in town for a meeting with Flemming Flindt. In the foreword to this book, Neumeier has described his last meeting with Volkova and her powerfully affecting gesture when she took his hand in both of hers and pressed it to her forehead, saying, 'You – love me...'

Neumeier was shocked to see how powerless the once-indomitable Volkova seemed, and how, for the first time since he had met her, he had the feeling that she needed him, not the other way round. Hugh Finch Williams described his wife that week as a Pre-Raphaelite painting. Her face was hollowed and had a tragic, hunted look. Her eyes had a pleading expression.

Jurij Moskvitin also came to see his 'surrogate mother' at St Lukas. He remembered that 'Hugh hardly dared to speak or look at Vera, the woman he had lived with for 50 years. He just paced up and down the room looking terrified.

'Vera was happy to see me', he recalled.

> She asked me to raise her up in the bed a little. As I lifted her and managed to push a couple of cushions under her neck, I realised how heavy a person's head is. She had moisture round her mouth, which came in fits and starts, but when it was wiped away she was lucid. We spoke Russian.
>
> Hugh continued to stalk to and fro like a wolf in a cage. 'Why am I always thinking of tea and strawberries – from my childhood. Isn't it strange, Jurij?' Volkova said. I supported her increasingly heavy neck, and kept wiping her mouth until she lost consciousness.[332]

In an unexplained note found after her death, Volkova confessed:

> Inside of myself I always have a suspicion that real, true life happens somewhere else. That it has always a different form.

One night when she was drifting in and out of awareness, between dream and reality, her soul rose in the darkness and took flight for the last time. She danced Giselle, the tragic heroine inspired by her ancestor's writings: the role she had identified most strongly with, and coveted since seeing Spessivtseva dance it in Petrograd. Giselle had, in a sense, followed her through her life, even if she had never danced her on stage. This night she 'heard every note of the music and remembered every step and gesture'.

In character, she reached desperately for the sky as her body slipped through the arms of her faithless lover, Albrecht. It was a last defiant attempt to resist the pull of the underworld, but her corpse crashed to the ground.

Damned and buried in unconsecrated ground, she rose from her grave to dance under the moon. On *pointe* – above but of the earth – and, wreathed in a long white dress, she arched her body against the wind like a lily, the flower of death. Vengeful spectres danced around her in the darkening forest, giving her no peace. An unquiet spirit, she battled her own anger and desire for revenge. She fought to save the betrayer she loved, and to save her own soul.

Volkova's vision was both a release and a catharsis. 'I felt free, so fluent', she told her husband. She felt 'blessed to be an artist, a dancer'.[333] Through Giselle, she experienced many of the conflicts, secrets and un-faced issues in her life without having to face them. In that dream-dance, she could, perhaps, see herself without confronting herself, and heal some of the pain she had suffered without feeling it.

Was the burial in unconsecrated ground her exile and search for belonging? Her coming to accept that her final resting place would be not in Russia but in Denmark – and that she would die alone, as her father, mother, brother and sister had done?

Were the tormenting spirits the demons of regret that haunted her when she gave up the dance to teach? Did Albrecht – the lover who betrayed her – represent the performing career that never came to fruition? Did Giselle's moment of doubt in saving Albrecht mirror Volkova's loyalty to her mentor, Volynsky? As Giselle found peace through forgiving Albrecht, did Volkova find peace through accepting that, as Volynsky had predicted, although her dream had been to dance, her destiny had been to enable others to do so?

It is no exaggeration to say that her entire life was spent seeking to recapture what she had felt when dancing: that her progression, thoughts and decisions were motivated by this goal. It was the phoenix that led her through the most difficult times of her life, and ultimately it was the dance, again, that saved her, that allowed her to let go, to see her life as fulfilled and to find peace.

As morning broke on 5 May 1975, Hugh Finch Williams was dozing in the sickroom, alone with Volkova. Suddenly he was awoken, not by a sound but by an awareness of silence. He knew that his wife was dead. *'Gone.'*

Afterword

This book was originally written in Danish and published in Copenhagen by Arvid Honoré and Schønbergske Forlag with a foreword by John Neumeier. My first thanks go to them.

It has only come out in English now thanks to two remarkable women. Paula Hostrup-Jessen who diligently and generously did a first draft translation of the full text, and Stephanie Lewis who literally sat me down, took me to task and made me rework it for an English readership. Stephanie, who is a dear friend and a brilliant editor and writer, was both patient and relentless in going through the manuscript with me over many days and nights in her kitchen in Fulham, questioning me and demanding clarification in the many places where I had been too garbled and failed to get across what I really wanted to say. I am infinitely grateful for all her help.

I must also thank David Leonard of Dance Books Ltd. who took on the biography after having read only the first four chapters in English and who waited so uncomplainingly for me to finish the remaining twelve – something I finally achieved in St Petersburg in July 2006. Working with his enthusiastic and knowledgeable editor Dr. Rod Cuff was a real pleasure and I appreciate his many insights and suggestions. They have bettered the book, as has the input of American critics Robert Greskovic, George Jackson, Alexandra Tomalonis, and Allan Ulrich, their British colleagues Patricia Daly and Katherine Sorley Walker, French-Canadian writer Katharine Kanter, and the Danish ballet experts Eva and Tove Kistrup, who all read it before publication.

My work on the Volkova biography began in earnest when two rich archives of information were made available to me. Firstly, the unpublished memoirs of Volkova's late husband Hugh Finch Williams, as well as Volkova's private correspondence, which he kindly entrusted to me before his death in 2002, and which his niece Elizabeth Rogers gave me permission to use and quote from. Secondly, the archives of Volkova's close friend David Arkell. Arkell, an English writer, had always had a deep interest in Volkova's life and career and had wanted to write a book about her himself. His cousin, Paula Hostrup-Jessen, and literary executor, Marabel Hadfield, made Arkell's research and papers available to me and they proved invaluable in my finally documenting Volkova's early years.

One other collection of letters was important and I would like to thank Colette Clark for giving me access to her private correspondence with Volkova. I would also like to acknowledge the Estate of Lady Diana Menuhin, which allowed me to publish a Letter to the Editor she had submitted to Dancing Times but which never appeared in print. Also William Earle and Christopher Pennington of The Jerome Robbins Trust and Foundation who allowed me to quote from Volkova's correspondence with Jerome Robbins, and Charles Perrier of the New York Public Library for the Performing Arts Dance Division, who dug out Volkova's letters to and from Lucia Chase and Ruth Page.

The written sources were substantiated, explained and put into context through the many conversations I had with Hugh Finch Williams and the late Danish ballet-master and Artistic Director Henning Kronstam in the 1990s, as well as through getting to know Henry Danton who shared Volkova's passion for dance yet claims she is still a mystery to him. I think in many important ways he was closer to her than anybody else I have met.

For obvious reasons, Volkova's formative years were the hardest to research but writers, historians and scholars Marc Haegeman and Tatiana Kassatkina, Marina Panfilovich from The Galina Ulanova Foundation, Maria Ratanova, Igor Reichlin, Mikhail Smondyrev, Elizabeth Souritz, and Alexander Trohachev were of great help to me in doing so. Nora Kijamova and Edward Chatov helped me translate a number of Russian letters and documents. Kijamova even travelled with me and photographer Charlotte Munch Bengtsen to St Petersburg, where we found and visited Volkova's childhood home, her favourite spots in the city and the schools she attended – and had a good time, too. Professor Emeritus Jeffrey L. Sammons of Yale University helped me with Volkova's genealogy, while Professor Wolf Moskovich of Slavic Studies Department, Jewish University of Jerusalem, and Stanley Rabinowitz, Professor of Russian and Director of the Amherst Center for Russian Culture, generously shared their knowledge of Volkova's mentor, the fascinating Akim Volynsky.

I would also like to thank the following for their help in specific areas. In London, the late Audrey Harman received me at the Royal Ballet School White Lodge in Richmond Park every Thursday one summer. She talked and talked and showed me the Volkova treasures she had amassed for the School's Archive, including a large collection of photographs which Anna Meadmore kindly let me reproduce in this book. Leo Kersley walked through London's West End with me and showed me Volkova's old haunts there. I visited the late Penelope Boscawen, former Social Secretary at the British Embassy in Copenhagen and a friend of Volkova's, at her country house and interviewed Michael Boulton, Clement Crisp, Colette Clark, Mary Clarke, Julia Farron, Maina Gielgud, Alexander Grant, Richard Ingram, Alexander Ingram, Julie Kavanagh, Brenda Last, Pamela May, Barbara Vernon, Gilbert Vernon, and Sir Peter

Wright, either in person or over the phone. In America, Henry Danton spoke to Mavis Ray and Celia Franca for me and recorded their conversations.

Volkova spent nearly 25 years in Denmark and my understanding of her time there comes from interviews with the Danish dancers Frank Andersen, Ib Andersen, Eske Holm, Mette Hønningen, Palle Jacobsen, Niels Kehlet, Mette-Ida Kirk, Margaret Mercier, Inger Mosfeldt Thøfner, Benedikte Paaske, Flemming Ryberg, Kirsten Simone, Eva Sømoed, Arne Villumsen, and Arlette Weinreich and the critics Erik Aschengreen, Knud-Arne Jürgensen, and Ebbe Mørk, who all knew Volkova in their youth. The late Danish philosopher and writer Jurij Moskvitin, who considered Volkova to have been a surrogate mother, shared his thoughts with me and let me quote from his memoirs, Skæbnens Nøgler.

A real Russian 'kosmopolit', Volkova worked all over Europe, in Africa, Australasia and America, and choreographers, teachers, dancers and writers Maurice Béjart, Dale Brauner, Yvonne Cartier, Francesca Falcone, Maria Fay, Kenneth Greve, Juan Guiliano, Marian Horosko, Jonathan Hurwitz, Bengt Häger, Finis Jhung, Deborah Jowitt, Keith Macintosh, David Moroni, Mimi Paul, Wilfrid Piollet, Anna Maria Prina, Francia Russel, Claire Sombert, Helgi Tomasson, Leigh Witchel, and Ann-Marie Wrange all helped me trace her across the world, and I am most grateful for their time and assistance.

While I was writing this biography people close to me took great interest in my work and helped and supported me in a number of ways. They are friends, and expect no thanks, but deserve them in full. They are, in alphabetical order, Suzanne Banki, Lars Bjørn, Dorte Barnow, Pierre and Lone Beskow, Luís Cardador-Pereira, Lars Dahl Pedersen, Anne-Marie Elmby, Simona Gouchanova, Majbrit Hjelmsbo, Jesper Meinertz, Charlotte Munch Bengtsen, Hanne Outzen, Jean Charles Roghi, Peter Thygesen, and David Vaneenoo. Finally, thanks to Ivan Grundahl, John N. Pepper, Philippe Cohen, Stephanie Lewis, and Miles and Rachel Lewis who opened their homes to me in Saint André de Sangonis, Saint Valery-sur-Somme, Castillon du Gard and Torcy in France where I found the space to write.

I am most indebted.

Alexander Meinertz,
ul. Gagarinskaya 25, St Petersburg, 4 July 2006

Notes

1. Vera Volkova, letter to David Arkell, 30 August 1967. Private collection, Paula Hostrup-Jessen.
2. Ibid.
3. Vera Volkova claimed to have been born in 1907, whereas various encyclopaedias and ballet dictionaries agree on her year of birth as 1904. The birth date and city given here, 1905, Tomsk, have been found in a grant application from the Archives of St Petersburg's Assembly of Nobles, St Petersburg, Russia.
4. Jeffrey L. Sammons, *Heinrich Heine*, Princeton University Press, 1979, p. 22.
5. Anna Nikolaevna Engelhardt, *The Memoirs of the Girl Students of Institutes of Noble Maidens*, New Literary Review, Moscow, 2003.
6. Ibid.
7. Major-General Sir Alfred Knox, *With the Russian Army 1914–1917*, Hutchinson, London, 1921, pp. 553–9.
8. Harold Williams, *Russia of the Russians*, Pitman, London, 1914.
9. Isaak Babel, *The Dead*, W.W. Norton, New York, 2002, pp. 495–7.
10. Vera Volkova, audio-recorded interview conducted by David Arkell. Private collection, Paula Hostrup-Jessen, and the Royal Ballet School Archives, London.
11. Audrey Harman, interview.
12. Elizabeth Souritz, *Soviet Choreographers in the 1920s*, Dance Books, London, 1990, p. 61.
13. Ibid.
14. Peggy Willis-Aarnio, *A. Vaganova*, The Edwin Mellen Press, New York, 2002, p. 339.
15. Ibid., p. 318.
16. Ibid.
17. Ibid., p. 320.
18. Ibid.
19. Ibid., p. 338.
20. A.L. Volynsky, quoted by Marietta Frangopoulo in *Stalin Prize Laureate of People's Artist of Russia – Professor Yakovlevna Vaganova – Fifty Years of Work in Ballet*, Leningrad, 1948.
21. Vera Volkova. Quote from a manuscript for a speech given to the Royal Academy of Dancing, Cape Town, South Africa, 11 December 1973. Private collection, Alexander Meinertz.
22. Ibid.
23. Vera Volkova, 'Agrippina Vaganova', *Ballet Annual* No. 7, 1953.
24. Ibid.
25. Ibid.
26. Ibid.
27. Doris Hering, 'America meets Vera Volkova', *Dance Magazine*, September 1959, p. 38.
28. Solomon Volkov: *St Petersburg – A Cultural History*, The Free Press, London, 1995, p. 295.
29. Peggy Willis-Aarnio, *A. Vaganova*, The Edwin Mellen Press, New York, 2002, p. 352.
30. Yuri Slonimsky, unknown source.
31. A.L. Volynsky, *Kniga Likovanii*, Leningrad, 1926, p. 320.
32. Ibid.
33. Vera Volkova, quoted by David Arkell.
34. 'The House of Arts', *Taleon Magazine*, St Petersburg, February 2003.
35. Stanley Rabinowitz, A Room of His Own: The Life and Work of Akim Volynskii, Russian Review, Vol. 50, No. 3, p. 306
36. Nina Berberova, *The Italics Are Mine*, Chatto & Windus, London 1991, p. 113.
37. Ibid.
38. In Serge Lifar, *History of Russian Ballet*, Putnam, London 1938, p. 135, Volynsky is quoted as saying: 'This swan has an appropriate heroism and a true exaltation, opposed to every form of mannered coquetry. The Russian woman is beautiful even when clothed in a simple white dress, without the luxurious rustle of magnificent lace. We know this from history, from life, and from literature. Under her heroic lineaments, she remains none the less the wondrous swan. This was understood plastically by Lev Ivanov when he created his dances for the second scene of the first act of *Le Lac des Cygnes*. Starting with a European legend, he has been able to refract its motives by

means of the prism of the purest Russian soul, and through that he has built along the path of Marius Petipa a monument whose importance makes us forget the seductiveness of French rococo.'

39. Nina Berberova, letter to David Arkell, 27 March 1977. Paula Hostrup-Jessen's collection.

40. A.L. Volynsky, *Kniga Likovanii*. Excerpt reprinted in *DanceScope*, vol. 5, no. 2, p. 24. New York 1971.

41. Peggy Willis-Aarnio, *A. Vaganova*, The Edwin Mellen Press, New York, 2002, p. 324.

42. John Gregory, *The Legat Saga*, Javog Publishing Associates, London, 1992.

43. N. Legat, *Zhizn' iskusstvo*, 27 June 1922.

44. Lopukhov, unknown source.

45. Elizabeth Souritz, *Soviet Choreographers in the 1920s*, Dance Books, London, 1990, p. 63.

46. Ibid.

47. Peggy Willis-Aarnio, *A. Vaganova*, The Edwin Mellen Press, New York, 2002, p. 385.

48. L. Rozdestvennskaja, *Agrippina Yakovlevna Vaganova – Recollections, Materials*, Leningrad, State Publishing House Iskusstvo, 1958.

49. Peggy Willis-Aarnio, *A. Vaganova*, The Edwin Mellen Press, New York, 2002, p. 384.

50. Orlando Figes, *Natasha's Dance*, Penguin Books, London, 2003, p. 449.

51. Ibid., p. 450.

52. Solomon Volkov, *St Petersburg – A Cultural History*, The Free Press, London, 1995, p. 285.

53. Ibid., p. 286.

54. Elizabeth Souritz, *Soviet Choreographers in the 1920s*, Dance Books, London, 1990, p. 274.

55. Ibid., p. 63.

56. Ibid., p. 273.

57. Ibid.

58. Ibid.

59. Ibid.

60. Solomon Volkov, *St Petersburg – A Cultural History*, The Free Press, London, 1995, p. 308.

61. Ibid., p. 300.

62. Ibid.

63. Ibid.

64. Natalia Roslavleva, *Era of The Russian Ballet*, London, 1966, p. 198.

65. John Gregory, *The Legat Saga*, Javog Publishing Associates, London, 1992.

66. Solomon Volkov, *St Petersburg – A Cultural History*, The Free Press, London, 1995, p. 298.

67. A.L. Volynsky, *Birzhevye vedemosti*, 22 March 1914. Published in translation in Tim Scholl's *'Sleeping Beauty' – a Legend in Progress*, Yale University Press, 2004, p. 205: '... various figures formed at a difficult tempo to a complex musical rhythm. The river nymphs in white tutus run to the front of the stage in two lines and immediately separate into four lines. Then, after a few bars, the Nereids form tight lines, as before, and the front line drops to its knees. The general adagio begins. The lines scatter across the stage without breaking their linearity. In one especially beautiful moment, two diagonal lines change places and the Lilac Fairy, Prince Désiré, and the Sleeping Beauty pass through the middle of them, as if playing blind man's buff. Finally, in conclusion of the wonderful adagio, a portion of the dancers with garlands in their hands form a circle with a shell in the shape of a shoe in the middle. Aurora places her foot in it and rises into attitude. The remainder of the corps de ballet then divides into two parallel lines.'

68. A.L. Volynsky, *Birzhevye vedemosti*, 22 March 1914. Published in translation in Tim Scholl's *'Sleeping Beauty' – a Legend in Progress*, Yale University Press, 2004, p. 205.

69. A.L. Volynsky, *Zhizn' iskusstvo*, 26 September 1922. Published in translation in Tim Scholl's *'Sleeping Beauty' – a Legend in Progress*, Yale University Press, 2004, p. 205.

70. Ibid.

71. A.L. Volynsky, Parthenon, Petrograd, 1922.

72. Nina Berberova, *The Italics Are Mine*, Chatto & Windus, London, 1991, p. 143.

73. Shostakovich, *Testimony*, Hamish Hamilton, London, 1979, pp. 10–11.

74. A.L. Volynsky, *Kniga Likovanii*, Leningrad, 1926, p. 320.

75. Konstantin Muller, quoted in a letter from Natalia Roslavleva to Hugh Finch Williams, 19 April 1976. Private collection, Alexander Meinertz.

76. A.L. Volynsky, *Kniga Likovanii*, Leningrad, 1926, p. 319.

77. Ibid., p. 295.

78. Ibid.

[79.] Programme from performances of the School of Russian Ballet, 16 and 23 May 1925. Private Collection, Alexander Meinertz.

[80.] Membership card for Vera Volkova to RABIS, issued 19 June 1925. Private Collection, Alexander Meinertz.

[81.] Contract between Vera Volkova and Stavrin, issued 12 February 1926. Private Collection, Alexander Meinertz.

[82.] Serge Lifar, *A History of Russian Ballet*, Putnam, London, 1938, pp. 293–4.

[83.] Stanley Rabinowitz, A Room of His Own: The Life and Work of Akim Volynskii, Russian Review, Vol. 50, No. 3, p. 308

[84.] 'The House of Arts', *Taleon Magazine*, St Petersburg, February 2003.

[85.] D. Shostakovich, *Testimony*, Hamish Hamilton, London, 1979, pp. 10–11.

[86.] Elizabeth Souritz, *Soviet Choreographers in the 1920s*, Dance Books, London, 1990, p. 62.

[87.] Maria Volkova, letter to Vera Volkova, undated. Private collection, Elizabeth Rogers.

[88.] Solomon Volkov, *St Petersburg – A Cultural History*, The Free Press, New York, 1995, p. 312.

[89.] Ibid.

[90.] Maria Volkova, letter to Vera Volkova, undated. Private collection, Elizabeth Rogers.

[91.] Meredith Daneman, *Margot Fonteyn*, Viking, London, 2004, p. 46.

[92.] V.A. Zhiganoff, *Russians in Shanghai*, Shanghai, 1936.

[93.] Irina Volkova, letter to Vera Volkova, 17 July 1930. Private collection, Elizabeth Rogers.

[94.] Irina Volkova, letter to Vera Volkova, 5 August 1933. Private collection, Elizabeth Rogers.

[95.] Ibid.

[96.] Maria Volkova, letter to Vera Volkova, undated. Private collection, Elizabeth Rogers.

[97.] Maria Volkova, letter to Vera Volkova, undated. Private collection, Elizabeth Rogers.

[98.] Margot Fonteyn, *Autobiography*, W.H. Allen, London, 1975, pp. 30–31.

[99.] Hugh Finch Williams, *Vera Volkova – A Biography*, unpublished.

[100.] Margot Fonteyn, *Autobiography*, W.H. Allen, London, 1975, pp. 30–31.

[101.] Hugh Finch Williams, *Vera Volkova – A Biography*, unpublished.

[102.] Maria Volkova, letter to Vera Volkova, 25 December 1936. Private collection, Elizabeth Rogers.

[103.] Irina Volkova, letter to Vera Volkova. Undated. Private collection, Elizabeth Rogers.

[104.] Irina Volkova, letter to Vera Volkova, undated. Private collection, Elizabeth Rogers.

[105.] Maria Volkova, letter to Vera Volkova, undated. Private collection, Elizabeth Rogers.

[106.] Advertisement in *Dancing Times*.

[107.] Michael Bayston, letter to the editor, *Dancing Times*, January 1986.

[108.] Ibid.

[109.] Scott Highton, interview with Igor Schwezoff, New York, 1979, published electronically as www.highton.com.

[110.] Ibid.

[111.] Michael Bayston, letter to the editor, *Dancing Times*, January 1986.

[112.] In January 1941 Volkova performed once with Mona Inglesby's International Ballet at the Cambridge Theatre, London. Volkova took the part of a cloud alongside Moira Shearer in a dance entitled *Endymion*, but was fired soon after for being 'out of the style of the company'.

[113.] Vladimir Forgency, *L'Adolescense*, 1966.

[114.] Vera Volkova, letter to Hugh Finch Williams, 1939. Private collection, Alexander Meinertz.

[115.] Ibid.

[116.] Claire Tomalin, Foreword to *Ententes Cordiales* by David Arkell, Carcanet Press, 1989.

[117.] Alain-Fournier, *Le Grand Meaulnes*, Penguin Books, London, 2000.

[118.] David Arkell, *Travelling Star*, unpublished manuscript. Private Collection, Paula Hostrup-Jessen.

[119.] Irina Volkova, letter to Vera Volkova, undated. Private collection, Elizabeth Rogers.

[120.] Ibid.

[121.] Ibid.

[122.] Diana Gould, Letter to the Editor, *Dancing Times*, 1975. Unpublished. Printed with permission from the estate of Diana Gould-Menuhin.

[123.] Ibid.

[124.] Ibid.

[125.] Ibid.

[126.] Private Memoirs, Mrs Peggy Ingram and Richard Ingram.

[127.] Fernau Hall, *Modern English Ballet*, Andrew Melrose, Ltd. London, 1950, pp. 245-7.

[128.] Ibid.

[129.] Godfrey Winn, 'Going My Way?', essay in a British newspaper. Date and publication unknown.

[130.] Leo Kersley, *Fonteyn's Teachers and Technique as Seen by Leo Kersley – or Fonteyn's Pedigree*, Fonteyn Seminar, London, September 1999.

[131.] Ibid.

[132.] Meredith Daneman, *Margot Fonteyn*, Viking, London, 2004, p. 156.

[133.] Ibid.

[134.] Barbara Wace, 'Madame V. Lives by her Toes'. *Everybody's Magazine*, 1950.

[135.] Margot Fonteyn, *Autobiography*, W.H. Allen, London, 1975, p. 89.

[136.] Ibid.

[137.] Vera Volkova, quoted in *The Observer*, 23 August 1953.

[138.] Margot Fonteyn, *Autobiography*, W.H. Allen, London, 1975, p. 89.

[139.] Gilbert Vernon, 'Margot Fonteyn: A Personal Tribute', *Dance Chronicle*, 1991.

[140.] Barbara Wace, 'Madame V. Lives by her Toes', *Everybody's Magazine*, 1950.

[141.] Gilbert Vernon, 'Margot Fonteyn: A Personal Tribute', *Dance Chronicle*, 1991.

[142.] Letter from Michael Somes to Hugh Finch Williams, 21 February 1976.

[143.] Margot Fonteyn, *Autobiography*, W.H. Allen, London, 1975, p. 89.

[144.] Vera Volkova, 'Frederick Ashton in Denmark', *Ballet Annual* No. 15, 1961.

[145.] David Vaughan, *Frederick Ashton and his Ballets*, Alfred A. Knopf, New York, 1977, p. 206.

[146.] Margot Fonteyn, *Autobiography*, W.H. Allen, London, 1975, p. 89.

[147.] Vera Volkova, 'Frederick Ashton in Denmark', *Ballet Annual* No. 15, 1961.

[148.] Vera Volkova, letter to Henry Danton, 2 March 1953. Private collection, Henry Danton.

[149.] Ibid.

[150.] Marian Horosko, 'Esprit de corps', *Dance Magazine*, November 1998.

[151.] Godfrey Winn, 'Going My Way?', essay in a British newspaper. Date and publication unknown.

[152.] Beryl de Zöete, 'Vera Volkova', *Ballet*, January/February 1951, pp. 40–41.

[153.] Information about the classes from Audrey Harman's unpublished manuscript, *The London Classes 1944–45 of Madame Vera Volkova, Distinguished Russian Classical Ballet Teacher*.

[154.] Mrs Peggy Ingram and Richard Ingram. Private memoirs.

[155.] William Chappell, *Fonteyn, Impressions of a Ballerina*, London, 1951, pp. 44–5.

[156.] Richard Buckle, *The Adventures of a Ballet Critic*, The Cresset Press Ltd., London, 1953, p. 271.

[157.] Ibid.

[158.] Ibid., p. 272.

[159.] Claire Bloom, *Limelight and After: The Education of an Actress*, HarperCollins, London, 1982, p. 62.

[160.] Mrs Peggy Ingram and Richard Ingram. Private memoirs.

[161.] Ibid.

[162.] Ibid.

[163.] Irina Volkova, letter to Vera Volkova, 22 July 1948. Private collection, Elizabeth Rogers.

[164.] Ibid.

[165.] Pigeon Crowle, *Enter the Ballerina*, Faber and Faber Ltd, London, 1955, p. 108.

[166.] Doris Hering, 'America Meets Vera Volkova', *Dance Magazine*, September 1959, p. 88.

[167.] William Chappel, *Fonteyn, Impressions of a Ballerina*, London, 1951, pp. 44–5.

[168.] Richard Buckle, *The Adventures of a Ballet Critic*, The Cresset Press Ltd, London, 1953, p. 65.

[169.] Gilbert Vernon, 'Margot Fonteyn: A Personal Tribute', *Dance Chronicle*, 1991.

[170.] Richard Buckle, *The Adventures of a Ballet Critic*, The Cresset Press Ltd, London, 1953, p. 64.

[171.] Vera Volkova, quoted in the unpublished biography by Hugh Finch Williams.

[172.] Beryl de Zöete, 'Fonteyn's Teacher', Letter to the Editor, *The Sunday Times*, undated.

[173.] Editorial, *Dance and Dancers*, Vol. 2. No. 1, January 1951.

[174.] Vera Volkova, letter to Hugh Finch Williams, 10 December 1950. Private collection, Alexander Meinertz.

[175.] Hugh Finch Williams, *Vera Volkova – A Biography*, unpublished, p. 195.

[176.] W.J. Turner, *The English Ballet*, Collins, 1944, p. 46.

[177.] Doris Hering, 'America meets Vera Volkova', *Dance Magazine*, September 1959, p. 88.

[178.] Vera Volkova, diary entry as quoted in Hugh Finch Williams, *Vera Volkova – A Biography*, unpublished, p. 193.

[179.] Ibid., p. 213.

[180.] Ibid., p. 203.

[181.] *Soviet Art*, 1951, August 7, p. 4.

[182.] Vera Volkova, quoted in connection with a postcard to David Arkell, 23 June 1951. Private collection, Paula Hostrup-Jessen.

[183.] Vera Volkova, letter to David Arkell, 25 August 1951. Private collection, Paula Hostrup-Jessen.

[184.] P.W. Manchester, 'The Ballet Season in Copenhagen', *Ballet Annual* No. 8, 1954, London.

[185.] Harald Lander, *Thi kendes for ret – ?*, Erindringer, Henning Branners Forlag, Copenhagen, 1951, p. 121.

[186.] Alexandra Tomalonis, *Henning Kronstam – Portrait of a Danish Dancer*, University Press of Florida, 2002, p. 73.

[187.] Vera Volkova, letter to David Arkell, 23 February 1952. Paula Hostrup-Jessen's Collection.

[188.] Vera Volkova, *The Danish Ballet and its Background*. Unpublished manuscript. Elizabeth Roger's Collection.

[189.] 'Den Kgl. Ballet er en af de førende i verden', *Politiken*, 20 January 1953.

[190.] Vera Volkova, letter to David Arkell, 23 February 1952. Paula Hostrup-Jessen's Collection.

[191.] 'Margot Fonteyn sagde "Bournonville" til Vera Volkova', *Politiken*, 19 January 1952.

[192.] Ibid.

[193.] Quote from Niels Bjørn Larsen's diary, published in his wife Elvi Henriksen's magazine for the students of the Royal Theatre, *Takt og Tone*, May 1975.

[194.] Ibid.

[195.] Tobi Tobias, 'The Quality of the Moment: Stanley Williams', *Dance Magazine*, March 1981.

[196.] Ibid.

[197.] John Gruen, *Erik Bruhn – Danseur Noble*, Viking, 1979.

[198.] Alexandra Tomalonis, *Henning Kronstam – Portrait of a Danish Dancer*, University Press of Florida, 2002, p. 82.

[199.] Vera Volkova, letter to David Arkell, 2 August 1952. Paula Hostrup-Jessen's Collection.

[200.] Henning Brøndsted, telegram to Vera Volkova, 8 July 1952. Author's Collection.

[201.] Letter from Vera Volkova to Jerome Robbins, 15 January 1955. The Jerome Robbins Collection, New York Public Library of Performing Arts.

[202.] Letter from Vera Volkova to Jerome Robbins, 2 March 1956. The Jerome Robbins Collection, New York Public Library of Performing Arts.

[203.] Letter from Jerome Robbins to Vera Volkova, 7 March 1956. The Jerome Robbins Collection, New York Public Library of Performing Arts.

[204.] Vera Volkova, 'Før Festivalen. Den Kgl. Ballets Traditioner og dens Fremtid', *Politiken*, 25 May 1954.

[205.] Ibid.

[206.] Ibid.

[207.] Ibid.

[208.] Ibid.

[209.] Alexandra Tomalonis, *Henning Kronstam – Portrait of a Danish Dancer*, University Press of Florida, 2002, p. 73.

[210.] Lillian Moore, 'Horizons of the Royal Danish Ballet', *Dance Magazine*, September 1955.

[211.] Ibid.

[212.] Ebbe Mørk, *Bag mange masker – Niels Bjørn Larsen fortæller*, Lindhardt og Ringhof, Copenhagen, 1974, p. 79.

[213.] Mia Okkels, *At danse med sjælen*, DR Multimedia 2002.

[214.] Vera Volkova, 'Før Festivalen. Den Kgl. Ballets Traditioner og dens Fremtid', *Politiken*, 25 May 1954.

[215.] Vera Volkova, letter to Audrey Harman, 9 January 1952. Audrey Harman's Collection.

[216.] Vera Volkova, letter to Audrey Harman, 16 September 1953. Audrey Harman's Collection.

[217.] Vera Volkova, 'Før Festivalen. Den Kgl. Ballets Traditioner og dens Fremtid', *Politiken*, 25 May 1954.

[218.] Henning Kronstam, quoted in Hugh Finch Williams, *Vera Volkova*, an unpublished biography, p. 293.

[219.] P.W. Manchester, publication unknown.

[220.] Lillian Moore, 'Horizons of the Royal Danish Ballet', *Dance Magazine*, September 1955.

[221.] Vera Volkova, 'Før Festivalen. Den Kgl. Ballets Traditioner og dens Fremtid', *Politiken*, 25 May 1954.

[222.] Ibid.

[223.] Ibid.

[224.] Vera Volkova, 'Frederick Ashton in Denmark', *Ballet Annual* No. 15, 1961.

[225.] Vera Volkova, 'Før Festivalen. Den Kgl. Ballets Traditioner og dens Fremtid', *Politiken*, 25 May 1954.

[226.] 'Den Kgl. Ballet er en af de førende i verden', *Politiken*, 20 January 1953.

[227.] Tobi Tobias, 'The Quality of the Moment: Stanley Williams', *Dance Magazine*, March 1981.

[228.] John Gruen, *Erik Bruhn – Danseur Noble*, Viking, 1979.

[229.] Ibid.

[230.] Svend Kragh-Jacobsen, 'International Choreography Takes the Lead In Copenhagen', *Ballet Annual* No. 10, 1956.

[231.] Vera Volkova: Confidential Report, December 1955. Elizabeth Rogers' Collection.

[232.] Ibid.

[233.] Ibid.

[234.] Ibid.

[235.] Ibid.

[236.] Ibid.

[237.] Ibid.

[238.] Ibid.

[239.] Ibid.

[240.] Ibid.

[241.] Ibid.

[242.] Vera Volkova, letter to David Arkell, 28 October 1956. Private collection, Paula Hostrup-Jessen.

[243.] Vera Volkova, letter to Colette Clark, 9 February 1958. Private collection, Alexander Meinertz.

[244.] Svend Kragh-Jacobsen, *Ballet in Denmark, 1956–67*, *Ballet Annual*, No. 12, 1958.

[245.] Vera Volkova, letter to Colette Clark, 8 December 1958. Private collection, Alexander Meinertz.

[246.] Vera Volkova, letter to Colette Clark, 9 February 1959. Private collection, Alexander Meinertz.

[247.] Eugene Palatsky: 'What's Ahead for the Royal Danish Ballet', *Dance Magazine*, July 1958.

[248.] Ibid.

[249.] Ibid.

[250.] Ibid.

[251.] Jerome Robbins, letter to Vera Volkova, 26 June 1956. The Jerome Robbins Collection, New York Public Library of Performing Arts.

[252.] Jerome Robbins, letter to Vera Volkova, 9 November 1956. The Jerome Robbins Collection, New York Public Library of Performing Arts.

[253.] Jerome Robbins, letter to Vera Volkova, 7 April 1957. The Jerome Robbins Collection, New York Public Library of Performing Arts. 'I'm very familiar with this material as I have produced the show here very successfully and I know it would make a really wonderful ballet.'

[254.] Jerome Robbins, letter to Vera Volkova, 1 October 1957. The Jerome Robbins Collection, New York Public Library of Performing Arts.

[255.] Vera Volkova, letter to Jerome Robbins, 22 November 1957. The Jerome Robbins Collection, New York Public Library of Performing Arts.

[256.] Vera Volkova, letter to Henning Kronstam, 8 July 1959. Private collection, Alexandra Tomalonis.

[257.] Doris Hering, 'America meets Vera Volkova', *Dance Magazine*, p. 88, September 1959.

[258.] Vera Volkova, letter to Colette Clark, 11 March 1961. Private collection, Alexander Meinertz.

[259.] Ibid.

[260.] Ibid.

[261.] Ibid.

[262.] Ibid.

[263.] Otis Stuart, *Perpetual Motion*, Penguin USA, 1996, p. 105.

[264.] Ibid., p. 106.

[265.] Nureyev, *An Autobiography With Pictures*, Dutton, London, 1962, p. 126.

[266.] David Arkell, letter to Vera Volkova, 8 February 1964. Private collection, Alexander Meinertz.

[267.] John Percival, *Nureyev: Aspects of the Dancer*, Faber and Faber Ltd., London, 1976, p. 160.

[268.] Margot Fonteyn, *Autobiography*, W.H. Allen, London, 1975, p. 214.

[269.] Vera Volkova, letter to Hugh Finch Williams, 18 September 1961. Private collection, Alexander Meinertz.

[270.] Julie Kavanagh, *Secret Muses*, Faber and Faber Ltd., London, 1996, p. 459.

[271.] Vera Volkova, letter to Hugh Finch Williams, 12 October 1961. Private collection, Alexander Meinertz.

272. Ibid.

273. Erik Aschengreen, *Mester*, Gyldendal, Copenhagen, 2005, p. 327.

274. Vera Volkova, letter to Hugh Finch Williams, 7 February 1962. Private collection, Alexander Meinertz.

275. Vera Volkova, letter to Hugh Finch Williams, 26 February 1962. Private collection, Alexander Meinertz.

276. Vera Volkova, letter to Hugh Finch Williams, 11 March 1962. Private collection, Alexander Meinertz.

277. Ibid.

278. Vera Volkova, letter to Hugh Finch Williams, 3 March 1962. Private collection, Alexander Meinertz.

279. Vera Volkova, letter to Hugh Finch Williams, 11 March 1962. Private collection, Alexander Meinertz.

280. Vera Volkova, letter to Hugh Finch Williams, 18 November 1962. Private collection, Alexander Meinertz.

281. Vera Volkova, letter to Hugh Finch Williams, 17 October 1961. Private collection, Alexander Meinertz.

282. Vera Volkova, letter to Hugh Finch Williams, 17 October 1961. Private collection, Alexander Meinertz.

283. Vera Volkova, letter to Hugh Finch Williams, 22 January 1962. Private collection, Alexander Meinertz.

284. Vera Volkova, letter to Hugh Finch Williams, 17 October 1961. Private collection, Alexander Meinertz.

285. Vera Volkova, letter to Hugh Finch Williams, 18 February 1963. Private collection, Alexander Meinertz.

286. Vera Volkova, letter to Hugh Finch Williams, undated, 1962. Private collection, Alexander Meinertz.

287. Vera Volkova, letter to Hugh Finch Williams, 4 March 1963. Private collection, Alexander Meinertz.

288. Vera Volkova, letter to Hugh Finch Williams, 15 October 1962. Private Collection, Alexander Meinertz.

289. Ibid.

290. Ibid.

291. Ibid.

292. Vera Volkova, *Some Fundamentals*, undated. Private collection, Alexander Meinertz.

293. Ibid.

294. Gretchen Ward Warren, *The Art of Teaching Ballet*, University Press of Florida, 1996.

295. A Volkova class in the early 1960s, described by Volkova to Marian Horosko in a radio interview, New York, 1964.

296. Vera Volkova, *Some Fundamentals*, undated. Private collection, Alexander Meinertz.

297. Vera Volkova, letter to Colette Clark, 11 December 1963. Private collection, Alexander Meinertz.

298. Ibid.

299. Vera Volkova, letter to Hugh Finch Williams, 19 October 1961. Private collection, Alexander Meinertz.

300. Vera Volkova, letter to Hugh Finch Williams, 22 January 1962. Private collection, Alexander Meinertz.

301. Vera Volkova, letter to Colette Clark, 17 September 1965. Private collection, Alexander Meinertz.

302. Ibid.

303. Ibid.

304. Ibid.

305. David Arkell, letter to Vera Volkova, 6 July 1966. Private collection, Alexander Meinertz.

306. Vera Volkova, letter to David Arkell, 26 July 1966. Private collection, Paula Hostrup-Jessen.

307. David Arkell, letter to Vera Volkova, 8 September 1965. Private collection, Alexander Meinertz.

308. Ibid.

309. Ibid.

310. Vera Volkova, letter to David Arkell, 2 October 1965. Private collection, Paula Hostrup-Jessen.

311. David Arkell, letter to Vera Volkova, 8 February 1964. Private collection, Alexander Meinertz.

312. Vera Volkova, letter to David Arkell, 9 June 1967. Private collection, Paula Hostrup-Jessen.

[313.] Vera Volkova, letter to David Arkell, 30 August 1967. Private collection, Paula Hostrup-Jessen.

[314.] Ibid.

[315.] Ibid.

[316.] Ibid.

[317.] Vera Volkova, letter to Hugh Finch Williams, 29 April 1973. Private collection, Alexander Meinertz.

[318.] Ibid.

[319.] David Arkell, letter to Vera Volkova, 14 May 1973. Private collection, Alexander Meinertz.

[320.] Vera Volkova, letter to David Arkell, 15 July 1973. Private collection, Paula Hostrup-Jessen.

[321.] Ibid.

[322.] Ibid.

[323.] Vera Volkova, letter to Fernau Hall, 10 June 1974. Private collection, Alexander Meinertz.

[324.] Hugh Finch Williams, *Vera Volkova*, an unpublished biography, p. 369.

[325.] David Arkell, letter to Vera Volkova, 23 February 1972. Private collection, Alexander Meinertz.

[326.] Ashton quoted in a letter from Vera Volkova to David Arkell, 14 October 1974.

[327.] Hugh Finch Williams, *Vera Volkova*, an unpublished biography, p. 415.

[328.] Ibid., p. 422.

[329.] Hugh Finch Williams, letter to Colette Clark, 12 March 1975. Private collection, Alexander Meinertz.

[330.] Alexander Pushkin: *Prologue, Ruslán and Ludmíla. The Penguin Book of Russian Verse*, introduced and edited by Dimitri Obolensky, 1962.

[331.] From *Anton Chekhov: Plays*, Penguin Classics, 1986.

[332.] Excerpts from Jurij Moskvitin's unpublished memoirs, *Skæbnens Nøgler*.

[333.] Hugh Finch Williams, *Vera Volkova*, an unpublished biography, p. 425.

Index